New Wealth for Old Nations:
Scotland's Economic Prospects

New Wealth for Old Nations: Scotland's Economic Prospects

Diane Coyle

Wendy Alexander

Brian Ashcroft

Editors

PRINCETON UNIVERSITY PRESS
PRINCETON AND OXFORD

Copyright © 2005 by Princeton University Press

Published by Princeton University Press,
41 William Street, Princeton, New Jersey 08540

In the United Kingdom: Princeton University Press,
3 Market Place, Woodstock, Oxfordshire OX20 1SY

Library of Congress Cataloguing-in-Publication Data

New wealth for old nations: Scotland's economic prospects / edited by Diane Coyle,
    Wendy Alexander, and Brian Ashcroft.
        p. cm.
    Includes bibliographical references.
    ISBN 0-691-12256-3 (alk. paper)
    1. Scotland—Economic policy. 2. Regional economics. I. Title: Scotland's economic
prospects. II. Coyle, Diane. III. Alexander, Wendy. IV. Ashcroft, Brian, 1947–

HC257.S4N45 2005
330.9411—dc22   2004061698

British Library Cataloguing-in-Publication Data

A catalogue record for this book is available from the British Library

This book has been composed in Times

Typeset by T&T Productions Ltd, London

Printed on acid-free paper ∞

www.pupress.princeton.edu

Printed in the United States of America

10 9 8 7 6 5 4 3 2 1

Contents

Preface

This book is dedicated to improving prosperity by advancing economic ideas and promoting better public policy.

The aim of the Allander Series of seminars, the origin of this book, was to bring together some of world's leading economists to assess how Scotland can best respond to the challenge of globalization, to investigate the policies to support higher sustainable growth, and to encourage the application of these insights in Scotland and beyond. This book reflects the contributors' outstanding work, the commitment of corporate Scotland and the dedication of the project team, notably project manager, Jo Armstrong, an independent consultant and Scottish Executive Policy Adviser, and John McLaren, an economist and former Scottish Executive Special Adviser. Both worked in advisory capacities to the First Minister in Scotland's newly devolved parliament. Both have made invaluable comments on the book.

While the collective efforts of the team were instrumental in creating this book, it would not have been possible without generous financial support from key sponsors. The University of Strathclyde and Professor Andrew Hamnett, its Principal, provided the platform to develop the concept and The Hunter Foundation provided the core funding. We are extremely grateful for their help and foresight. Many Scottish corporations, entrepreneurs and foundations provided the finance to secure the contributions from our authors. They also supported the Allander Series of Seminars held in Scotland in the winter of 2003–04. Many thanks for their generosity and support to Atos Origin, BP plc, City Refrigeration Holdings Limited, Clyde Blowers, Ernst & Young, McGrigor Donald, Scottish & Newcastle plc, Scottish Equity Partners, Scottish Power plc, The Hamilton Portfolio Limited and The Royal Bank of Scotland plc. Our special thanks also go to Adair Turner, who presented the final paper in the Allander Series, and to Kirsty Wark, Susan Rice, Ian Russell and Tom Hunter, who facilitated a number of the Allander Series of Seminars.

Thanks are also due to the many academics and commentators who reviewed individual chapters, helping our overseas contributors to engage with the Scottish scene. Particular thanks are due to David Bell, Richard Blundell and his colleagues at the Institute for Fiscal Studies and University College London, Alex Christie, David Heald, Peter Jones, Arthur Midwinter, Douglas Osler, Lindsay Paterson, Christine Stephen, Kim Swales and Andrew Walker.

We would also like to give special thanks to Malcolm Scott of Scottish Power, Kylie Forrest of the Beattie Media Group and Maurice Smith and John Morton of TVI for their assistance during the Seminar Series. Finally, vital administrative support was provided by Isobel Sheppard and Linda Kerr of the Fraser of Allander Institute as well as Jake Humphreys, Xavier Solano di Bello, Lorraine McFarlane, Agnes Robertson and Vanessa Ewing.

Contributors

Wendy Alexander is a Member of the Scottish Parliament, former Minister for Enterprise, Lifelong Learning and Transport and a Visiting Professor at the University of Strathclyde.

Jo Armstrong is an independent economist and consultant after working for 18 years as a senior manager in leading UK companies.

Brian Ashcroft is Professor of Economics and Policy Director of the Fraser of Allander Institute at the University of Strathclyde.

William J. Baumol is Emeritus Professor of Economics at Princeton University and Professor of Economics at New York University.

John Bradley is Research Professor at the Economic and Social Research Institute in Dublin.

Nicholas Crafts is Professor of Economic History at the London School of Economics.

Diane Coyle is Visiting Professor at the University of Manchester's Institute of Political and Economic Governance, and a member of the UK Competition Commission.

Edward L. Glaeser is Professor of Economics at Harvard University.

C. Paul Hallwood is Professor of Economics at the University of Connecticut.

James J. Heckman is the Henry Schultz Distinguished Service Professor of Economics at The University of Chicago. He won the 2000 Bank of Sweden Prize in Economic Sciences in Memory of Alfred Nobel.

Heather E. Joshi is Professor of Economic Demography and Director of the Centre for Longitudinal Studies at the Institute of Education, London.

Paul R. Krugman is Professor of Economics at Princeton University.

Ronald MacDonald is Professor of International Finance at the University of Strathclyde.

John McLaren, formerly an adviser to the Scottish and UK governments, is a political economist and consultant, and Honorary Research Fellow at the University of Glasgow.

Dimitriy V. Masterov is a researcher at the University of Chicago.

Robert E. Wright is Professor of Economics at the University of Stirling.

New Wealth for Old Nations:
Scotland's Economic Prospects

Introduction

This book asks how to improve growth in a small economy, specifically growth in advanced industrial regions and nations which also have a commitment to social justice and sustainability. The case study is Scotland. To paraphrase Adam Smith, one of the country's most famous sons, the task is to identify sources of new wealth for old nations. The challenge of understanding what makes economies grow, and how governments can help or hinder, is hardly new; but contemporary challenges provided the impetus for this book. First, how do the long-standing EU members compete after the Union's enlargement in 2004? Secondly, what forces drive growth in small economies, whether a sovereign state or a region? This question is particularly pertinent now Europe has a common monetary policy and growing pressures for greater fiscal coordination, and is relevant everywhere because of the impact of globalization in intensifying competition with much lower cost locations. For these reasons, there is a renewed interest in what local levers can affect growth. Our contributors focus on Scotland but their policy prescriptions demonstrate just how general are the political economy challenges for any advanced, industrial region.

AIMS OF THE BOOK

We asked the contributors to consider three themes. The first is simply *growth*: what enhances and what limits the growth rate? The second is *opportunity*: in a small country like Scotland, with just over five million people and an essentially social democratic political consensus, what is the nature of the trade-off between growth and fairness, and can its terms be improved? The third theme is *governance*: how can the productivity of the public sector be improved and how can a consensus for policy change be developed and implemented?

The book regards the need for a specific commitment to growth as a policy priority in Scotland, where recent growth rates have been mediocre in international terms (see Chapter 1). Such a growth priority has wide relevance in many developed economies exhibiting sluggish performance in the recent past. All now face the challenges posed by ageing, static or declining populations and the ever-rising demand for better public services and superior infrastructure. Improving growth is important to managing the trade-offs inherent in the popular desire for both low taxes and high-quality services. In Scotland, as elsewhere in Europe, there is a strong social democratic aspiration for the policy process to deliver fairness in economic outcomes. How can both improved allocative efficiency and redistribution objectives be addressed in a small economy

1

highly sensitive to factor flows in a world of ever-increasing capital and labour mobility? These dual aims of growth and opportunity raise pressing questions of governance. How can limited public funds be used more efficiently and what political and administrative structures help rather than hinder economic performance?

By focusing on the three challenges of faster growth, improved opportunity and better governance, we are not denying that there are many other pressing issues confronting public policy. However, achieving higher sustainable growth by increasing the resources available would ease many other policy challenges, both social and environmental. This book is a contribution to creating a renewed climate of ambition for public policy. We aim to spark a debate about the use of microeconomic instruments. Structural economic reform in the European Union and elsewhere may find that its best hope lies at the regional level, where significant powers have been devolved.

Inevitably, given its ambitions, there will be inappropriate emphases, misperceptions and errors of judgement in this book. However, all the authors are eminent academic economists known for applying their analytical insights to the policy realm. Most of our contributors are based outside Scotland, a choice which reflects a desire to ensure the analysis both drew on international evidence and stepped outside partisan domestic sensitivities and prescriptions. We invited them to apply their external perspective to challenge the received wisdom within Scotland about the right economic strategies.

THE GROWTH PROCESS

The issues at stake in the developed world are less urgent than those in the developing world, but nevertheless small improvements in productivity and growth can make a big difference to the quality of life in a small economy such as Scotland. However, neither economics as a discipline nor this book offers an easy answer to the question of how the long-term growth rate can be raised. The more complex but richer appreciation of the growth process in modern economic theory considers improvements in growth as self-reinforcing. Central elements in the growth process include innovation, investment, human capital, the institutional context and 'social capital' (i.e. the network of relationships and institutions, both formal and informal, underpinning the organization of the economy), openness to trade, and incentive structures created by government policy.

How these all fit together is another matter. Certainly, increasing returns to scale and spillovers mean the specifics of place and time play an important part. They also mean that economies are subject to virtuous and vicious circles. This places a greater emphasis on aspects of culture, political institutions, social norms and even historical accidents.[1] But it also makes it much harder to draw simple policy conclusions. The old machine metaphor, of policy levers to change the economy's gear and getting the engine ticking over faster, has been abandoned to rust by the side of the road.

---

[1] There is a voluminous recent literature on growth. A classic theoretical statement is by Romer (1986); an overview is given by Aghion and Howitt (1998).

Instead, the focus is on policy as a means of coordinating collective behavioural change such as encouraging more entrepreneurial attitudes or convincing people of the desirability of extra years of education and workforce training. Government intervention in the growth process can therefore be best understood in terms of either promoting market efficiency or redressing the consequences when markets fail (Balls et al. 2004, Chapter 1). Encouraging competition is an example of the former, while an example of the latter is the provision of tax credits when the social return to investment in R&D is higher than the private return due to external spillovers. Policy makers need to set incentives to influence the behaviour of key groups and individuals, creating a collective commitment to national economic priorities and setting a framework where fear of failure does not hinder innovation.

The importance of ideas in stimulating growth in advanced economies also creates new policy challenges. While economies have always depended on knowledge, adding value now depends more heavily than in the past on intangibles including the exploitation of human capital, tacit knowledge and personal networks. The 'knowledge economy' has entered the lexicon of policy without economists having provided a full account of why and exactly what role 'knowledge' per se plays in growth (Coyle 1996; Quah 2002). Even so, it is apparent that in some countries at least, trend growth rates have increased due to the importance of information and communication technologies (OECD 2003). The growing body of evidence suggests investment in human capital, investment in new technologies, and international openness all play an important role. Case studies also point to important aspects of organizational change (Brynjolfsson and Hitt (2000, pp. 23–48) offer a survey).

The processes underpinning economic growth are becoming better understood, particularly the importance of achieving behavioural change in a specific historical, geographic and institutional context. But one corollary of this is that economic policy needs to be viewed as less technocratic and more 'political'. In practice, good policies need to be persuasive to many thousands or even millions of individuals, with incentives set appropriately, rather than winning over a handful of senior politicians and officials. Thomas Schelling suggested many years ago that the ideal for effective policies was the traffic light, a self-enforcing convention (Schelling 1976). The role of government is to establish the convention but not to enforce individual compliance, which is rewarded automatically. Growth theory has come around to effectively the same conclusion about policy design, recognizing the importance of incorporating appropriate incentives in policies and the importance of the incentives faced by the policy makers and politicians themselves.

The chapters that follow demonstrate considerable consensus among the contributors about the issues that need to be tackled. But a natural concern[2] is whether politicians are willing to pursue structural reforms in the face of opposition from powerful vested interests. Resistance to change is likely to be stronger in circumstances where any adverse consequences of a failure to act are unclear, and when the available evidence can be interpreted in conflicting ways.

---

[2]Often raised in the seminars held by the authors in Scotland in 2003–04.

Recent Irish experience suggests that achieving sufficient consensus for radical action is important in improving growth (Alexander 2003). However, a robust debate is required to crystallize the choices and the implied trade-offs associated with different policy options. Achieving a balance between conflict and consensus goes to the heart of effective leadership. Political leadership must ensure that policies are shaped by evidence, and then harness the best available expertise in both the public and private sectors to secure the implementation of reforms. Those regions and nations which are able to engage both public and private sectors successfully in a common purpose will have a head start.

WHY SCOTLAND?

Scotland is a country of just over five million people who have recently acquired political autonomy over their domestic affairs from the rest of the UK (nearly 60 million people in total) and are also part of the newly enlarged European Union (455 million). This recent policy autonomy makes it an excellent case study. There are lessons for many small, developed economies in its recent experience and current challenges.

In common with other parts of Western Europe, Scotland, with its impressive industrial and intellectual history, has known considerable past economic success. Such legacies can be both inspiring and debilitating. Indeed, a challenge for the new Scottish Parliament, created in 1999, is how to reconcile past splendours with contemporary mediocrity. As Paul Krugman notes in Chapter 2, Scotland's 'first wind' created such a powerful legacy that it has been hard to muster the momentum for a second and now a third wind. However, the new Parliament's powers offer the scope to implement fresh policy proposals, stimulating widespread interest in the regional growth and productivity performance.[3] The next few years therefore mark a window of opportunity to steer the economy onto a higher path.

This book draws on a series of seminars commissioned by the University of Strathclyde's Fraser of Allander Institute and funded by 13 Scottish businesses, entrepreneurs and foundations. Many Scots share an aspiration to combine the American spirit of enterprise with the European commitment to solidarity. In the seminars a number of the contributors noted complacency, contentment with a satisfactory underperformance and the absence of a single-minded strategic intent on the part of the policy elite in Scotland. This contrasts with many successful small nations and regions. Other participants detected an appetite among many Scots, in all walks of life, for an effort to create a nation which, although small, is both 'smart' and 'successful' (to borrow the phrase chosen for the Scottish Executive's 2001 policy document, *Smart, Successful Scotland*). The desirability of creating a consensus about the economy's future direction is recognized by a wide swathe of Scottish society. Yet Scotland's economic concerns are far from unique. How to thrive locally in the global economy lies at the heart of the policy challenges facing all small advanced economies.

---

[3]The powers and responsibilities of the Scottish Parliament are listed in the appendix.

THE EUROPEAN CONTEXT

Many of the lessons in this book therefore have wider applicability. For example, many central and eastern European economies are still experiencing the difficulties of transition, with extensive public ownership and an over-reliance on traditional manufacturing industries. The accession of many of these economies to the EU in 2004 suggests that conventional policy formulations, such as competing for foreign direct investment (FDI) in leading sectors, cannot possibly work in every case. The Irish success in convergence after joining the EU might well turn out to be a strategy viable only in its specific historical context. With more competing locations and presumed limits on the quantity of FDI, other regional economies in the new Europe will need to assess carefully their own chances of attracting inward investment, its character and the nature of potentially beneficial spillovers.

Many aspects of the Scottish experience chime with other parts of Western Europe, particularly the devolution by central government of many of the instruments of structural economic policy. All of the major countries of the EU15—Germany, Italy, Spain, Britain and France—have opted for greater subsidiarity in domestic affairs, whether it be the fully fledged federalism of Germany or the more cautious, uneven decentralization in Italy. This is of particular interest in the context of the Lisbon Agenda, the economic priorities identified by EU leaders at their summit in Lisbon in June 2002.[4] They committed the EU to becoming the world's most competitive and dynamic knowledge-based economy by 2010. Yet it is already apparent as the mid-point review in 2005 approaches that Europe is in fact falling further behind the US.

Progress on structural reform has been agonizingly slow, arguably because the process failed to address the political framework needed to introduce difficult economic reforms. A recent report prepared for the European Commission by a group of experts led by André Sapir (2003) offers this concise statement of the problem:

> Faster growth is paramount for the sustainability of the European model, which puts a high premium on cohesion. Sustainability is nevertheless under threat from rapid developments in demography, technology and globalisation, all of which increase the demand for social protection. Failure to deliver on the commitments of the Lisbon Agenda would endanger the present European contract and could lead to its fundamental revision, thereby threatening the very process of European integration. Fortunately, however, technology and globalisation, like enlargement, also hold the potential for faster growth throughout Europe.

Sapir's report emphasizes decisions taken at the EU and national levels, with the regional dimension of Europe's structural reform agenda rarely noted.[5] This is

---

[4] See http://europa.eu.int/comm/lisbon_strategy/index_en.html.

[5] In addition, although both national governments and the Commission have produced a plethora of reports on the Lisbon Agenda, member governments are not obliged to present to their national parliaments a coherent overview of how they plan to meet the targets.

particularly disturbing given that more balanced regional growth can lead to faster overall national growth (Balls et al. 2004, Chapters 1 and 5). Moreover, the Sapir report dwells on a number of measures which do lie in the hands of the Scottish Executive and other regional European governments. Many of the powers needed to deliver structural reforms rest with regional rather than national authorities. Finding the right balance between competitiveness and cohesion, the needs of the economy and those of society and the environment, goes to the heart of the debate taking place in many small European countries and regions, which may be politically autonomous but are increasingly tightly woven into the fabric of the European and global economy.

THE STRUCTURE OF THE BOOK

The book begins with a chapter offering non-Scottish readers an overview of the political economy of Scotland. The chapter was written by the editors along with Jo Armstrong and John McLaren, making up the team which ran the Allander Series. An overview of Scotland's political and constitutional past provides the context for an analysis of recent economic performance and policy. The remaining chapters are arranged in three parts corresponding to the themes of growth, opportunity and governance.

PART 1: GROWTH

In Chapter 2, Paul Krugman sets out the analytical framework with a discussion in the light of recent theories on growth and economic geography of the challenge of raising the trend growth rate in a regional economy such as Scotland. He examines the distinctive characteristics of regional growth. Unlike growth in a large economy such as the US, the EU or large nations—where, of necessity, the primary market is domestic and growth is driven by productivity gains—regional growth is more export-dependent. Hence, a region's overall openness to international markets matters. However, in small economies the attraction of significant flows of mobile capital and labour can stimulate a rapid rate of growth whatever the domestic productivity performance.[6] Exploiting this opportunity can lead to spillovers which can snowball in a virtuous circle of growth. But this requires a deep understanding of a regional economy's competitive advantages and how they might be exploited to generate factor inflows on a big enough scale. Key areas of potential advantage include higher education to ensure the availability of a skilled labour force, the quality of life (for the same reason) and public infrastructure. Securing domestic productivity improvements, whether by encouraging spillovers from FDI or by direct attempts to improve the efficiency of domestic industry, cannot be neglected if growth is to be sustained.

---

[6]Ireland is a case in point. Location, tax incentives, macro-stability, a favourable exchange rate and labour availability together stimulated the attraction of US multinationals which fuelled the Celtic Tiger phenomenon. Yet the domestic economy still faced huge productivity challenges concerning research, innovation and structural reform.

The other chapters in this part turn to the specifics of policies that could help Scotland achieve faster growth. William Baumol addresses enterprise and innovation, emphasizing the need to tailor policies to the varying roles played by both large and small firms and by other institutions, notably universities and government. Scotland's record on entrepreneurship and innovation is relatively weak, and the institutional capability of the economy to innovate lags competitor economies. Baumol puts the spotlight firmly on microeconomic instruments such as investment in basic research, corporate R&D, the provision of finance, competition and patenting policies, and education and training. He also echoes Krugman on the importance of openness to technology, ideas and people from overseas—a lesson for small economies too rarely understood at the regional level. He therefore stresses the need for the Scots to become skilled imitators as well as excelling at 'blue-skies' research. This may be particularly relevant in economies such as Scotland where the capabilities of the corporate sector to undertake R&D and innovate appear weak.

In Chapter 4 Edward Glaeser looks at the role of the major cities in attracting the skilled workforce needed for economic growth. He notes that for knowledge-intensive activities there has been an increasing concentration in cities—unlike the pattern in manufacturing where the trend has been dispersal to cheaper, less-congested areas or relocation overseas. The message is clear: if future economic success depends on attracting knowledge-intensive activities, then those economies wishing to compete effectively will have to offer successful city regions where people want to live. Increasingly city regions are competing to attract and retain talented people and businesses. Glaeser crystallizes the choice: does Glasgow want to be a Boston or a Detroit? He argues that Scotland's urban core has managed the transition from traditional manufacturing to services reasonably successfully, but a fresh approach is now required. Edinburgh and Glasgow need to operate as one city region to achieve the scale necessary to succeed in the global marketplace. Attracting skilled workers requires: providing education and amenities to grow the skilled workforce; tackling urban social problems without driving the better-off elsewhere; making affordable housing readily available; and managing the inevitably growing use of cars in cities. He characterizes his prescriptions as 'sun, skills and sprawl'. And if sun is too often absent, as in Scotland, the greater the importance of skills and sprawl.

In the final chapter in this part, Paul Hallwood and Ronald MacDonald turn away from structural policies to look at an issue with great political salience in Scotland, as in many other regional polities, namely the characteristics of an effective financing mechanism for regional governments. Hallwood and MacDonald start with an analysis of what recent economic theory suggests about how to align revenue and expenditure powers across multiple tiers of government in order to maximize allocative efficiency and growth without jeopardizing macroeconomic stabilization or redistribution objectives. They then examine how other states have approached these challenges. They conclude that the asymmetric nature of devolution within the UK (expenditure but not taxation) and institutional considerations may have limited the potential efficiency gains. They suggest a different equity/efficiency trade-off is needed in an optimal financing system for subnational governments.

Part 2: Opportunity

Higher economic growth is the priority for many European regions, especially in the context of demographic change and the pressure that is likely to place on pension provision and government expenditures. At the same time, most also value social cohesion extremely highly, and the political centre of gravity in Scotland is certainly squarely in this tradition. This part of the book looks at the ambition for greater opportunities for all citizens in the context of a dynamic economy. Both chapters conclude that investing in the young is where growth and opportunity meet.

James Heckman and Dimitriy Masterov assess the evidence on the formation of human capital. Their central insight is that families, not schools, are the key sites of skill formation. Hence, any commitment to equity of opportunity for all children must involve ensuring the acquisition of skills through support for appropriate parenting. Both cognitive and non-cognitive skills are formed in the early years of life. Cognitive skills are largely determined by the age of eight while non-cognitive skills remain more malleable into the teenage years. Remedial interventions thereafter are both costly and less effective. The policy implications of this analysis are significant, notably that where there are scarce funds, returns to society are maximized by focusing expenditures on the early years rather than universal university tuition fee support, since only a small proportion of the tertiary student population is truly income constrained. Investments in schooling should be subject to rigorous cost–benefit analysis and the focus should shift to improving teacher quality.

Chapter 7, by Heather Joshi and Robert Wright, sets the demographic scene in Scotland. The main factor contributing to its ageing population, as in the rest of Europe, is a low fertility rate. Broadly speaking, this is lower the further south and east one travels in Europe but Scotland stands out from the rest of the UK, and from near neighbours such as Ireland and Denmark, in having a low fertility rate, typical of the Mediterranean. The chapter introduces the first results from the Millennium Cohort Study, a new dataset tracking a large sample of children born mainly in 2001 in Scotland and the rest of the UK. The striking result is evidence of a social and economic polarization between women who start childbearing early, often having relatively few labour market prospects, and those with better educational attainments and earning power, who start their families when they are near or into their 30s. There appears to be a hollowing-out of the birth rate among women in their 20s. The results make the case, the authors argue, for public policies to offer more support to families with working parents. Whether or not this would succeed in stabilizing or raising the fertility rate, as evidence from Scandinavia and France hints, better support for all children is a necessary response to the social polarization apparent in the data. Nurturing the nurturers is vital because of the impact they have in shaping the skills, well-being and productivity of the next generation.

Part 3: Governance

Both Chapters 6 and 7 in Part 2 imply the need for a substantial reconfiguration of existing public policies, especially government spending priorities. The final part turns to what is arguably the most important question of all for anybody interested in policy, namely *how* to implement the recommendations that follow from the first two parts of the book. This in turn can be divided into two issues. How can we ensure that the delivery of public policies is as effective as possible and offers value for money, given both the growth and opportunity objectives? And how can we improve, within a particular institutional and political framework, the set of policies chosen to improve growth and enhance opportunities, given the need to develop a consensus among many participants and stakeholders whose interests may conflict?

Nicholas Crafts sets out the evidence that public services, especially health and education, are valued extremely highly and can also make a greater contribution to economic growth than is widely appreciated. In Scotland, as elsewhere in Europe, the public sector accounts for a large share of GDP, making value for money paramount. However, the evidence is that the efficiency and effectiveness of health and education services are often disappointing. One reason is the providers of services often have little incentive to deliver the outcomes users want, in the absence of the profit motive and competition which align managers' and owners' incentives more closely in the private sector. In the UK, including Scotland, the government has placed much emphasis on setting targets to monitor and improve the productivity and quality of public services. Crafts argues for two alternative approaches: better measurement of the value of services, to allow greater use of social cost–benefit analysis and to emphasize how much is at stake for citizens; and greater competition or contestability in the provision of public services in order to improve incentives in the public sector and stimulate innovation. Both approaches can assist in overcoming institutional hurdles to reform within the organization of the public sector.

John Bradley draws on the experience of Ireland, often eyed enviously in Scotland as a model for Celtic growth, but in fact facing from the 1950s onwards the simpler task of economic convergence from a low level of GDP per capita rather than renewal. However, the lesson of the Irish experience in its transition from a protectionist, agricultural economy to a highly open, hi-tech economy is that the conceptual framework for policy is decisive. Ireland and Scotland are archetypes of two types of European economic unit—the region of a large nation and the small nation state—and now face similar economic policy challenges. Bradley argues that while the politics of institutional design and implementation are different in the case of regions and nations, both need to combine economic analysis with insights from business research to get the right conceptual framework for a renewal of growth, a second or third wind. The task of policy makers is to create a favourable economic environment, and this involves close alignment between government and business.

Finally, we highlight the principal conclusions and challenges emerging on policies to grow small economies in general and the Scottish economy in particular. The conclusion emphasizes the role of greater openness, incentives and capabilities in stimulating future growth. But it also stresses the importance of winning the battle for people's hearts and minds in support of good policy, because if the politics do not make sense, the policy will rarely change.

REFERENCES

Aghion, P. and P. Howitt. 1998. *Endogenous growth theory*. MIT Press.

Alexander, W. 2003. *Chasing the Tartan Tiger*. The Smith Institute.

Balls, E., G. O'Donnell and J. Grice (eds). 2004. *Microeconomic reform in Britain*. HM Treasury, Palgrave Macmillan.

Brynjolfsson, E. and L. Hitt. 2000. Beyond computation: information technology and organisational transformation. *Journal of Economic Perspectives* 14(4):23–48.

Coyle, D. 1996. *The weightless world*. Capstone/MIT Press.

OECD. 2003. *ICT and economic growth: evidence from OECD countries, industries and firms*. Paris: OECD.

Quah, D. 2002. Technology dissemination and economic growth: some lessons for the new economy. CEP Discussion Paper 522. (Available at http://econ.lse.ac.uk/staff/dquah/dp0522.html.)

Sapir, A. (chair). 2003. *An agenda for a growing Europe: making the EU economic system deliver*. (Available at http://europa.eu.int/comm/dgs/policy_advisers/experts_groups/ps2/docs/agenda_en.pdf.)

Schelling, T. 1978. *Micromotives and macrobehavior*. W. W. Norton.

Romer, P. 1986. Increasing returns and long run growth. *Journal of Political Economy* 94:1002–1037.

The Political Economy of Scotland, Past and Present

By Wendy Alexander, Jo Armstrong, Brian Ashcroft, Diane Coyle,
John McLaren

INTRODUCTION

This chapter provides an overview of Scotland's political and constitutional past as well as its economic performance. In the first part of the chapter, we review the political and cultural history of modern Scotland. Scotland's past success still weighs heavily as both a benefit and a burden, casting a long shadow over the present.[1] As the Scottish commentator Carol Craig (2003) has noted, the Scots have long been an active, outward-looking people. Fighting, exploring, colonizing, inventing, engineering, building, preaching, shipbuilding and coal mining are just some of the roles that Scots have for centuries played in the world. Late eighteenth-century Scotland was not only home to the Scottish Enlightenment but arguably Europe's first modern literate society (Herman 2001, p. 20).[2]

The second part of the chapter examines Scotland's economic performance given this historical context. At the start of the nineteenth century Scotland was experiencing a social and economic transformation unparalleled among European societies of the time in its speed, scale and intensity (Devine 2000, pp. 107 and 108). From these foundations, nineteenth-century Glasgow became the second city of the British Empire. The spirit of invention continued into the twentieth century, with Scottish inventors pioneering the technology behind television and penicillin and later medical resonance imaging and the birth of Dolly the sheep. But the earlier glory had begun to fade. Traditional industries declined, new, lighter industries failed to become sufficiently well-established and Scotland became a problem region of the UK. Policy success in attracting foreign investment, the discovery and development of North Sea oil and the blossoming of financial services, meant GDP per capita rose to parity with the UK by the mid 1990s. But as our analysis shows, this revival began to falter, especially so after the downturn in the electronics and information

---

[1] In 2007 Scotland will mark the 300th anniversary of the Act of Union of the English and Scottish Parliaments, which resulted in the creation of Great Britain in 1707.

[2] Herman (2001, pp. 21 and 22) contends that in no other European country did education count for so much, or enjoy so broad a base. Devine (2000, pp. 92, 97, 98) recognizes that by 1790s the network of parish schools in the Lowlands was virtually complete and, although contesting the myth of universal literacy, he notes the achievements of Scottish schooling were impressive by international standards, and rivalled perhaps only by Denmark and Sweden. Moreover, access to universities was certainly more open than in most European nations with a strong emphasis on education in the professions and practical sciences.

and communication technology (ICT) industries post-2000. If Scotland's past glories still attest to vital intellectual and other assets which could fuel future economic success (as Paul Krugman suggests in Chapter 2), we must also understand inherited weaknesses as well as strengths.

THE SHADOW OF SCOTLAND'S PAST: CULTURE, HISTORY, POLITICS

The political Union in 1707 between Scotland, England and Wales catalysed early economic success. As the historian Tom Devine (2000, p. 55) has argued, the Union could have doomed Scotland to becoming England's economic satellite, a supplier of foods, raw materials and cheap labour but with little possibility of growth and diversification in her own right. However, instead of being the prelude to dependency and stagnation, it ushered in a new age of progress and prosperity. From around 1760 there was a social and economic transformation unparalleled in Europe. Scotland underwent its early agricultural and industrial revolutions on the back of the lead nation, England.[3] By the late eighteenth century virtually every parish in Scotland had a school; and Scotland's five universities of long standing were by contemporary standards democratic in their admissions policies and modern in their outlook.

The Scottish Enlightenment was no freakish coincidence whereby a constellation of genius happened to be born in the same century in the same small country. Nor was it a chance byproduct of the Union. Rather, the Scottish Enlightenment had deep roots in the culture of late seventeenth-century Scotland and it flourished not as an exotic outgrowth of the universities but as part of the fabric of educated Scotland (Kidd 2002, p. 24). The core of the European Enlightenment was the France of the Encyclopaedists, but Roy Porter has offered convincing evidence for the intellectual importance of the English Enlightenment as well (Porter 2000, pp. 480 and 481). The view that Scotland invented the modern world (Herman 2001) may be exaggerated, but it does have a claim to be recognized as the most significant provincial outpost of the new learning.

Some fields of enquiry were virtually founded in eighteenth-century Scotland. Taken together Adam Ferguson, Lord Kames and John Millar acted as midwives to the new subjects of sociology and anthropology (Kidd 2002, p. 24). And of course Adam Smith's masterpiece (*Inquiry into the Nature and Causes of the Wealth of Nations*, first published in 1776), along with David Hume's writings on political economy (*A Treatise of Human Nature*, first published in 1739–40, and *Enquiry Concerning the Principles of Morals*, first published in 1751), laid the foundations for the development of economics as a social science. Smith was the first person to identify the principles of specialization and competition, summed up in his 'invisible hand', as the key factors in the development of trade. This did not amount to an argument for unrestricted laissez faire but viewed the ethical and institutional context of the market as vitally important (Adam Smith, *The Theory of Moral Sentiments*, first published in 1759). The Enlightenment represented, above all, freedom from

---

[3]Devine demonstrates how three factors were turned to national advantage: leadership by landed elite and business classes manifested as a commitment to economic growth as a national priority; abundant coal and iron ore near water routes; and Scotland's cultural and educational inheritance.

prejudice (Kidd 2002, p. 25). When Hume described the 'spirit of accuracy' which takes all the sciences 'nearer their perfection, and renders them more subservient to the interest of society' (David Hume, *An Inquiry Concerning Human Understanding*, Chapter 1, first published in 1745), he summed up the spirit of the age.

The defining characteristic of the first 200 years after the political merger was Scotland's enthusiastic participation in both the Union and in the British Empire. Scotland's domestic affairs also became more integrated with the rest of Britain, with the eighteenth-century dominance of the parish giving way in the nineteenth century to vibrant local government and civic leadership, and culminating in 1886 in the establishment of the Scottish Office in Edinburgh. From then until 1999, 113 years in all, Scotland was administered by a department of the UK government, albeit one operating with considerable autonomy. The process of political centralization arguably not only enhanced Scotland's integration into the UK but also intensified the sense of dependency. As Britain's economic self-confidence and performance waned in the twentieth-century, Scotland was not immune. Indeed, Scotland, along with the north of England and Wales, suffered more than the rest of Britain in the first half of the century due to structural economic change and outward migration.

Scottish politics also changed with the nineteenth-century hegemony of the Scottish Liberal Party giving way to the progressive rise of the Labour movement at the start of the twentieth century. Labour's rise drove Scottish middle class voters from the Liberals towards the Conservatives, who became the dominant political party from the 1920s to the 1950s, so the left–right politics of class interest dominated throughout the twentieth century. This effectively masked the Scottish dimension of domestic politics until the late 1960s. The political frustration spawned by relative economic failure and the discovery of North Sea Oil then became contributory factors in the growth of the Scottish National Party (SNP), seeking Scottish sovereign statehood. The SNP's popularity in a general election peaked at 30% of the vote in October 1974, only to decline at the end of the decade. It regained popularity with the decline of the Conservative Party in Scotland from the 1980s and today remains the principal opposition party in the Scottish Parliament.[4]

Yet ever since that electoral high water mark, the question of whether national sovereignty could unlock greater economic success has frequently dominated the political agenda, in a 40-year debate about statehood and national identity. In 1979, given the chance to vote for a devolved parliament, the country split near evenly, narrowly favouring devolution but too narrowly to pass the required threshold for constitutional change.[5] Thereafter despite four successive UK general election victories between 1979 and 1992, the Conservatives never succeeded in securing the

---

[4]Since devolution support for both SNP and Labour has fallen, with the SNP's share of the vote in the 2003 falling by 6% points on the 1999 election, while Labour experienced a fall of 4% points. These changes in part reflected growing support for minor parties, particularly the Scottish Socialists and Greens.

[5]This vote was soon followed by the fall of the UK Labour government and although Margaret Thatcher, the new Conservative Prime Minister from 1979, began by professing a commitment to devolution, her opposition to it quickly hardened.

largest number of votes in Scotland.[6] This generated a profound debate about the legitimacy of political decision-making and also intensified support for devolution. It is a deep irony of Scottish politics that devolution's most virulent opponent, Margaret Thatcher, became its best recruiting sergeant. When Labour was elected in the UK general election in May 1997 and held a new referendum barely four months later, the endorsement of a Scottish Parliament was decisive: 68% in favour, with 65% in favour of powers for the new Scottish Parliament to vary income tax at the margin.

The establishment of the Scottish Parliament and Welsh Assembly in 1999 and, subsequently, the Northern Ireland Assembly, marked a decisive break with the past, taking the highly centralized United Kingdom towards the political mainstream of other major European states.[7] Since 1999 Scottish domestic affairs have again been debated and decided in Scotland. The achievements are real: Scottish law has been modernized and public spending is allocated more democratically through a Scottish Parliament.[8] The early years of devolution have marked a transition from the *administration* of Scotland to the *governing* of its domestic affairs by a Parliament accountable to Scottish voters. The new relationship between Scotland and the other devolved administrations in Wales and Northern Ireland and in the rest of the UK has an implicitly federal character.

But for three decades from the late 1960s until 1999, while the constitutional question was unresolved, the quest for economic renewal was forced to the margins of public debate or policy discussion. The constitutional preoccupations often fed the legacy of dependency. Too often, indigenous political, social and economic shortcomings were blamed on the rest of the UK, characteristic of a nation too preoccupied with its nearest neighbour and insufficiently global in its outlook. The new constitutional arrangements are catalysing change. But expectations of the long-awaited Parliament were understandably but unrealistically high. Some disappointment was perhaps inevitable. Scotland still seeks a dialogue about the economy that fully transcends past preoccupations with borders and boundaries. But what will it take for Scotland to succeed? We now turn to Scotland's recent economic performance.

THE ECONOMIC CONTEXT: PERFORMANCE AND POLICY

Textiles gave Scotland its 'first wind' of industrialization in the eighteenth century, giving way in the nineteenth century to successful industrial clusters in textile machinery, shipbuilding and later in steel, marine engineering and coal mining. By 1913, the Glasgow region produced half of British marine engine horsepower, a third of its locomotive and rolling stock, a third of its shipping tonnage (a fifth of

---

[6]The party's share of the vote in Scotland declined from 31.4% in 1979 to 25.6% in 1992 (see Seawright 2002). In the 1997 general election, the Tories failed to win a single constituency seat in Scotland.

[7]By the late 1990s Britain was the only major EU state not to have decentralized or recognized the reality of interdependence of sovereignty between different jurisdictions.

[8]The Scottish Parliament is elected by proportional representation and in turn it elects a First Minister who forms an Executive, hitherto a coalition of the Labour and Liberal Democrat parties that together command the support of a majority of members in that Parliament.

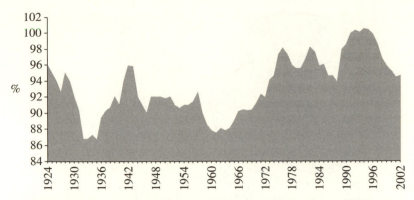
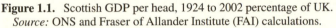

Figure 1.1. Scottish GDP per head, 1924 to 2002 percentage of UK.
Source: ONS and Fraser of Allander Institute (FAI) calculations.

the world's) and a fifth of the specialty steel (Devine 2000, pp. 250 and 251). Yet this appearance of economic might was deceptive. The weaknesses that would lead to relative decline during the next wave of industrialization were already present, above all over-specialization in heavy engineering, particularly shipbuilding. This led to a failure to generate and attract the lighter, consumer-based industries such as motor vehicles, electrical engineering, chemicals, cycles, and furniture and uphol-stery. Rearmament for World War I in fact intensified the concentration of activity in the heavy industries. As consumer goods took the place of heavy industry in generating growth, many of Scotland's natural advantages became redundant, while it lacked many of the attributes, such as sizeable and wealthy markets, needed for success (Ashcroft 1997, pp. 7–11).

Following World War II, the lack of incentive to restructure was reinforced by massive state intervention, with the nationalization of coal (1947), railways and elec-tricity (1948), and iron and steel (1949). In 1951, shipbuilding was still Scotland's biggest industry, producing 15% of the world's tonnage (Devine 2000, pp. 556 and 557). But the decline continued, reaching a nadir in the late 1950s when Scottish GDP per capita dipped below 90% of the UK average. It remained there until the mid 1960s. But as Figure 1.1 shows, the low of the late 1950s (like a similar dip in the 1930s) was untypical. For most of the twentieth century (1924–2002) Scot-land's GDP per capita has ranged from 93% to 98% of the UK's GDP per capita. Only once has Scottish GDP per capita risen to parity and beyond, from 1992 to 1995.

Figure 1.1 also highlights the start of a significant economic turnaround from the 1960s, which reflected a strengthening of UK regional policy, flows of inward investment particularly from the rest of Britain and the US, the development of North Sea oil and the growth of financial services. There was a pause relative to the UK in the early 1980s when high oil prices and a monetarist macroeconomic policy cause the pound to appreciate. The subsequent recession cut a swathe through Scottish manufacturing industry and increased unemployment significantly. From the late

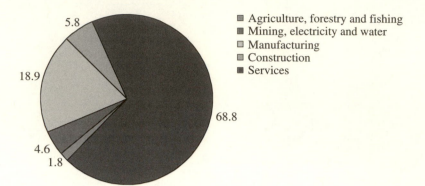

Figure 1.2. Scottish sectoral GVA shares in 2000. *Source:* Scottish Executive.

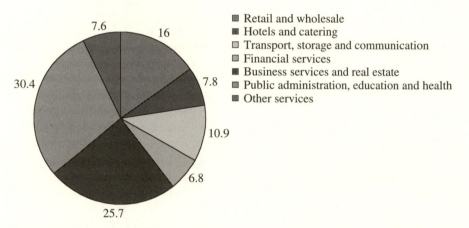

Figure 1.3. Sectoral GVA shares in services in 2000. *Source:* Scottish Executive.

1980s the impact of a new wave of inward investment[9] and continuing rapid growth in the financial services sector is apparent. The structure of the Scottish economy has shifted to a more service-based economy, with manufacturing sector heavily reliant on FDI, particularly in electronics. Figures 1.2 and 1.3 show the sectoral composition of the modern Scottish economy by shares of GDP, gross value added, in 2000.

The service sector dominates the economy accounting for almost 70% of GDP, while manufacturing accounts for less than 20%. The share of the value added in services is shown in Figure 1.3. What is clear from this figure is that the public sector has the biggest share of services at 30.4%, or 20.9% of overall GDP. Business services accounts for just under 26% of service sector value added and 18% of

---

[9] A distinct Scottish industrial policy began to emerge in the mid 1970s with the creation of the Scottish Development Agency in 1976 and its later offshoot, Locate in Scotland (LIS). LIS's one-door approach to marketing Scotland internationally, particularly in North America, put her out in front of other UK regions, which had to rely on the more-fragmented activities of the Invest in Britain bureau within the UK's Department of Trade and Industry.

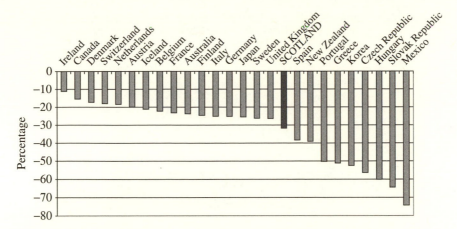

Figure 1.4. GDP per capita (at purchasing power parity).
Difference from United States, 2002. *Source:* OECD and FAI calculation.

Table 1.1. Absolute GDP growth rates, Scotland and UK
(annual average per cent), constant basic prices, 1970–2000.

Year	Scotland	UK	Year	Scotland	UK
1970–1980	1.5	1.5	1990–1995	1.8	1.6
1980–1990	1.9	2.6	1995–2000	2.1	3.1
1990–2000	2.0	2.3	2000–2002	1.6	1.5
1970–2000	1.8	2.2			

Source: Scottish Executive and Office for National Statistics (ONS).

overall GDP, while financial services accounts for about 7% of the service sector
and just under 5% of total GDP.

Scottish GDP per capita not only improved relative to the UK but also rose in line
with the OECD average. Scotland was a low-growth economy in the 1970s, but a
medium-growth performer in the 1980s and 1990s (McLaren 2003). However, after
a strong performance in the early 1990s, growth per capita began to falter after 1995,
and weakened further after 2000 when electronics production dropped markedly as
a result of the worldwide ICT downturn. By 2002, as Figure 1.4 indicates, GDP per
head in Scotland languished nearly 32 percentage points adrift of the US and in the
third quartile of 26 OECD countries.[10]

The trend rise in GDP per head relative to the UK since the early 1960s masks
a weaker growth rate overall, averaging 2.1% a year between 1963 and 2002 in
Scotland compared with an annual average of 2.3% in the UK. Absolute real GDP
growth rates in selected periods between 1970 and 2002 are shown in Table 1.1.

---

[10]For some countries GNP per head is a better indicator of domestic income because it includes net
overseas income. Ireland is a case in point, where GNP per head is below GDP per head due to the
repatriated profits of multinationals operating there.

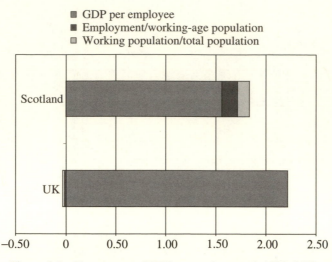

■ GDP per employee
■ Employment/working-age population
▢ Working population/total population

Figure 1.5. Components of GDP per capita growth 1990–2000.
Average annual percentage change. *Source:* ONS and FAI calculations.

The reason for Scotland's relatively stronger GDP per capita growth up to the mid 1990s is that it was buttressed by persistent net out-migration.[11] Scotland is a nation with an extraordinary history of emigration. Between the early nineteenth and twentieth centuries, Scotland exported more people per head than any other European country except Ireland and Norway. In the 1920s and 1930s Scotland rose to the very top of this unenviable league table, with over 400 000 leaving in these decades, an extraordinary number for a country with a total population of five million (Devine 1992, pp. 1–3). This pattern of net outward migration has persisted throughout the postwar period, with only a couple of blips, until the 1990s. For the past few years net migration has been in balance, although there is little diversity in the population.[12]

UNDERSTANDING SCOTTISH ECONOMIC GROWTH

To gain some insight into Scotland's middling economic growth, and the economy's underlying strengths, weaknesses and prospects, we begin by examining the components of GDP per capita growth in the 1990s, shown in Figure 1.5. Between 1990 and 2000 GDP per capita[13] grew at an annual average of 1.83% in Scotland and

---

[11] In 2001, the Scottish share of UK Gross Value Added (GVA or GDP at basic prices) was 8.1% and her share of UK population was 8.6%.

[12] Most in-migrants to Scotland come from elsewhere in the UK. Overall only 2% of the Scottish population are of non-white ethnic origin, compared with 29% in London and 9% in England overall. Indeed, Scotland has the most ethnically homogeneous population of any part of the UK except for Northern Ireland. (Table: Distribution of ethnic groups within regions, April 2001, Census, April 2001, Office for National Statistics.)

[13] As measured using the income-based regional GVA estimates produced by ONS, 30 April 2004. The growth estimates for Scotland derived from this source differ from the Scottish Executive's GDP estimates, which measure GVA output growth.

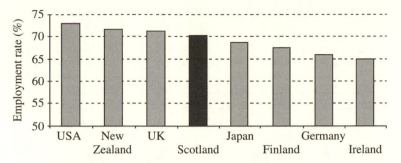

Figure 1.6. Employment rates in 2001. *Source:* OECD and LFS for Scotland. Scotland is 11th in a 31-country OECD sample, placing it in the second quartile. A figure for Scotland comparable with the OECD data was not available due to differences in the definition of the working-age population, so instead the figure for Scotland from the Labour Force Survey was used to scale Scotland relative to the UK. This gives Scotland an employment rate of 70.3% against the UK figure of 71.3%, the LFS rates being 73.4% and 74.4%, respectively.

2.19% in the UK. To the extent that comparisons are possible, this would place the UK in the second quartile and Scotland in the third quartile of 26 OECD countries, with both countries displaying middling growth performance. Irish growth, bringing rapid convergence up towards average EU prosperity, was 6.4% a year and Switzerland's 0.2%.

The breakdown of growth in Scottish and UK GDP per employee differed considerably. While GDP per employee rose by 2.22% per annum in the UK, this measure of labour productivity grew at an average of just 1.56% in Scotland. However, the Scottish employment rate rose by 0.15%, while the ratio of its working to total population grew by 0.12% each year.[14] In the UK labour market, both the employment rate and working population ratio fell slightly, by 0.01% and 0.02% a year, respectively. Figure 1.6 shows the relatively high level of Scotland's recent employment rate in comparison with key OECD nations.

Scotland's focus on inward investment from the 1970s was ambitious compared with the innovation record of the industry it was displacing, but by the 1990s the nature of the inward investment Scotland was attracting was decidedly low-tech in the broader European context. However, since this inflow of FDI successfully re-employed many of those displaced by structural change in other older industries, there was little political momentum to move on to higher-value-added activities. After 2000 when ICT sectors worldwide went into recession, electronics production in Scotland almost literally collapsed.

Figure 1.7 identifies the key growth sectors in the Scottish economy during the period 1996–2003. Until the third quarter 2000, the electronics sector played a key role, expanding by more than 70% from 1995. However, the figure reveals the scale

---

[14]It is possible that the contribution of labour productivity to growth is understated in this analysis because we are considering GDP per employee and not GDP per hour worked. Average hours worked have tended to fall in OECD countries in recent years. However, this is not the case in Scotland, where in 2002 the average for all workers was only marginally lower than in 1993 at 33.3 hours compared with 33.7 in 1993, *Scottish Economic Report 2004*, and Scottish Executive.

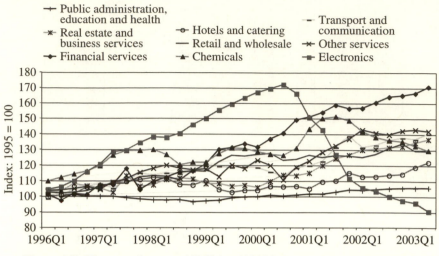

Figure 1.7. Key growth sectors 1996Q1 to 2003Q2. *Source:* Scottish Executive.

of the collapse after 2000, with electronics production volumes falling by more than 40%.[15] Other key sectors in manufacturing such as chemicals also began to cut back production as world trade slowed and export demand for their products faltered. Scottish manufacturing was in recession for three years from 2000 and was much weaker than UK manufacturing, principally because of the greater significance of electronics and its vulnerability to the world ICT downturn. Following the collapse of electronics, growth was clearly supported by the service sector which expanded by 13% in Scotland compared with growth of only 6% in UK services between 2000Q3 and 2003Q2.

Figure 1.7 also indicates the robustness of the Scottish service sector, during the whole period, particularly banking and financial services but also retail and wholesale, transport services and business services. From 1995 to 2003Q2 financial services grew by more than 70% in volume terms, while other services and transport and communication grew by around 40%, business services by 37% and retail and wholesale by 30%. During the same period (1995 to 2003Q2) manufacturing contracted by around 12%.

Figure 1.8 highlights the implications of these sectoral shifts for the components of Scottish GDP per capita growth between 2000 and 2002. During the ICT downturn Scottish GDP per capita growth fell from an annual average of 1.83% in the 1990s to 0.92% while per capita GDP growth in the UK fell from 2.19% to 1.20%. The difference between Scotland and the UK was that while UK labour productivity growth faltered, dropping to 0.97% a year in 2000–2002 from 2.22% in the 1990s, Scottish labour productivity actually declined, the growth rate collapsing from an annual average of 1.56% during the 1990s to −0.08% a year. Growth in Scotland

---

[15]From 2003Q3 the Scottish Executive introduced a new chain-linked quarterly aggregate GVA, with revised subsectoral weights and 2000 as the base. On these new weights the fall in electronics production is 40% to 2003Q3, a little less than under the old series.

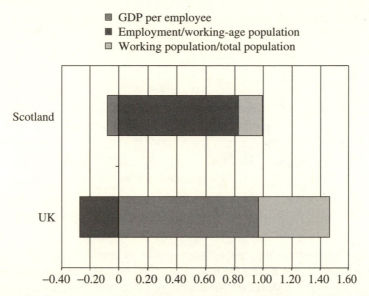

■ GDP per employee
■ Employment/working-age population
□ Working population/total population

Figure 1.8. Components of Scottish GDP per capita growth between 2000 and 2002. Average annual percentage change. *Source:* ONS and FAI calculations.

was positive during the later period because of improved labour utilization; the employment rate rose by an average of 0.83% each year and the working to total population rate rose by 0.17% a year.

What can we conclude? First, Scotland's labour productivity performance (growth of GDP per person employed) over the past decade appears to have been weaker than in the UK. Putting this into the context of 26 OECD countries, with labour productivity growth ranging from 0.7% (Switzerland) to 4.6% (Luxembourg)[16], the UK lies in the second quartile and ranks 9th, while Scotland would be in the third quartile, ranking 16th. Yet during the early 1990s Scotland attracted much inward investment which undoubtedly boosted productivity growth. However, Scotland appeared to be undergoing a form of catch-up in the labour market during the 1990s as the employment rate and working population rate rose both absolutely and relative to the UK. The interrelationship between labour utilization and labour productivity reflects the fact that the people taken into employment as utilization rises generally have lower education levels and thus probably lower productivity than those already in employment (see, for example, OECD 2003, p. 35). Another factor perhaps dampening productivity growth was the strong performance of the service sector, in the latter part of the period at least.

Secondly, the fall in productivity since 2000 was largely the result of the loss of FDI, and electronics production in particular. This also highlights the apparent lack of significantly favourable externalities or spillover effects from FDI to domestic business activities. Recent Scottish Executive data show that Scotland's most

---

[16]After Luxembourg, Korea (4.5%), Ireland (3%), Finland (2.9%), Sweden (2.5%) and Turkey (2.5%) were the top six labour productivity growth performers (OECD 2003).

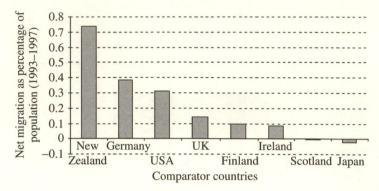

Figure 1.9. Net migration as a percentage of the population (1993–1997). *Source:* OECD Statistical Compendium, GROS, Census of Population, ONS and Central Statistics Office for Ireland.

productive[17] manufacturing establishments were, in terms of GVA per employee, around 5.3 times as productive the least productive, and this variation was common to a number of sectors. Moreover, the relative productivity of foreign manufacturing plants in Scotland was on average 1.8 times greater than their Scottish counterparts, and much more so in food and drink, and in electrical and optical engineering.

Thirdly, improved labour utilization has been important to Scottish economic growth but it has limits as a source of growth. The most obvious limits are the size of population and its age composition. During the 1990s, Mexico, Korea, Turkey and Ireland all enjoyed a significant boost to growth from favourable demographic factors, with Ireland also reversing its long-term trend of net outward migration. But increasingly population growth in Scotland (and many other OECD economies) is slowing and the share of persons above working age rising (OECD 2003). In Scotland, the significance of population trends is hotly debated, particularly when the character of outward migration is analysed. As Figure 1.9 shows the net outflow of Scots has now halted, but Scotland is behind several other OECD economies in attracting migrants.

Moreover, Scotland's population is still forecast to both fall and age—it has one of the lowest birth rates in Europe.[18] On current projections Scotland's population is forecast to fall below the psychologically important figure of five million in

---

[17]The most productive firms are defined as those whose productivity lies at the 90th percentile of the distribution and the least productive firms at the 10th percentile. Furthermore, the ratio of the 10th to 90th percentile points varies between 3.3 and 6.2 for most sectors, with a couple of sectors (15, food and beverages, and 35, other transport equipment) showing larger differentials. Source: *Productivity in Scottish Manufacturing Plants 1994–1997*, Scottish Economic Report, Scottish Executive, June 2001.

[18]In 2002, Scottish fertility reached an historic low. The total fertility rate (TFR) fell to 1.48 births per woman. Scotland is now a very low fertility country with a TFR below 1.5%. Scotland's TFR is now below Ireland, France, Northern Ireland, Denmark, Finland, Netherlands, Belgium, the rest of the UK and Sweden. It remains above Germany, Spain and Italy. Since a TFR of 2.1% is the rate required for population replacement in the absence of migration, the shortfall has provoked worries about Scotland's demographic future, and prompted the Scottish Executive to launch a Fresh Talent Initiative to attract new migrants into Scotland as well as to retain current residents (Graham and Boyle 2003, Chapters 2 and 3).

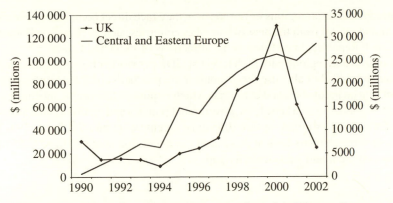

Figure 1.10. Inward investment to UK versus Central and Eastern Europe.
Source: United Nations and Scottish Economic Report, March 2004, Scottish Executive.

2009. This decline, of around 15%, in the next 50 years, is comparable with the prospect facing some other developed nations such as the Czech Republic and Japan, and lower than the decline predicted for Switzerland (−19%) and Italy (−22%). It is unlikely indeed that demographic trends and utilization of labour could bring about a significant improvement to Scotland's trend growth rate. So we turn now to Scotland's productivity 'gap'.

SCOTLAND'S PRODUCTIVITY CHALLENGE

Productivity growth can be divided into growth due to changes in the volume and quality of the inputs to production (capital and labour) and remaining, or residual, productivity growth. This latter is frequently known as *total factor productivity* or *multi-factor productivity* growth, and is usually taken to reflect technological progress (Solow 1957).

The UK Treasury, which is engaged in a drive to increase national productivity, identifies five key drivers of labour productivity growth: investment, skills, competition, innovation and enterprise (Balls et al. 2004, pp. 9 and 10). But this approach disguises the distinction between factor accumulation and total factor productivity growth. In addition, at the regional scale higher productivity may—through inward investment, the attraction of talented people and spillovers—be the *consequence* rather than the *cause* of growth.[19] On the first point, diminishing returns will eventually set in unless offset by technological progress or other unspecified determinants of total factor productivity growth (Jones 2002, pp. 43 and 44). So investment per se, unless accompanied by innovation and technological progress, will not foster long-term GDP per capita growth. On the second, if higher productivity can be the consequence of growth fuelled by inflows of capital and labour, as was the case in Scotland through significant inflows of FDI and consequent spillovers, then the key influence on regional productivity might be the extent to which the economy is attractive to mobile inputs. As Figure 1.10 illustrates, this is an acute issue for the

---

[19]Paul Krugman develops this point in Chapter 2.

traditional industrial regions of Europe now they face direct competition for mobile labour and capital from the new EU member countries such as Hungary, Poland and the Czech Republic, in addition to the attractions of India and China.

Countries and regions with high levels of GDP per worker not only invest more in capital and skills but also use these inputs more productively. Productivity depends essentially on innovation and enterprise which requires a favourable incentive structure. An economy's markets, laws, government policies and institutional framework, both formal and informal, in turn determine incentives (Jones 2002, pp. 194–196). The following chapters look at these issues in detail. But some stylized facts hint at the roots of Scotland's productivity gap.

Low Investment

Much of the UK productivity gap compared with France and Germany is due to lower investment in physical capital (plant and machinery) (Balls et al. 2004, p. 100). Data are limited on investment in capital in Scotland and the English regions but the latest figures (for 2000) suggest that gross fixed capital formation was 20.3% of GVA in Scotland and 19.1% in the UK (Cope and Flanagan 2003). As William Baumol discusses in Chapter 3, Scotland is in the third quartile of 30 OECD countries with business R&D just over 0.5% of GDP, over 1.5% less than the leader Finland and 0.75% behind the UK as a whole. Both the UK as a whole and Scotland compare well in terms of R&D investment by the government and higher education sectors. Investment in education in Scotland would also appear to compare well with the UK and many other countries. In 2001–02 Scotland spent nearly £5 billion on education, which amounts to 7.2% of Scottish GDP compared with 5.6% of GDP in the UK.[20] This is reflected in high participation in higher education: in 2001–02 51.5% of Scots under 21 entered tertiary education compared with 35% in England. However, Scotland is 17th in a 31-country sample in terms of graduate employment, with 16% of the workforce (ages 25–64) having tertiary qualifications. Scotland expanded the rate of participation in higher education significantly since the early 1990s, to one of the highest participation rates in Europe, but the age composition of the workforce means this rise is only slowly feeding through into the qualifications of the workforce. The best-performing country is the USA, where 31% of the workforce are graduates. Scotland is a net exporter of tertiary skills. It appears that there are insufficient attractive jobs for graduates in Scotland, another facet of the productivity problem.

There are also concerns about Scotland's infrastructure, with calls for increased investment from business organizations.[21] There have, though, been substantial efforts to improve Scotland's electronic infrastructure, particularly broadband access. In 2002, around 53% of the Scottish population, and 66% of the UK popu-

---

[20]Investment in skills is more difficult to establish since it is the sum of both public and private training programmes by external training providers and in-company training. However, Scotland's rank is 9th of 12 UK regions in the proportion of employees receiving training, although the differences are small (DfES, Statistics of Education: Education and Training Statistics for the United Kingdom, 2002).

[21]Institution of Civil Engineers, *State of the Nation Report, 2004.*

lation, had access to mainstream broadband services, while the costs of connection and use were in the middle of the range for the EU15 countries.[22]

Innovation and Enterprise

The picture on Scottish innovation and enterprise is mixed. The evidence is reviewed in detail in Chapter 3. However, the low rate of investment by business in Scotland on R&D is reflected in a low percentage of innovative firms, and a low share of UK patents filed.[23] Moreover, when compared with the key German regions of Bavaria and Baden-Wurtemberg, for example, take-up of new technologies also tends to be slower in Scotland. Scottish manufacturing firms also appear less likely than international competitors to form alliances to improve products and processes.[24] The result is that for much of 'traditional' manufacturing in Scotland competition is still too much focused on the basis of price rather than on product differentiation and innovation. In contrast, Scotland does quite well in the share of value added contributed by knowledge-intensive industries ranking 6th out of 28 countries.

In addition, the fact that higher-education R&D spending in Scotland is high by international standards is reflected in the number of companies created by university academics per head of the population, where Scottish performance is better than the UK, Canada and the USA.[25] The numbers are small, however, and the commercialization of ideas from the Scottish universities is a continuing concern of policy makers.[26] This concern extends to the business birth rate and entrepreneurship generally (Ashcroft 1997).

Scotland's record in generating new firms is poor by UK standards. Between 1980 and 1999 the creation in Scotland of VAT registered business per 10 000 resident adults averaged around 75% of the UK figure. By international standards also, Scotland does not have a strong entrepreneurial record.

Incentives

Stability, open, competitive markets and institutions that favour production over diversion and rent seeking are beneficial to economic growth (Jones 2002, pp. 143–147; OECD 2004, pp. 34–43). The macroeconomic situation in the UK is very favourable, although the long-term impact of remaining outside the Euro zone remains a matter of considerable debate.[27]

Scotland is an open economy with respect to trade, with exports accounting for around 70% of GDP; but trade with the rest of the UK accounts for around 50% of

---

[22] Scottish Executive, *Measuring Smart Successful Scotland, 2003.*

[23] The Patent Office Annual Facts and Figures 2000–2001 and 2001 Census.

[24] Fraser of Allander Institute, *Innovation Activity in Manufacturing: A Comparison of Scotland, Bavaria And Baden-Wurttemberg*, report of research sponsored by Scottish Enterprise and the Scottish Executive (2001).

[25] *Measuring Smart Successful Scotland*, Scottish Executive, 2003.

[26] *Smart Successful Scotland*, Scottish Executive, 2001.

[27] Since 1997, interest rates have been set by the Monetary Policy Committee of the Bank of England.

exports and 65% of imports. Of the exports not going to the rest of the UK, 57% go to the EU15, about 12% to the US, and 10% go to the rest of Europe. The Scottish economy is also marked by the large flows of capital and, to a lesser extent, labour, in the latter case principally to and from the rest of the UK. However, as other contributors discuss, the economy could be more open to ideas and knowledge from overseas. In addition, the extent of competition within the small domestic Scottish market for non-tradables has been brought into question in recent years.[28] A related issue is the significant loss to Scotland of corporate HQ functions and independent Scottish firms through a process of takeover and relocation over the past 40 years (Ashcroft and Love 1993).

The role of Scotland's formal and informal institutional structure in limiting or enhancing incentives to promote economic activity and growth is unresearched. Informally, there may be cultural inhibitors to starting new businesses, taking risks or risking failure, although business birth-rate initiatives by the enterprise agencies, networking efforts among key entrepreneurs and initiatives in schools to promote enterprise have all recently sought to tackle these attitudes. Formal institutions such as the civil service, universities and all the social partners face the challenge of evolving a proper policy-making capacity in the newly devolved Scotland. For example, Scotland's civil servants have to adjust from managing a region of the UK to aiding elected politicians govern a devolved nation. Indeed, counteracting the centripetal pull of London and the South East in the culture, business and ideas may be an important ingredient in creating a new mindset more favourable to risk-taking and growth.

Economic Policy Initiatives

In 2000 the Scottish Executive launched a *Framework for Economic Development in Scotland* (FEDS). FEDS follows mainstream economic growth theory, recognizing that it is the private sector that plays the key role in promoting economic change while stressing the importance of the public sector in dealing with market and institutional failures as well as in the promotion of fairness and equity.

FEDS was followed in 2001 by *Smart, Successful Scotland* (SSS), which provided the operational direction to economic development policy. The launch of SSS signalled a development strategy focused on a high-value-added, high-skill agenda for the knowledge economy. The strategy had four thrusts: fiscal stability; recognition of the value of skills and human capital, symbolized by bringing enterprise and lifelong learning together in one ministry; a commitment to the development of a knowledge economy; and a recognition of the impact of globalization on future flows of the most mobile factors of production, notably highly skilled labour. This strategy attracted considerable support from the business and policy community, but success also required a commitment to growth across the whole range of government activities.[29] The wider implications of prioritizing growth for policies towards reg-

---

[28]Fraser of Allander Institute, Quarterly Economic Commentary, December 2003.

[29]The Scottish Enterprise and Highland & Islands Enterprise networks in the Scottish case.

ulation, planning, infrastructure, education, innovation policy and public services do not appear to have been fully recognized in these other areas of Executive policy.

The Executive's Fresh Talent initiative to attract new immigrants to Scotland is an encouraging sign in view of the growth implications of Scottish population decline.[30] However, recent research by Harrison and Mason (2003) indicates that migration is often endogenous to economic opportunity rather than an exogenous element in economic development.[31] The research reveals that the primary considerations for high-skilled migrants are company reputation and job challenge, with lifestyle and place considerations being secondary. Scotland has too few jobs of appropriate quality to attract or retain talent.

The public sector, finally, plays a direct part in Scotland's productivity gap. Scotland is more dependent than the rest of the UK on the public sector for jobs and output: 27% of Scottish employees work in the public sector, which accounts for 21% of GVA. The equivalent figures for the UK are 24% and 18%, respectively. So concerns about the greater risk in Scotland of public-sector activity crowding out private sector employment or willingness to start businesses appear to be valid. However, while government expenditure as a proportion of GDP is a little higher in Scotland than in the UK, 46% as against 45%, the tax burden is less, 41% compared with 45%. Scottish taxpayers bear a lower burden because a significant proportion of Scottish public expenditure constitutes a transfer payment from UK taxpayers.[32] Still, Scotland is not out of line with international averages on either the revenue or expenditure side.[33] The crucial issue is the efficiency of the public sector (see Chapter 8).

CONCLUSIONS

Some parts of Scotland's business community display a real commitment to global success. Major Scottish-headquartered companies such as the Royal Bank of Scotland and HBoS in banking, Scottish Power in energy, the Wood Group and Cairn Energy in oil and the Weir Group in engineering are examples. There are also new business organizations, such as the Entrepreneurial Exchange, which look to promote mutual support among entrepreneurs over government assistance. Such success stories are balanced by concerns about the sector diversity of Scotland's largest

---

[30]The Fresh Talent initiative was launched by the First Minister in 2003 to retain talent in Scotland, attract back Scots from overseas, act as a magnet for relocation within the UK, and attract fresh talent from elsewhere, especially overseas students once they graduate. Specific initiatives include a Relocation Advisory Service, the promotion of work permits to employers and a scheme to allow overseas graduates to remain in the UK for two years while seeking employment.

[31]Research by Florida (2003) offers evidence for the US to contradict this view.

[32]As discussed by Hallwood and MacDonald in Chapter 5, Scotland benefits from fiscal transfers from the rest of the UK through the Barnett Formula. While the fiscal balance has been a subject of significant controversy, Scottish expenditure levels are appreciably higher than those in the English regions, and are not fully met by equivalent Scottish contributions to the Exchequer (Heald 1994).

[33]In terms of international comparisons, Tanzi and Schuknecht (2000) estimate for 1996 for general government expenditure 43% as a % of GDP for UK, compared with an OECD 17-country average of 45.6% and for general government revenues 38% for UK, compared with OECD 17-country average of 43.5%.

27

companies, the slow emergence of major new entrants, and the performance of the so-called 'mid caps', the smaller quoted sector and the overall size of Scotland's corporate base. In essence, recent progress has been piecemeal.

The sharp contraction from 1980 of Scotland's large manufacturing sector caused a major adjustment problem. Despite that the relative catch-up of GDP per head vis-à-vis the UK begun in the early 1960s, continued into the mid 1990s, and followed by a few relatively less impressive years at the end of the century, there are now signs of renewed optimism with business and financial services providing the motor for this growth as they have since 1990. Hence the big-picture Scottish growth per head story is one of relative failure in the 1950s moving to catch up from the 1970s, until the mid 1990s. After 1995, while absolute Scottish growth rose, UK growth increased by considerably more. This led to a temporary slipping back in Scotland's relative GDP per head. However, Scottish employment rates rose relative to the UK in the 1990s to just below the UK level and are higher than in most of Europe. We return to the importance of high employment levels for overall well-being in the concluding chapter (see Frey and Stutzer 2002).

Scotland today is an average European economy achieving average per capita growth, although this has historically been achieved through continued emigration since the 1990s. Scotland's weaknesses should not be exaggerated. The Scottish economy has real areas of strength, including banking, oil and gas, tourism, whisky and speciality foods, bioscience, electronics and retailing. Edinburgh is a significant European financial services centre. Glasgow has arguably become the UK's second best shopping centre after London. Three of the initial public offerings (IPOs) of new Scottish companies anticipated in 2004–05 are in biotechnology, reflecting a regional expertise in this field and raising the question as to whether such companies can continue to grow from a Scottish base. In oil and gas, activity and prospects remain strong with global oil services centred on Aberdeen. The relatively thick labour markets in the financial services have helped grow Scotland's banking capabilities, but elsewhere in the sector continuing consolidation provides challenges that cannot be underestimated.

Scotland also has other inherent advantages. These include extensive administrative capabilities associated with having its own Parliament, civil service, legal system, financial tradition and educational system. While orientated towards the public sector, these capabilities nevertheless both attract and cultivate significant management skills and add to employment and output. Scotland's universities increasingly attract overseas students and have world-class research strengths—capabilities that would be difficult to replicate elsewhere. High-quality higher-education institutions are a key element of environments in which highly skilled people want to live. There has been a relative fall in transportation costs and spread of new communications technologies. These mean Scotland may be less disadvantaged by locational factors than in the past. Scotland also possesses a rightly famous natural environment and a relatively high quality of life, assets which do have an economic value but, as subsequent chapters indicate, these factors are increasingly important in creating an environment in which skilled people wish to live and work. The strength of Scotland's brand identity, its scenery, heritage, sports, music, culture, food and beverages are all important elements in ensuring Scotland is an attractive place to live and work, as well as visit.

However, these areas of Scottish strength do not always seem to have translated into the kind of growth performance that one might have expected. For a few years in the mid 1990s the economy did move to parity with UK GDP per capita but this relative success was not long sustained. Scotland, like other developed nations, should aspire to achieve GDP per capita growth of at least 2%, which is the long-run norm for such nations. Hitherto it has tended to grow at just below 2% per capita. As Adair Turner observed at the final Allander Series lecture, the US in the last decade in particular has outpaced European GDP per capita, a phenomenon explained almost entirely by realizing productivity growth through the successful application of IT. While the structural pattern is bound to be different in Europe, the US performance does emphasize the need to realize productivity gains in all sectors, including the public sector.

Like many other European economies, Scotland does need to improve its performance. The ageing and declining population mean a rising economic burden of pensions and many local services. In this demographic context, slow growth could become self-reinforcing, due to diminishing rates of investment, weak entrepreneurship, and perhaps also a dilution of social and economic dynamism. And like other regional or small national economies in the EU, Scotland is competing for highly mobile labour and capital. Policy choices can skew the economy towards either dynamism or stagnation, either high-skill, high-value activities or to low-skill, low-value ones. The remaining chapters look at how to affect this outcome.

APPENDIX: SCOTTISH GOVERNANCE

A devolved Scottish Parliament within the UK was created in 1999, following a referendum in 1998 in which a majority of Scots voted for its establishment. The division of powers is shown in Table 1.2.

There are 129 Members of the Scottish Parliament (MSPs) elected by the Additional Member System form of proportional representation. There is no second (revising) chamber, unlike Westminster, which has the House of Lords. However, an extensive committee system provides both pre-legislative scrutiny of bills and of the work of the Executive and its officials.

At local government level there is a single-tier structure of 32 local councils responsible for delivering providing major services, such as education, planning, housing, leisure and recreation, parks and libraries, refuse collection and social services. They also have shared responsibilities in partnership with central government and other local bodies for police and fire services and local transport. Local government is financed mainly by grants from central government; although significant revenue also accrues from council tax (a local property tax levied on capital values of each dwelling) and centrally pooled revenues from non-domestic rates, a property tax on business premises.

The European Union's policies have distinctive Scottish dimensions in agriculture, fisheries and in development funds. The Common Agricultural Policy domi-

Table 1.2. Division of powers: devolved powers, devolved to the Scottish Parliament; reserved powers, reserved to the UK Parliament.

Policy powers	
Devolved	Reserved
Education	Social security
Road and transport	Defence
Health	Foreign Affairs
Law courts	Constitutional issues
Police	Immigration
Local government	Ethical issues
Social Work	
Housing	
Forestry	
Joint Responsibility	
Environment	
Energy	
Agriculture and Fisheries	
Culture and sport	

Economic powers	
Devolved	Reserved
Local taxation	Fiscal and monetary policy
Skills and training	EU relations
Inward Investment	International trade and currency
Economic development	Consumer protection
Grant support	
Export promotion	Competition law
Tourism development	Employment law
Planning	Health and safety
Higher education	Industry regulation
Careers development	

nates any UK or Scottish policy and determines most subsidy levels. Development funds for a variety of economic and social development purposes are now declining.

REFERENCES

Ashcroft, B. 1997. Scotland's economic problem: too few entrepreneurs, too little enterprise? Department of Economics, Fraser of Allander Institute, University of Strathclyde.

Ashcroft, B. and J. H. Love. 1993. *Takeovers, mergers and the regional economy*. Edinburgh University Press.

Balls, E., G. O'Donnell and J. Grice (eds). 2004. *Microeconomic reform in Britain*. HM Treasury, Palgrave Macmillan.

Cope, I. and S. Flanagan. 2003. Regional and subregional gross fixed capital formation. Economic Trends, ONS.

Craig, C. 2003. *The Scots' crisis of confidence*, pp. 39 and 40. Big Thinking.

Devine, T. M. (ed.). 1992. *Scottish enterprise and Scottish society*. Edinburgh University Press.

Devine, T. M. 2000. *The Scottish nation 1700–2000*. Penguin.

Florida, R. 2003. *The rise of the creative class*. Basic Books.

Frey, B. and A. Stutzer. 2002. *Economics and happiness*. Princeton University Press.

Graham, E. and P. Boyle. 2003. *Scotland's Population 2002: the Registrar General's Annual Review of Demographic Trends*. General Register Office for Scotland.

Harrison, R. and C. Mason. 2003. The attraction and retention of high skilled labour. Final Report to Scottish Enterprise.

Heald, D. 1994. Territorial public expenditure in the United Kingdom. *Public Administration* 72:147–175.

Herman, A. 2001. *The Scottish enlightenment: the Scots' invention of the modern world*. London: Fourth Estate.

Jones, C. I. 2002. *Introduction to economic growth*. New York: Norton.

Kidd, C. 2002. A nation betrayed. In *Scotland on Sunday: the story of a nation*. Part 1. *Union and enlightenment 1690–1780*.

McLaren, J. 2003. Scotland's real economic performance. *Quarterly Economic Commentary*. Fraser of Allander Institute, University of Strathclyde.

OECD 2003. *The sources of economic growth*. Paris: OECD.

Porter, R. 2000. *The Enlightenment: Britain and the creation of the modern world*. Penguin.

Seawright, D. 2002. The Scottish Conservative and Unionist Party. In *Tomorrow's Scotland* (ed. G. Hassan and C. Warhurst). Lawrence & Wishart.

Solow, R. 1957. Technical change and the aggregate production function. *Review of Economics and Statistics* 39:312–320.

Tanzi, V. and L. Schuknecht. 2000. *Public spending in the twentieth century: a global perspective*. Cambridge University Press.

PART 1
Growth

PART 1
Growth

CHAPTER TWO

Second Winds for Industrial Regions?

By Paul Krugman

I approach the question of growth in Scotland by reviewing the issues facing regions that flourished during the era of heavy industry, and must now reinvent themselves as postmodern economies. As a group, advanced nations are fairly similar today in productivity, real wages and other measures of economic development. There are, however, large divergences in regional growth rates. I will not try to define 'region' precisely, but will simply note that by and large it means a relatively geographically compact area with a population measured in millions rather than tens of millions, and usually with high internal mobility of labour. Some regions are sovereign states, like Ireland. At the opposite extreme are regions that are not only not sovereign, but may have no common government at all, and not much cultural differentiation from the rest of their country, but nonetheless have a distinct economic identity—for example, broadly defined metropolitan areas like greater Boston, which extends across three states and contains almost five million people. In between there are regions such as Scotland with some significant degree of political autonomy and/or cultural distinctiveness.

I will argue that these distinctions do not matter much for the strict economics of regional growth. Where they may matter a lot is in the political economy; regions with a strong government may have a lot more ability to shape their own destiny. In any case, the key question is what do we know about why some regions grow so much more quickly than others? And to what extent can policy help a region do relatively well rather than relatively poorly?

It is important to say that I am not talking about the big questions of development economics—why some countries have vastly higher per capita income than others, why some countries are at the cutting edge of the digital age while others have near-Malthusian economies. The issues at stake here are far smaller. Advanced countries seem to be more or less at the same level of technological development. Regional differences in per capita income within Western Europe or North America are fairly modest, and are driven in large part by differences in employment–population ratios and average working hours rather than large differences in output per man-hour. I am addressing a smaller, less profound question: why is employment growth so much greater in some regions than in others? Another way to say this is that Bertil Ohlin was wrong. In his classic book, Ohlin (1933) insisted that international and interregional economics were more or less the same subject. At a deep level, of course, that is true. But an attempt to explain why South Korea has grown so much faster than the Philippines will look quite different from an attempt to explain why metropolitan Atlanta has grown so much faster than metropolitan St. Louis—and almost, though not quite, as different from an attempt to explain why Ireland has grown so much faster than Scotland. For it turns out that the latter question is best viewed as largely, though not entirely, one of regional economics.

INTERREGIONAL OR INTERNATIONAL ECONOMICS?

The standard models of both international trade and economic growth presume an economy that must rely on its own resources—its own working-age population, educated and trained *in situ*, capital accumulated through its own saving, and so on. In other words, the standard models assume no inward or outward movements of the factors of production, labour and capital. This assumption has two main consequences. Firstly, in the absence of factor movements, differences in growth rates can arise from differences in savings rates, differences in fertility or differences in rates of technical progress—and that's about it. (Rates of labour force participation can also change.) In practice, the story told by such models tends to be dominated by differences in technical progress, as measured by total factor productivity (TFP), or in other words the level of output produced with all the given inputs. Despite almost 20 years of endogenous growth theory, we still do not have a very good handle on what causes TFP to grow so much more rapidly in some countries than in others. Secondly, in the absence of factor movements in standard models, it makes almost no sense to talk about national 'competitiveness'. The ability of a country to export a particular good reflects comparative advantage, not absolute advantage, and each country has a comparative advantage in some goods, a comparative disadvantage in others, no matter how efficient or inefficient it may be on average.

The assumption of zero factor mobility is reasonable for big economies, like the US or the EU as a whole—yes, there is significant capital mobility between them, but it rarely accounts for more than a fifth of investment, and labour mobility is very low. It is even a pretty good approximation for medium-sized economies like the UK, mainly because international labour mobility is for the most part small among EU countries, despite the Single European Act—presumably reflecting cultural and linguistic barriers.

At a regional level, however, the story changes dramatically. It is reasonable to assume that capital mobility within the United States is near perfect—that is, there is probably near-equalization of risk-adjusted rates of return across states and metropolitan areas. Fragmentary evidence suggests that fast-growing US states may have current account deficits of 15 or more per cent of gross state product—in other words, they may well be financing half or more of their gross investment with inflows of funds from other regions, while slow-growing states export much of their saving. Meanwhile, a line of empirical work dating from a classic paper by Blanchard and Katz (1992) suggests that labour mobility among US states is also near-perfect, once a few years of adjustment have taken place. Sustained shocks to state-level employment are offset by inflows or outflows of labour, with no sustained effect on either relative unemployment or relative wages.

To what extent is this true of European regions? Capital mobility between these regions is probably very high. Labour mobility is more questionable, although higher between UK regions than between regions of some other European economies (see Atkeson and Bayoumi 1993). Partly because of public housing and income support programmes, and partly because of cultural and linguistic differences, Europeans are less mobile than Americans. Indeed, most European countries show large, persistent intra-national differences in unemployment rates that are not visible in US data. (Italy and post-unification Germany are the most dramatic examples, but even the UK data show much more in the way of persistent regional unemployment gaps than the US.)

Yet labour mobility is still significant, and is a key factor in allowing very large growth differentials. A case in point—applying to a small country that is in effect (and also in terms of the formal definition by the EU) a region—is recent Irish growth. The 'Celtic Tiger' grew at a remarkable annual pace of 7.7% between 1990 and 2001, five percentage points faster than the UK. This did in part reflect more rapidly rising real GDP per worker. But about two-thirds of the growth difference between Ireland and the UK reflected employment growth: employment in Ireland grew at a 3.7% annual rate over that period, compared with only 0.5% in the UK. The very high rate of Irish employment growth was possible because of the country's shift from its historic role as a supplier of émigré labour to other countries to a new role as destination for immigrant labour. In this sense Ireland was more like a fast-growth region within an advanced country—like a rapidly growing sunbelt state in the United States—than like the second-fastest growing OECD economy, South Korea, which had only slightly above-average employment growth.

Success for a regional economy, then, would mean providing sufficiently attractive wages and/or employment prospects and return on capital to draw in labour and capital from other regions. It makes sense to talk about 'competitiveness' for regions in a way one would not talk about it for larger units. Scotland, of course, is a region for these purposes. Scotland has high labour mobility with the rest of the UK, and is part of Europe, which at least in principle is becoming a unified labour market. So it is helpful to think about Scotland differently from the way you might think about the United States as a whole, or the European Union. In other words, it is sensible to talk about the *competitiveness* of Scotland's economy.

This is not just a linguistic distinction: it makes interregional growth rates much more sensitive than international growth rates to differences in efficiency. Consider two countries, one of which is for some reason 15% more efficient than the other—that is, total factor productivity (TFP) is 15% higher. In the absence of factor mobility, this difference would translate directly into a 15% difference in per capita income, and would then have some secondary effects via capital accumulation. But that would be the end of the story.

If we are considering two regions, however, that large a difference in TFP would lead to sustained movements of capital and labour out of the less productive region and into the more productive region, probably leading to very large differences in growth rates over a long period. A 15% difference in regional productivity can mean the difference between a region that is rapidly gaining jobs, gaining population and one that is steadily losing them. Regional growth is much more sensitive to differences in productivity performance. The converse is that for regional economies in a well-integrated larger economy these differences do not necessarily translate into large differences in per capita income.

So the stakes are higher when factor mobility is high. The potential role for policy is also considerably enlarged. When factor mobility is low, the difference between policies that raise TFP by a few per cent and policies that lower it by a few per cent is, guess what, a few per cent. When factor mobility is high, such policy differences can be make or break for regional development.

Do such growth differences matter? Suppose we are talking about two different destinies for a regional economy, a somewhat rainy northern portion of the United Kingdom, either 20 years in which the working-age population declines at 0.1% or 0.2% a year, and 20 years in which it rises at 0.5% or 1% a year. What difference does it make, since it is probably true that in either case per capita income would be not very far from the UK average? Moreover, Anthony Venables of the London School of Economics and Patricia Rice of the University of Southampton make, among other points, a reasonable case that the regional differences in per capita income in the UK correspond to much smaller and possibly near-zero differences in utility, that is, in the actual standard of living (Venables and Rice 2003). This is because the price of houses and other amenities are higher in high per capita income regions. Thus we are not really talking about huge differences in standards of living, certainly between Scotland and the UK average. So why should we be worrying about it?

One reason is that equilibrium never quite happens; that, although there is a tendency for things to level out, it does matter whether you are rising or falling. In a region with growing employment and a growing economy, things are going to feel better, job opportunities at the margin are going to be better. It is simply a happier place. I can attest to that, having lived in New England most of my adult life, during periods when it was relatively declining and during periods when it was relatively rising. Although at no point was it ever poor and at no point was it ever particularly rich, by US standards, it felt a whole lot better between 1980 and 1987 when the economy was growing than it did between 1987 and 1993. There is a very large difference in sentiment and in the opportunities offered, especially to young people. The other reason is that it does matter how much employment there is in a particular region for the provision of social services for those who are not working. They tend to be the least mobile, particularly the elderly and it is helpful to have a large vibrant working-age population around them.

Sources of Advantage: Fundamentals or External Economies?

Given that modest differences in total factor productivity can have large growth consequences at the regional level, what accounts for such differences? A broad division would be between 'fundamentals'—differences rooted in a region's characteristics—and 'external economies' that are themselves a consequence of a region's pattern of economic development. Examples of fundamentals would be a well-educated local population, the result of a strong tradition of good schooling; a local culture of entrepreneurship; natural advantages of climate or resources; and sustained public policy differences such as differences in tax rates and quality of infrastructure. These can clearly be sources of regional advantages or disadvantages. They can also play a catalytic role in promoting virtuous circles based on external economies.

External economies are the spillovers that result from regional concentrations of industry, and explain the snowball effect of a virtuous circle of growth. Such external economies have been the main subject of the *new economic geography* which attracted the attention of international trade theorists in the 1990s. A central theme of economic geography, both new and traditional, is the way these external economies drive the evolution of regional economies. An industry or cluster of industries generates spillovers which reinforce that industry's local advantage, or in some case spillovers to other industries which are thereby encouraged to locate in a particular region.

A key point about external economies is that they give a large role to history. On one side, accidents can have lasting consequences, so that, to take the most famous example, the vision of Stanford's dean of engineering played a decisive role in creating Silicon Valley. On the other side, historical industrial patterns can, in unpredictable ways, provide a favourable environment for new industries to grow and then establish self-reinforcing external economies; thus the New England textile machinery industry created a base of skills that proved crucial for the high-tech industries of the 1980s.

The traditional analysis of external economies stresses Alfred Marshall's trinity of local externalities. First is the ability of a large local concentration to support specialized suppliers of intermediate inputs, both goods and services. Second is the presence of a 'thick' labour market in specialized skills, with skilled workers benefiting from the job security provided by a variety of potential employers who in turn benefit from the flexibility of a deep pool of potential employees. Third is the existence of pure knowledge spillovers resulting from personal contact among people working on closely related projects. To these we might add a fourth, which is in the same tradition. Although it is hard to judge its importance, anecdotal evidence suggests that venture capital has become an important determinant of regional industrial success. This capital depends on the existence of pools both of locally knowledgeable investors and of potential entrepreneurs, both with sufficient technological knowledge—so it is related both to the thick market and knowledge spillover stories.

Market access also becomes very important in this context. The question of what kind of access you have to markets, what is the size of your own market, conditions the possibilities of self-reinforcing growth in which being a large market in itself attracts businesses, and attracts jobs which lead to that market in turn growing in size. In addition, there is the issue of peripherality, which is important in Scotland.

The role of history in external economies means existing geographies of economic activity create a pattern of externalities and factor prices which dictate where new industries locate, generating over time new geographies that form the baseline for further change. Thus New England's textile industry, exploiting the readily available water power of the region, provided the basis for a continuing industry even after most mills were powered by steam. This industry provided a market for a textile machinery production, service and repair industry; the technical skills of this industry provided the basis for the minicomputer industry that powered a revival in New England after textile production had moved to lower-wage regions. And though minicomputers lost much of their market with the rise of the personal computer, experience with timesharing technology allowed New England to get another boost when networked computing became crucial. External economies are probably a secondary issue for the growth of large national economies, but for regional economies they can be decisive one way or the other.

However, it is not just past successes that pave the way for future industries. Past failures, too, sometimes seem to be the source of success.

HISTORY AND LEAPFROGGING

General observation suggests that there is a distinctive pattern within advanced countries in which the last becomes first. That is, some of the biggest recent success stories have come in regions that were relatively unindustrialized 50 years ago. These are regions that did not share much in the heavy industries, largely coal-based, which formerly dominated European and North American manufacturing, but have now become major centres of newer leading industrial sectors.

A few obvious examples would include the following: the rise of manufacturing in the southeastern United States, even as it declined in the northeast and the Midwest; the regional reversal in Belgium, with the Flemish-speaking areas leapfrogging the French-speaking zone; the relative decline in the UK's industrial north, and the rise of the southeast; the relative rise of Bavaria and decline of the Ruhr. Ireland can be cast as a similar story, with formerly backward Eire turned into a tiger while industrial Northern Ireland languishes.

To the extent that this is a real pattern, why might it be happening? More than a decade ago Elise Brezis and I suggested a simple, maybe simplistic model (Brezis and Krugman 1991). Suppose that one region has, for whatever reasons, got a head start on a particular suite of industries which yield mutually reinforcing external economies. Then as long as those industries remain dominant, this region will be the industrial 'core'. Suppose also that not all factors are mobile. Then immobile factors, perhaps including labour, will be paid higher returns in the core than in the 'periphery'. This may be a stable situation for a long time.

But now suppose that there is fundamental technological change, which obviates the old external economies—electric power replaces coal-fired steam engines in the basement, road transport replaces railroads, or whatever. The important point would be that the old advantages of locating in an established industrial centre would cease to exist, or at least be reduced in importance. And the lower factor prices elsewhere would encourage industries based on new technologies to locate away from the old industrial centres. Then, once established, these new industries would create their own self-reinforcing external economies. The result would be that the former industrial centre becomes a rust belt, a declining region, while areas formerly less industrialized take a leading role. It is a very stylized story, but it makes sense as an account of why the very places that were the engines of western economies circa 1920 or even 1950 are now, in many cases, depressed, while formerly relatively backward areas thrive. I am, of course, suggesting it as a story that applies to industrial Scotland.

The late Mancur Olson (1965) would have suggested an institutional side to the story as well. Leading industrial areas develop institutions—corporate structures, unions, work rules, and so on—which can become a hindrance to their transformation when technologies and markets change. A formerly underdeveloped region, starting with a clean slate, may be better placed to take advantage of new opportunities.

Prospects for Second Winds

Given this story of decline in formerly successful industrial regions, what are the prospects for a revival? This chapter is entitled 'Second Winds for Industrial Regions'. But it could be argued that, in a way, Scotland has already had a second wind. As Chapter 1 explained, we are really talking about a third wind, which might be a little more durable than the second. The story is familiar. A great manufacturing centre declined with the shift away from heavy industry in the advanced countries in general. A considerable revival followed based upon incoming lighter industries, especially electronics, largely benefiting from UK regional policy. But these have proved to be less of a source of sustained growth than one might have hoped.

William Baumol, in the next chapter, argues against excessive pessimism, which is certainly right. Scottish growth overall has been a little slower over the long term than the UK average. GDP per capita has been in line with the UK average, sometimes a little bit below, but never seriously so. There is really nothing that would lead you to say this is an *unsuccessful* economy. Scotland has never been as poor a relative to the UK average as parts of the southern United States have been relative to the US average. It has never underperformed as badly as the US Rust Belt during its bad years. So it is not a disastrous performance by any means. It is, however, a little bit disappointing and the example that springs to mind by comparison is of course the Irish boom, which started in the late 1980s and continued until recently. How much does Ireland suggest a path that Scotland could or should follow?

The Irish example is certainly very heartening. John Bradley looks at it in detail in Chapter 9. But on closer inspection, the more you look at the current Scottish background, the less Ireland seems like an example which offers very strong lessons. The parallels are not particularly strong in terms of starting points and potential. For the Irish, the starting position was one of a low-cost, low-wage environment, although not, of course, at third-world levels. That created an opportunity to launch a take-off. In some sense, Ireland did not get its first wind until 1987 or so. The Irish expansion was in very large part based on a very rapid growth in employment in a way that is probably not replicable in Scotland, which does not have the same problems that Ireland had 20 years ago. Ireland had high unemployment so could simply pull people out of the pool of unemployed. It had low female labour force participation, too, another source of potential rapid employment growth. It also had a large émigré diaspora, some of whom were drawn back to their country of origin.

So, in the case of Ireland, it turns out that while there was growth in GDP per worker above the OECD average, the bulk of the difference between Irish and average OECD performance is actually faster Irish employment growth. Even the total GDP growth gap is a little bit less compelling than it seems to be. Ireland is one of the few places where the difference between GDP and GNP is significant. GNP can be lower than GDP if capital income is repatriated overseas, and in Ireland there was a lot of external investment and some interesting issues involving transfer pricing. It therefore had productivity growth which was enviable by OECD standards, but was not enormous.

Ireland's was therefore less of a miracle and more of an understandable boom. Reasonable, sustainable booms are of course welcome, but again, because Scotland is not in as weak a situation as Ireland was in the 1980s, it cannot expect 15 comparably good years. However, what we did see at play in Ireland was the external economies that matter so much in economic geography. There were self-reinforcing clusters of industries and that is what Scotland can hope to replicate. There was also, at least to some extent, policy-driven success due to investment in infrastructure, especially telecommunications, a good educational system, and the use of tax incentives to attract business, and these too offer lessons for Scotland.

So, if one looks at Scotland in the mirror of Ireland, Scotland does not start from a particularly low-wage situation or from seriously high unemployment. It has neither the ability to attract business on the basis of low wages nor the reserve army of the unemployed to be drawn into work. That is all to the good. But it does mean that Scotland cannot expect a similar growth take-off. There is a Scottish diaspora, and if Scotland were doing very well, it would draw people back. But overall it seems unlikely we would see the kind of 3% or 4% annual employment gains experienced during the Irish boom. This is not a problem, as long as one does not set a standard of achieving Irish growth rates over an extended period. Such hopes would be disappointed, because Ireland was a very special case.

Let me nevertheless offer some hopeful thoughts for second, or third, winds in old regions, for one can certainly hope that Scotland can do better than it has. The first point is that factor prices in old industrial regions can quite quickly become an advantage, rather than a disadvantage. The clearest example is housing prices, which are often low in old industrial heartlands, and thereby make them attractive locations for firms that do not need to exploit localized external economies. This then gives an opportunity to rebuild an economic base, and possibly to get a new cycle of self-sustaining growth going. Scotland should consider its potential price advantages carefully.

The second point is that even when old industries no longer generate important spillovers, the physical legacy of previous industrial centrality can often be valuable. This includes infrastructure, such as fixed-rail transit systems, which are very expensive to create in new centres but already exist in old ones. (This is a partial explanation of the remarkable fact that in the US, traffic congestion is actually considerably worse in places like Los Angeles and even Atlanta and Houston than it is in the old urban centres of the northeast and Midwest.) Again, there is scope for reflection on the legacy of infrastructure in Scotland, and how it might best be leveraged in the future.

Even the seemingly trivial, like the architectural heritage of an established centre, can become an asset. Certainly, a remarkable number of old urban centres on both sides of the Atlantic have managed to turn old city centres and their buildings into significant sources of cultural promotion, tourism, and so on. Several of these issues are discussed in Edward Glaeser's chapter in this book and by Glaeser et al. (2000).

One might also speculate that the character of technical change in recent decades—very high rates of progress in a relatively narrow range of industries—is more likely than technology in the past to bypass existing advantages, due to the importance of external economies. Will Silicon Valley's reign in information technology last as long as Manchester's in textiles? It seems unlikely.

So, the moral here is that leapfrogged regions have a pretty good chance of getting a second or third wind, winning new industries in a competition with regions that have displaced them. The goal of regional development policy should be to enhance that second chance.

The Role of Policy

The reason policy can matter so much is the combination of factor mobility, which magnifies the effect of small differences in efficiency, and external economies, which allow a small push in the right direction at the right time to have lasting effects on efficiency. If the initiative of a Stanford dean or the accident of Bill Gates's place of birth can make or break economies not much smaller than Scotland's, what might a clever policy of sectoral promotion backed by the resources of a semi-autonomous government not achieve?

On the other hand, Stanford's engineering faculty did not realize how important it was to stake a few graduates in the semiconductor industry; it is only in retrospect that the significance of those actions became apparent. And sometimes it is not clear even in retrospect what did the trick. Ireland's economic miracle has been extensively studied, yet there is as far as I know no consensus on which particular pieces of policy—tax holidays? investment in telecommunications? general education?—were crucial. (Or was it just about being English speaking and having somewhat lower wages than the UK?)

At least one major axis of debate in Scotland involves the fiscal question (covered in more detail in the chapter by Paul Hallwood and Ronald MacDonald below). To what extent could greater fiscal autonomy permit better management of the Scottish economy? There are three dimensions. One is to use taxation as a way to attract business. The second is the possibility of being able to retain tax revenues as opposed to sending them on to London and then getting them back again, and the third is a shorter-term issue, which is the management of the business cycle: in the face of a recession, would you be able to do something about it with your own fiscal policy? So let me consider these three issues.

First is the use of tax incentives as a major tool of development. The Irish certainly did do so and others have tried and are trying to do it. But, in my view, the Irish experience was a one-off event, which is not going to be feasible or desirable as a major tool of development in the future, for a couple of reasons.

First, it seems unlikely the EU will stand for it. Ireland doing this in the 1980s was one thing, but today it is not likely that a reasonably well-off region in the EU would be permitted to try a beggar-thy-neighbour policy on corporate taxes, particularly in the face of competition from new member states. It is unlikely to be acceptable longer term.

Secondly, while costs always matter, a bid to be a low-cost region within Europe is probably a less viable strategy in general nowadays than it would have been a couple of decades ago, simply because of globalization. If low cost is what you are looking for as a business, highly cost-sensitive decisions are always going to lead you to Bangalore or Shanghai. That margin has largely disappeared within the advanced world. Looking at the US position, surveys of businesses show actual business decisions do not in practice respond a lot to differences in state tax rates—and there are wide differences in state tax policies. In practice, when it comes to location decisions, the tax issue tends to be much less important than concerns about the availability of an educated labour force, quality of life and infrastructure. In practice, businesses do not go racing off to Alabama, which has very low tax rates on business, because Alabama ranks 49th in terms of educational attainment in the United States, and that is more important for someone considering relocating a business there than the fact that business taxation is almost non-existent. If you were to look back at the US in the 1950s, you would have discovered that low tax, low wage was a big attraction, with businesses moving south from the old industrial heartland but that is no longer true. If low tax, low wage is what you want now, you will go to South East Asia. So, while it does not make sense to ignore complaints from businesses if they say they want lower taxes, equally you should not think of tax policy as a prime development tool.

On the second issue, concerning the ability to retain local tax revenues, it might be helpful to provide a US perspective. The US has a very strong geographic political division between red states and blue states. By tradition the electoral map colours states that went Republican red and those that went Democratic blue. And the red states tend to be in the middle of the country and the blue states along the coast. The red states tend to be relatively rural, low population density and the blue states tend to be more urban and denser. The red states have a very strong ideology of self-reliance and paying your own way, while the blue states are all for social insurance. And the blue states subsidize the red states enormously. So, New Jersey receives about a dollar in federal spending for every dollar and a half that it pays into Washington and Montana receives about $1.75 of federal spending for every dollar that it pays in, which is a heavy subsidy. It would turn out that the mountain states are in fact receiving net subsidies of between 5% and 10% of GDP from the Federal government.

Scotland is receiving red state levels of net subsidy from London. There will eventually be a tendency for spending to converge within the UK, but it is meanwhile worth pointing out the current direction of the net flow of resources. To be fair, it is true that sparse population does tend to lead in various ways to increased national spending demands, and so to some extent existing flows reflect the effect of geography. But this compensation for sparse population is not automatic.

The third point with respect to the fiscal question is about cyclical management. Clearly, if the region were at a different phase of the business cycle than the nation as a whole, then one would like the means to provide some fiscal boost when needed. Does fiscal autonomy permit that? The lesson from both the United States and at the national level within Europe is that it does not work. You might think that having your own budget would allow you to have your own fiscal policy and would therefore allow you to cope better with the economic cycle. In the United States about 40% of total spending is raised and spent locally through state and local taxation. It still turns out that, far from being able to use their budgets as business cycle stabilizers, local governments in fact end up being seriously pro-cyclical in their fiscal policy. In the recent downturn they have been laying off school teachers and fire fighters and raising taxes even in the face of serious unemployment problems. And the reason is that almost all of the states have in their constitutions the requirement that they balance their budgets on an annual basis.

One response is to ask why should it not be possible to borrow. But the answer is that, because the future growth of a state-level or regional economy is so uncertain due to the effect of labour mobility, investors do not know the long-term outcome, or at least much less so than at the national level. One cannot be sure that a downturn in a state economy is going to be reversed. (For econometricians, there is a unit root in output at the state level.) For example, Massachusetts had a very severe downturn in the late 1980s. The unemployment rate doubled to twice the national level. Five years later the unemployment rate had returned to the national level but there had been no gain in employment in that intervening period. The change in the rate was all due to the outward migration of labour. So a fall in output may never be reversed, which means that a prudent lender would not lend money to a state that tried to run large budget deficits in the face of a downturn. At a national level, however, downturns do get reversed. In practice, the best stabilizer against a regional downturn is to have a federalized budget, so that social insurance benefits come from the centre when payments to the centre fall. Fiscal autonomy is not helpful in responding to the business cycle.

How best can an autonomous region stimulate a second, or third, wind, in that case? There is nevertheless a lot to be said for public investment, tangible and intangible, in projects that are likely to enhance a region's attractiveness. It is hard to avoid platitudes here—but sometimes platitudes are the truth. A well-educated population is a good thing; so are leading institutions of higher education that can be nuclei for development. Good infrastructure for transportation and communication is important; and infrastructure projects can make a difference in terms of the ability to have a growing local economy. Everything we know suggests that high-quality public services are definitely important: employment creation is promoted by having good local transport, well-maintained roads, good basic education, and that the garbage gets picked up; and so on.

Most, though not all, of the success stories in the United States revolve around higher education, not basic education. Higher education seems to play a crucial role. Silicon Valley was centred upon Stanford University. It now probably doesn't need Stanford any more, though clearly the university played a crucial role. Most of my adult life was spent in the Boston area, which has a similar population to that of Scotland, and the complex of educational institutions there has clearly been at the heart of the local economy. If we look at the export sectors for New England for the past 20 years, they have shifted. It is actually a little hard to pin down now exactly what the shift is, but it clearly involves high technology of various kinds. Medical care is a major export industry, at least to other parts of the United States. Earnings come from people seeking high-end medical care in the Boston area and that, in turn, is closely related to the higher-education complex. And higher education itself turns out to be a surprisingly large generator of 'foreign exchange'—that is, dollars from the rest of the United States. The research triangle in North Carolina is another example of the creation of a high-tech complex in a previously unexpected area, which also relies a lot on higher education. So, given the historic strengths of Scottish higher education, it is certainly something to build on. The subsequent chapters by William Baumol and James Heckman both touch on different aspects of this issue.

What about the active promotion of clusters by government? This is worth pursuing, as long as one does not have exaggerated expectations. Michael Porter (1985) and others have persuasively argued that it is possible to identify some of the external economies that are central to how a complex local economy succeeds and sustains itself; and hence government intervention on a modest scale on behalf of those linkages can be useful. As long as one is talking about tens of pounds per capita, not hundreds of pounds per capita, it is worth developing as a regional strategy.

I have already mentioned the physical legacy of previous industrial strength as a stimulus to a second wind. In the US some older industrial centres have flourished to a surprising degree in recent years because they still have some of the advantages of the established centre with none of the external diseconomies of some of the really big centres. To take one example, we are seeing a surprising resurgence in Philadelphia. The city is a classic steel, shipbuilding, coal-based centre, which went a long way downhill and is now coming back because it is a pretty big city with great cultural attributes and some very good housing for people who want to live in an old-fashioned style. But above all it is not New York and therefore a lot easier to live in. High-quality amenities of the kind offered by cities such as Philadelphia or Boston appeal to people, and that is certainly one reason for hope in regional economies whose one-time glory is a bit faded, but may have an opportunity to be restored. This again highlights the importance of the quality of the local infrastructure.

Finally, there are some important generic lessons for old regions keen to stimulate renewed success. First, in terms of spending priorities, for any government there is always the issue of how much to spend in providing directly things that people want or need, and how much to spend on trying to promote future growth. This is sometimes put as current versus capital expenditures. It is important not to go to extremes here. The provision of services for the people is ultimately the purpose of government and so one should avoid drastic steps that are based on, say, forgetting health care for the indigent in order to focus on business. But it is equally important to keep the priorities clear, bearing in mind the region's long-term development needs, particularly when one has to make hard choices. For example, in the current state fiscal crisis in the US, many states are in the process of making decisions between medical care and road maintenance. The answer is that you cannot completely neglect road maintenance on behalf of medical care for the poor. Unfortunately, both have to share the cuts.

Turning to the issue of business incentives and attempts to promote business development, it is always important to take the views of business into account. Of course, businesses talking about what they need are not exactly objective sources of advice. So their views might need to be discounted, although never ignored. In the US there has been a definite problem of state development agencies getting bullied into subsidies, tax breaks and dedicated infrastructure for particular headline-making firms to keep them in the region. This leads to a kind of zero-sum competition among the states, which costs them revenue without actually adding net jobs anywhere. Regions should avoid getting into this sort of trap. By all means, be prepared to spend a little bit of money to help promote industrial clusters, but try to avoid, for example, the multi-billion dollar deal to keep Boeing from moving out of Seattle. I am suspicious of deliberate attempts to foster particular industries, let alone subsidies to particular firms. The reason is that external economies are difficult to identify even after the fact, and harder still to predict. Selective policies are all too often shaped by wishful thinking at best, undue influence at worst. This is why making policy recommendations can be agonizing, and policy makers must be aware of these challenges.

Still, there is good reason to think that policy can make a very big difference to regional development even though at the same time it is very hard to know exactly what the right policy is. So, the challenges for Scotland and other regions of Europe are real, but there is international evidence that regions can find a second or third wind by understanding their factor price advantages, by examining their historic legacy, by judicious public spending, and by an appreciation of the role of an educated labour force, of quality of life and of infrastructure in influencing future prosperity.

REFERENCES

Atkeson, A. and T. Bayoumi. 1993. Do private capital markets insure regional risk? Evidence from the United States and Europe. *Open Economies Review* 4:303–324.

Blanchard, O. and L. Katz. 1992. Regional evolutions. Brookings Papers on Economic Activity, pp. 1–75.

Brezis, E. and P. Krugman. 1991. Leapfrogging: a theory of cycles in national technological leadership. NBER Working Paper 3886.

Glaeser, E., J. Kolko and A. Saiz. 2000. Consumer city. NBER Working Paper 7790.

Ohlin, B. 1933. *International and interregional trade*, revised edition, 1957. Harvard University Press.

Olson, M. 1965. *The logic of collective action*. Harvard University Press.

Porter, M. 1985. *Competitive advantage: creating and sustaining superior performance*. New York: Free Press.

Venables, A. and P. Rice. 2003. Equilibrium regional disparities: theory and British evidence. *Regional Studies* 37:675–686.

Four Sources of Innovation and the Stimulation of Growth in the Scottish Economy

By William J. Baumol[1]

GROWTH AND INNOVATION POLICY

The recent enhancement of Scotland's policy autonomy, together with its reportedly lacklustre performance in innovation and growth, invite re-examination of the country's options and opportunities. In what follows, whenever I venture to offer any statement about the Scottish economy, it must be recognized as derivative from the very illuminating materials that have been provided to me.[2]

The key observations I will offer in this chapter stem from the all-too-obvious conclusion that a reliable stream of innovation is the most important requirement of the remarkable long-run economic growth that has been experienced by the industrialized economies in the past two centuries. The Scots should need little to persuade them of the validity of this contention, they having provided an impressive share of the revolutionary innovations that were crucial for this historically unprecedented growth. Yet only in the last 10 years or so have entrepreneurship and innovation begun to receive a great deal of attention.

Recent study of the free-market growth mechanism emphasizes the rivalry among oligopolistic firms (i.e. large firms in markets dominated by a small number of sellers) and has given less attention to the contribution of the public sector. Yet the government plays two critical roles, one active and the other passive. The passive contribution is provided primarily through the legal infrastructure that encourages entrepreneurship, the formation of new firms and investment in the innovation process by larger competing enterprises. That entails well-recognized provisions such as property rights and enforceability of contracts. It also entails the absence of government interference in the exchange of technical information and access to patented intellectual property, as well as avoidance of rules on employment and rental that inhibit the formation of new firms. On the active side, government support of basic

[1]As always, I must express my gratitude to my colleague, Sue Anne Batey Blackman, for her editing and contribution of sense to this chapter.

[2]I am particularly indebted to Brian Ashcroft, who, in addition to supplying the data that I requested, also sent me his very illuminating articles on the subject. But I owe even more to Diane Coyle, who edited, abbreviated and added to this chapter, masterfully, and whose unexceptional encouragement and cooperation made preparation of this piece pleasurable and easy. Much of the discussion in this chapter is based on my recent book (Baumol 2002).

research has proved to be invaluable: with its uncertainties and unpredictable beneficiaries, such research is not highly attractive to private enterprise, though it can be
critical for innovation and growth in the long run. Important innovations continue to
flow from two groups outside the market sector: the government and the universities.

In this chapter, I will also discuss the difference in, but complementary relationship between, the characteristic innovative contributions of large and small firms,
pointing out that these two groups have tended to specialize in different components
of society's innovation process. The major breakthroughs have tended to come from
small new enterprises, while the invaluable incremental contributions that multi-
ply capacity and speed, and increase reliability and user-friendliness, have been the
domain of the larger firms. Together, the two have contributed far more than either
would have by itself.

I will point out some of the truly astonishing contributions that have come from
each of the four sectors: large firms, small enterprises, government and universities.
The implication is that to ensure that the pertinent arrangements and institutions are
really effective in the promotion of economic growth, each must be provided with
the appropriate incentives to undertake its role in the process. For Scotland, as for
any other modern economy concerned with this issue, understanding of the roles of
the four key sectors and of the requisites for their effectiveness constitutes a road
map for public sector growth policy. For Scotland, a crucial first step in designing
such a policy will be to determine, examining each of the four contributory sources,
whether these requisites are indeed met and whether significant improvements are
possible. I will offer some observations on these matters in the conclusion.

INDICATORS OF THE MAGNITUDE OF THE FREE-ENTERPRISE GROWTH MIRACLE

The improvement in the growth performance of the industrial economies is so enormous that it is difficult to comprehend. Average growth rates for about one and a
half millennia before the Industrial Revolution are estimated to have been approximately zero, and while there was undoubtedly some growth starting around the tenth
century, it proceeded at a snail's pace by modern standards. But in the eighteenth
century, with the advent of capitalism in Great Britain, GDP per capita is estimated
to have grown some 20–30%. In the nineteenth century, this figure rose perhaps ten-
fold, to some 200%. In the twentieth century, growth in the US has conservatively
been estimated at about 700%, with some qualified observers arguing that this is a
substantial *underestimate*. Elsewhere, the twentieth-century growth rate was even
more spectacular. The British record is described in Figure 3.1, which reports Angus
Maddison's (2001) estimates of per capita income since the sixteenth century. The
negligible rate of increase during the first three centuries is evident. The explosive
growth path since that time is equally striking. Early in the rising trajectory, Marx and
Engels (1848) made their cogent observations: 'The Bourgeoisie [i.e. capitalism]
cannot exist without constantly revolutionizing the instruments of production....
Conservation of the old modes of production in unaltered form was, on the contrary,
the first condition of existence for all earlier industrial classes.... The Bourgeoisie,
during its rule of scarce one hundred years has created more massive and more

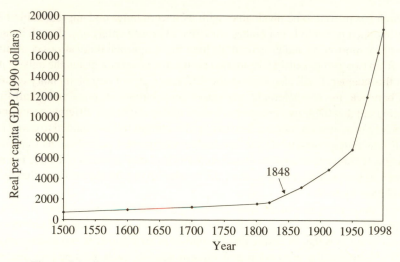

Figure 3.1. Real per capita GDP in the United Kingdom, 1500–1998.
Source: Maddison (2001).

colossal productive forces than have all preceding generations together.' (Published in 1848, marked on the chart.) Since then the pace of innovation has grown into a flood. The arrival of new products and processes has become commonplace.

Outlays on research and invention, like GDP per capita, have also been exploding. In real private (business) expenditures on research and development activity in the US for nearly half a century after World War II, there is again a near-exponential growth path. It is also worth saying how small was the effect of the recessions of the postwar period in holding back the growth in real expenditures on the invention process. The intervals of decline in R&D outlays are merely small deviations from what appears to be an inexorable rising path.

MARKET PRESSURES FOR AN ENHANCED LARGE-FIRM ROLE IN TECHNICAL PROGRESS

Free competition, that is, competition not handicapped by severe government regulations or tightly enforced customary rules, has arguably played a critical role in the growth of the capitalist economies. Of particular significance is rivalry among large firms in industries with a relatively small number of enterprises. And crucial here is the fact that many of these rival *oligopolistic* firms use innovation as the main weapon with which they protect themselves from competitors and with which they seek to beat those competitors. The result is precisely analogous to an arms race, to the case of two countries, each of which fears that the other will attack and therefore feels it necessary at least to match the other country's military spending. Similarly, either of two competing firms will feel it to be foolhardy to let its competitor outspend it on the development and acquisition of *its* battle weapons. Naturally, a constant stream of innovations can be expected to appear, because these giant warring firms dare not relax their innovation activities.

The entrepreneur is naturally associated with the small, start-up firm; indeed, widespread usage simply *defines* entrepreneurs as the creators of new enterprises. For the reasons just indicated, the apportionment of the resources invested in innovation has been changing materially. Increasingly, at least in the United States, the funding for innovation has been supplied by large enterprises with a small number of large rivals, hardly the sort of firms that one associates with the entrepreneur. Today some 70% of R&D expenditure in the US is carried out by private business, and most of it is spent by the larger firms (National Science Board 2002). In these enterprises, innovative activities are carefully designed to keep risks to a minimum. As a result, there is little of the free-wheeling, imaginative, risk-taking approach that characterizes the entrepreneur. Instead, the large firm's top management often keeps a tight rein on the activities of the company's laboratories, with budgets determined by the upper managers, who may also determine how many persons and what sort of specialists at what levels will be employed on R&D endeavours. It is not unusual for persons untrained or inexperienced in research to determine what new products and processes the laboratories should next seek to discover. Sometimes large firms try to unleash their employees by organizing a subsidiary operation that is more inviting to the free exercise of entrepreneurship, but often without much success.

It is natural for a bureaucratically governed enterprise to run research and development in accord with rules and procedures. All of this leads to the conjecture, voiced by Joseph Schumpeter (the twentieth-century's prime contributor to the economic analysis of entrepreneurship and innovation), that the work responsibilities the economy assigns to the entrepreneur are narrowing and are destined to shrink even further. One can easily surmise what prompted Schumpeter to foresee a limited future for the entrepreneur if industry and its innovation processes are widely characterized in the manner just described. Yet I will argue next that this is fundamentally a mischaracterization. Rather than being condemned to obsolescence, a vital role remains for independent entrepreneurs.

REVOLUTIONARY BREAKTHROUGHS: A SMALL-FIRM SPECIALTY

It is convenient here to divide up inventions into two polar categories: revolutionary breakthroughs and cumulative incremental improvements. Of course, many new products and processes fall into neither extreme category, but are somewhere in between. Still, the distinction is useful. Moreover, there are many examples that clearly fit into one category or the other quite easily. For instance, the electric light, alternating electric current, the internal combustion engine, and a host of other advances must surely be deemed revolutionary, while successive models of washing machines and refrigerators—with each new model a bit longer-lasting, a bit less susceptible to breakdown and a bit easier to use—constitute a sequence of incremental improvements.

The relevance of the distinction should be evident, given what has been said about the structure of R&D in the large business organization. Their inherent conservatism naturally leads to the expectation that these firms will tend to specialize in the incremental improvements and tend to avoid the risks that the revolutionary breakthrough entails. The latter is left most often to the small or newly founded enterprise. Though that is to be expected, the actual degree of asymmetry in the specialization of activity between large and small firms is striking. The US Small Business Administration has listed the breakthrough innovations of the twentieth century for which small firms are responsible, and its menu of inventions literally spans the range from A to Z, from the airplane to the zipper, and includes many other breakthroughs of enormous significance for our economies, such as the microprocessor, oral contraceptives, FM radio and the microscope.

A recent study, also sponsored by the US Small Business Administration (2001), provides more systematic and powerful evidence to similar effect.[3] This report examines technical change through patenting and it defines 'small firms' as 'businesses with fewer than 500 employees.'[4] Most notably, the study finds that 'a small firm patent is more likely than a large firm patent to be among the top 1% of most frequently cited patents.' Among other conclusions, in the words of its authors, this study reports that' (US Small Business Administration 2003, p. 2):

> Small firms represent one-third of the most prolific patenting companies that have 15 or more US patents.
>
> Small firm innovation is twice as closely linked to scientific research as large firm innovation on average, and so is substantially more high-tech or leading edge.
>
> Small patenting firms are roughly 13 times more innovative per employee than large patenting firms.

One is led to the plausible conjecture that most of the revolutionary new ideas of the past two centuries have been, and are likely to continue to be, provided more heavily by independent innovators who, essentially, operate small business enterprises. Small entrepreneurial firms have come close to monopolizing the search for revolutionary breakthroughs. But now we seem to have leapt to the opposite conclusion, that rather than the likely disappearance of the innovative role of the entrepreneur and the small firm, little would appear to be left for the large firm to do. That, as we will see next, is also a very misleading conclusion.

---

[3] Quoting the press release describing the study, 'A total of 1,071 firms with 15 or more patents issued between 1996 and 2000 were examined. A total of 193,976 patents were analysed. CHI [the firm that carried out the study] created a data-base of these firms and their patents. This list excluded foreign-owned firms, universities, government laboratories, and nonprofit institutions' (US Small Business Administration 1995, p. 2).

[4] It may strike the reader that a firm with 500 employees is not particularly small. However, in 2000 in the US, 46% of total R&D spending by business was spent by 167 firms with more than 25 000 employees each. 81% of the total was spent by 1990 firms with more than 1000 employees each, while 32 000 R&D-performing firms with less than 500 employees each accounted only for 15% of total R&D spending by business (National Science Board 2000, Chapter 2, p. 24). The pattern of R&D spending in Scotland by firms of different size was not that dissimilar, though of course the firms were much smaller. In 2001, Scottish business enterprises spent £512 million on R&D; 76% of that was spent by firms with 400 or more employees, 15% was spent by firms with 100–399 employees, and 9% by firms with 0–99 employees (Scottish Executive 2003c).

REVOLUTIONARY CONSEQUENCES OF AGGREGATED INCREMENTAL IMPROVEMENTS

As we have seen, the type of innovation in which the giant enterprises tend to specialize is primarily devoted to product improvement, increased reliability and enhanced user-friendliness of products and the finding of new uses for those products. The bureaucratic control typical of innovative activity in the large firm serves to ensure that the resulting changes will be modest, predictable and incremental. However, having recognized the critical role of the smaller enterprises, one should not go to the other extreme and undervalue the incremental contribution of the routine activity that at least sometimes adds more to growth than do the more revolutionary prototype innovations. Though each such small improvement may be relatively unspectacular, added together they can become very significant indeed. Thus, consider how little computing power the first clumsy and enormously expensive computers provided, and what huge multiples of such power have been added by the many subsequent incremental improvements.

For example, according to a recent report by Intel Corporation (Markoff 2003), over the period 1971–2003, the 'clock speed' of its microprocessor chips, that is, the number of instructions each chip can carry out per second, has increased by some *three million per cent*, reaching about three billion computations per second today. During the period 1968–2003, the number of transistors embedded in a single chip has expanded more than *10 million per cent*, and the number of transistors that can be purchased for a dollar has grown by *five billion per cent*. These are obviously no minor contributions. Added up, they surely contribute far more computing capacity than was provided by the original revolutionary breakthrough of the invention of the electronic computer. Of course, that initial invention was an indispensable necessity for all later improvements. But it is only the combined work of the two together that made possible the powerful and inexpensive apparatus that serves us so effectively today.

ON THE ROLE OF GOVERNMENT AND THE UNIVERSITY IN INNOVATION

I have so far omitted two key players, the universities and the pertinent government agencies, which have also made major contributions to technological progress. Here, one need only think of the electronic computer and the Internet. But the contributions of these institutions have also tended to be rather specialized and different from those discussed above. It is to them that we must look primarily for the results provided by basic research as distinguished from applied research. The reasons for this division of labour with private industry are well understood, and only a few words need be said on the subject here.

From the point of view of the unthinking market mechanism, expenditure on basic research is a 'wasteful' expenditure, because the outlay promises no addition to the profits of the firm. By its very nature, it is nearly impossible to predict whether basic research will yield any financial benefit at all and, if so, who will ultimately be the beneficiary. Certainly, it need not be the enterprise that carried it out. That is why governments and universities have had to step in, if basic research of any magnitude was to be carried out.

The importance for technological progress of the conjunction of public sector, academia and business was dramatically confirmed in an American Philosophical Society symposium[5] on recent and projected biomedical advances (for more on this, see also John Curtis's interview with Richard M. Satava (Curtis 2003)). There, it was strikingly demonstrated that the contributions of universities, government (notably the military) and (apparently small) private firms have produced a truly mind-boggling array of medical breakthroughs, such as surgery carried out by computer-guided robots; the growth of replacement bodily organs in specially maintained groups of animals (pigs favoured currently) for use in human transplantation; artificially induced hibernation and what can only be described as 'reversible pseudo-death' of patients as a substitute for anaesthesia; and the use of certain insects (notably butterflies, cockroaches and sphinx moths with their very specialized and powerful senses) to transmit information about the presence of dangers such as buried land mines or anthrax spores.

This list, surely, must suffice to stir the imagination to overload, to indicate that the end of innovation is nowhere in sight and to confirm that the large corporations cannot do it alone. These examples are drawn just from the arena of medicine, but much technological upheaval is under way elsewhere as well.

DISSEMINATION OF INVENTION AND RAPID TERMINATION OF THE OBSOLETE

I turn next to another feature of the innovation process under a free-market regime that is critical for growth: the speed with which use of improved products and production techniques becomes widespread. One of the attributes of an effective economic arrangement for the encouragement of technological change is the innovator's financial gain, derived from the temporary acquisition of monopoly power through the improved product or process. However, encouragement of growth also requires rapid *dissemination* of any improved techniques and products and their widespread adoption by others. These two desiderata would appear to be in conflict. After all, rapidity and ease of dissemination can threaten the innovator's reward. While the free market has hardly eliminated this conflict, it has nevertheless ameliorated it. My discussion will turn briefly to this issue because it will play a substantial role in the possible programmes that merit consideration for improving Scotland's growth.

As is to be expected, many businesses do guard their proprietary technology and strive with the aid of patents, secrecy and other means to prevent other firms from using the new products and processes. This is unfortunate for economic progress because it means that consumers who purchase from other firms are forced to accept obsolete features in the items they buy.[6] Moreover, two firms that deny one another access to their proprietary improvements in the firms' common product can both

---

[5]American Philosophical Society Meetings, 24–26 April 2003, Philadelphia, PA.

[6]It is, however, not always recognized that patents are not designed to *prevent* the spread of information about novel technology. On the contrary, patent holders are required to make full information on their inventions public so that others can profit from the ideas even if they cannot replicate the patented products themselves without the patent holder's permission.

survive, marketing their somewhat differentiated outputs, each of which is inferior in terms of what is currently possible technologically.

Happily, however, that is hardly the norm. On the contrary, voluntary licencing of access to proprietary technology is widespread. Many firms derive substantial incomes from the sale of such licences. The logic is straightforward. Suppose firm A invents a new widget and expects to make a net profit of X dollars per widget of the new type that it produces. Then if rival firm B offers firm A a licence fee of Y dollars $(Y > X)$ for each unit of the new widget it is able to sell, then A obviously can be better off letting B do so, even if every widget sold by B means one less sale for A. Of course, B will generally be able to afford so high a fee only if it is a more efficient *producer* of widgets than A, even though it may be an inferior inventor. In this way the price mechanism will not only encourage licencing, but will, as usual, elicit efficient specialization: inventive activity will be undertaken primarily by the more effective inventor, while production of the resulting products will be undertaken predominantly by the more efficient producer. This sort of unreciprocated licencing does take place in practice, but it seems most frequently to entail the sale of licences by large firms that are in a position to undertake extensive R&D activity, the licensees being smaller enterprises that cannot afford to carry out such activity and do not possess personnel qualified to do so.

There are a number of other incentives for such profitable voluntary exchanges in the free market. For example, the most straightforward and common reason is the very high cost of R&D activity. By entering into some sort of sharing consortium this burden can obviously be reduced for each participant. Given the public-good attribute of the resulting information, it is far less expensive (per user) to provide such information to several firms than only to supply it to one. Another reason is reduction of risk. In any given year, a single firm's R&D division may fail to come up with any significant breakthroughs. Technology-sharing agreements serve as effective insurance policies, protecting each participant from such catastrophes.

A further, and less obvious, reason for voluntary trading of technology is that it protects the firm from market entry by new rivals. Consider, for example, an industry with 10 firms of identical size, each with an R&D division with similar staffing and similar funding. Each firm in such a consortium will then have available to it not only the discoveries of its own R&D establishment, but those of nine other firms in addition. Now suppose an eleventh firm wants to enter the market, but is not invited to join the technology-sharing consortium. Having only the products of its own R&D division at its disposal, while the other firms each obtain the outputs of ten R&D establishments, the entrant can evidently find itself at a severe competitive disadvantage.

This type of arrangement has its pros and cons. It can be shown to stimulate innovative effort (provided that anti-competitive conspiracy is absent), for it helps to internalize the externalities generated by the innovative efforts of each firm. It can also be shown that the formation of such a consortium tends to be welfare-enhancing (Baumol 2002, Chapter 7). Yet there are dangers against which the authorities must be vigilant. Such consortia *can* serve as vehicles or as camouflage for anti-competitive behaviour. For example, the contract discussions could serve as a disguise for price fixing by the competitors. Or they could enter into an agreement for mutual restriction of their R&D expenditures, each firm knowing that it can safely limit its innovative efforts if it can rely on its rivals to do the same. Similar perils for the public interest arise in the last of the reasons for voluntary technology sharing—the problem of 'patent thickets' and the widespread patent pools that have been formed to deal with the thicket problem. A complex piece of equipment, such as a computer, characteristically is made up of components each of which is covered by patents,[7] and the patents pertinent for such an item are usually owned by several different firms, many of them direct competitors in the final-product market. This puts many of these firms in a legal position that permits each to bring the manufacturing process of the others to a halt. The most effective way to prevent the catastrophic consequences this threatens is the formation of a patent pool in which each makes the use of its patents available to the other members of the pool, and even to outsiders (as a step to avoid intervention by the anti-monopoly authorities). There are many such pools in the US.

In the US the Department of Justice and the Federal Trade Commission have recognized the two sides of the issue, the benefits of coordination in the arena and the attendant danger of anti-competitive behaviour. Their 2000 *Guidelines for the Licensing of Intellectual Property* very explicitly discusses the substantial pro-competitive benefits of licencing, coordination of research efforts and trading of proprietary technology. What is significant for us here is that licencing as the prime instrument for technology dissemination has become sufficiently important to merit this sort of attention by the anti-trust agencies.

The Invaluable Contribution of 'Mere Imitation'

Most of the innovation that Scotland can expect to introduce will not have been contributed by the country's own R&D activities, but by those of other countries. This is not to be regarded as a deficiency, nor is Scotland alone in this respect. In a world in which almost all major technological development takes place in some 25 countries, and in which technology licencing and trading is increasingly common, it is a tautology that if none of the countries falls significantly behind, then the average country should expect some 24/25ths of its new technology to come from abroad.

Other routes for technology transfer include, of course, international trade and foreign direct investment (FDI). Scotland has, over the last 50 years or so, benefited from a significant inflow of FDI, particularly by US multinationals as well as by Japanese, Korean and German firms. However, it is arguable that there has been much less technology transfer from these companies to domestic Scottish firms than many would have wished. Similar reservations have been raised about the role of FDI elsewhere, and though it may serve as a disincentive for such investment, the use of regulations requiring technical training and occupations that provide experience to

---

[7]Peter N. Detkin, vice president and assistant general counsel at Intel Corporation (the world's largest semiconductor company), estimates, for example, that there were more than 90 000 patents generally related to microprocessors held by more than 10 000 parties in 2002 (Detkin 2002, p. 667).

a minimum share of native employees may help the recipient countries to capitalize on such investments.

There is a significant misapprehension about the imitation process that is important in transferring technologies from abroad, which is that the imitation process has few or none of the attributes of a truly innovative activity. But that is simply incorrect. History is replete with examples of substantial improvements that were contributed by imitation. In part, these improvements are elicited by the need to adapt the technology to local conditions, including differences in size of the market, in the nature of consumer preferences, in climatic conditions and in the character of available complementary inputs. Thus, there is nothing inherently inferior about a process of organized imitation of foreign technology.

Moreover, as just noted, every economically advanced nation can be expected to run the risk of falling behind if it does not imitate. Even the US and Japan, the two leading contributors to the world's stock of new products and processes, derive a substantial proportion of their latest technology from elsewhere. For Scotland, as for every other advanced economy, innovation will continue to be of prime importance for economic growth. But a substantial proportion of that innovation will be obtained from foreign sources. And to be an effective user of such foreign technology, it is important for the country to ensure that it is a skilled imitator as well as an effective innovator.

Given the four contributory sources that play critical roles in expanding an economy's innovation and growth—entrepreneurs and small firms, large firms with internal R&D capacity, universities, and government—one is driven to conclude that effective programmes for facilitation and stimulation of entrepreneurship are important, but that there is more that can be done for this purpose. Below, I will turn to some illustrative policy suggestions. I hope that some of these proposals may at least draw attention to a broader range of promising options than might otherwise have been considered. Since the subject here is public policy, all of what will be said will relate to the role of government, as facilitator of the innovative work of others. But before turning to policy issues, in the following section I will briefly lay out some of the data for the Scottish economy.

EMPIRICAL EVIDENCE ON GROWTH, ENTREPRENEURSHIP AND INNOVATION IN SCOTLAND

The data for Scotland are often aggregated into the statistics for the United Kingdom, so particular indicators of Scotland's performance are sometimes less easy to obtain. Nevertheless, it may be useful to summarize some of the available data on entrepreneurship, innovation and growth in Scotland. Brian Ashcroft's (1997, pp. 27 and 28) thorough research of the facts has led him to conclude that

> Scotland's innovation rate in manufacturing and the rate of formation
> of new firms still remain abysmally low. Our current research on the
> determinants of innovation performance and the entrepreneurial choice
> decision, suggests that Scottish companies have failed to develop an

innovation culture, while Scottish individuals are less likely to be interested in forming their own firm and have greater difficulties in translating interest into action when such interest emerges.

Scottish companies are generally much less willing, compared with the UK, Ireland and particularly Germany: to undertake R&D; to formalise the innovation process; to involve key employee groups, such as designers, marketing/sales and engineering and technical staff, in all phases of the innovation process; and to collaborate with other companies and organisations.

Scottish individuals in the labour force are much less likely to run their own business and much less likely to want to run their own firm, with, in 1992, approximately 30% of the Scottish labour force found to be interested in setting up their own firm, compared with 43% in the UK.

The available evidence appears to confirm the bulk of these conclusions and, perhaps, to suggest more.

Growth in Scottish GDP and Per Capita GDP

What has been described as Scotland's 'perennially low' economic growth rate has put it in the bottom third of the industrial world's standings in per capita GDP (Ashcroft et al. 1999). But Figure 3.2, which charts the growth rates of GDP per capita for Scotland and 19 countries between 1990 and 2000, shows Scotland in the fifth highest position after Norway, Australia, the Netherlands and the US, and just behind the UK. For a longer period (1964–1998), the Scottish Executive reports that Scotland's average annual growth was slightly lower than the UK rate, 2.1% versus 2.4%, respectively (Scottish Executive 2003a); while the period 1973–2001 saw an average annual growth rate of 1.6% (versus 2.1% for the UK as a whole). Since the UK record of growth was not impressive over the postwar period, this suggests that Scotland might seek a higher goal.

Scottish Productivity Performance

The growth rate of an economy's productivity, that is, the speed with which technical change and other influences are able to increase the output obtainable from a given set of input resources, is a key variable for the determination of growth. Here, the longer-run record of the UK and Scotland is mixed. The UK productivity growth performance had been behind that of many other industrial countries for a considerable period, but in the last decade of the twentieth century it began to pull ahead, with Scotland performing correspondingly. The Scottish Executive (2001, p. 1) reports

> In Scotland, 'unadjusted' productivity growth (defined on the basis of total employment) was low from the mid 1980s through to the early 1990s—less than 1 percent per annum in most years—but was higher

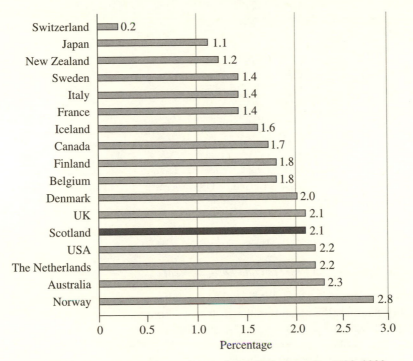

Figure 3.2. Average annual growth rate of real GDP per capita, 1990–2000, selected countries. *Source:* OECD (2003) and Scottish Executive (2003b).

in the period to 1999. ... Estimates suggest that the average rates of productivity growth in Scotland and the UK were very similar between 1995 and 1999. However, there was a deceleration in Scotland in 2000, partly due to the stronger than average growth in employment. The 4-year moving average to 2000Q4 was 1.2 percent.

Scottish Entrepreneurial Activity

Scotland's entrepreneurial activity, relatively speaking, is not outstanding. The proportion of 'new and nascent entrepreneurs stating they would employ 20 or more people in five years' suggests that while Scotland's performance is behind that of the UK, it is ahead of New Zealand, Finland and Ireland (Levie et al. 2002). A longer term (1994–2001) comparison of the UK and Scotland in new business starts per 10 000 population or new VAT registered businesses for Scotland and UK (for the period 1981–1999) both show that Scotland is clearly behind the UK. In Figure 3.3, from the 2002 Global Entrepreneurship Monitor (GEM) Scotland report, we see that Scotland's 'total entrepreneurial activity' (TEA) measures up well against Japan, Finland, Germany and the UK as a whole, but falls well short of the record of Ireland, the US and New Zealand. TEA scores for a much larger sample of countries show Scotland at 10th from the bottom among the 37 countries that are ranked.

59

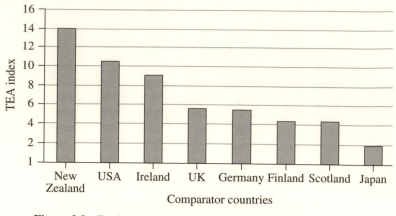

Figure 3.3. Total entrepreneurial activity (TEA) by country (2002).
Source: Levie et al. (2002).

Scottish Spending on Research and Development

R&D expenditure is a useful indicator of an economy's commitment to innovative activity. And here the standing of the Scottish economy varies considerably by sector. Scotland's relative performance in business spending on R&D seems particularly weak. One problem here is that companies with activities in Scotland may well allocate a considerable portion if not all of their R&D spending to the location of their headquarters, very often in England. Business R&D investment as a proportion of GDP in 2000 is shown in Figure 3.4, in which Scotland occupies penultimate place (ahead of Italy) behind 10 of the 12 other countries reported. Its share of GDP devoted to R&D is about one-quarter that of the two leaders, Sweden and Finland, and less than half that of Japan and the US. For a longer-term period, comparing Scotland with four other countries in terms of business R&D expenditures as a percentage of output for the period 1990–1998 shows Scotland in last place. A more recent three-year average indicates the same ranking. However, R&D spending by Scottish institutions of higher education and by the Scottish government indicate that university spending on R&D was relatively high, while that of government was considerably lower, although still respectable by international standards. This is an arena in which the government can improve performance directly and in a straightforward manner.

Scottish Secondary and Higher Education

Figure 3.5 presents data on graduates (of tertiary institutions) as a percentage of the workforce for Scotland and seven other countries, with only two of those countries behind Scotland. Scotland's relative performance is better in its secondary school students' mean scores in reading, scientific and mathematical literacy for Scotland and other countries. Here Scotland is fourth in the set of eight countries reported and its position is impressive, being ahead of the UK, Ireland, the US and Germany (Fraser of Allander Institute 2003).

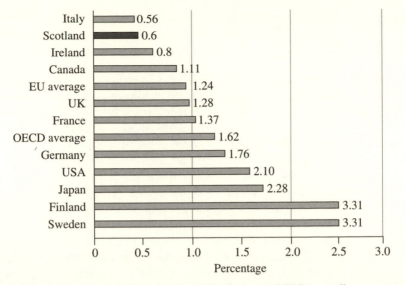

Figure 3.4. Business enterprise research and development (BERD) spending as a percentage of GDP, selected countries, 2001. *Source:* OECD (2003) and Scottish Executive (2003c).

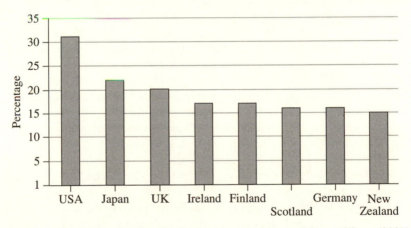

Figure 3.5. Graduates of tertiary institutions as a percentage of the workforce (2001). *Source:* Fraser of Allander Institute (2003).

Scottish Patenting Activity

Patent applications filed per 10 000 population for Scotland and other British regions show Scotland clearly ranking low on this measure of converting knowledge into products or processes (Patent Office 2001). In terms of US utility patents[8] per million population by inventor country of residence (for the period 1996 through February

---

[8]A utility patent is a patent of invention; it can cover a useful process, machine, article of manufacture or composition of matter, as distinguished from a design patent that covers cosmetic appearance, or a copyright that covers an original expression of an idea.

2002), Scotland also lags substantially behind. As MacRae (2002, p. 25) puts it, 'Is Scotland being left behind in innovation? For a country that produced Andrew Carnegie, James Watt and Dolly the sheep, the disconcerting answer appears to be "yes".'

But these numbers do not tell the whole story. Another measure of success in innovation, at least in the universities, is the rate of commercialization of the knowledge produced by academic institutions. A recent study by Bob Smailes (2002) at the University of Edinburgh compared the per-dollar efficiency of US and Scottish universities in terms of patents granted and number of so-called 'spin-out' businesses started. On average, between 1995 and 2001 Scottish universities actually spent fewer research dollars per patent ($3.2 million) and per 'spin-out' firm created ($20.2 million) than did a group of 11 top American universities during a similar time period ($5.3 million and $77.4 million, respectively). And, according to MacRae (2002), Scottish higher educational institutions account for 19% of all UK academic spin-out companies. The conclusion suggested by this limited evidence seems to be that, while Scotland's universities are relatively efficient and effective in carrying out the innovation process, the country's overall innovative activity is limited and yields correspondingly limited results. While the universities' research and innovation performance is indeed commendable, they seem much less effective in arranging for widespread adoption and commercialization of the results.

In sum, while there are bright spots, Scotland's overall performance in productivity, innovation and growth leaves a good deal to be desired. As explanation, Ashcroft (2002) suggests that indigenous Scottish industry is not sufficiently flexible or entrepreneurial, and that it continues to be characterized by low rates of new firm formation, R&D expenditures and product and process innovation within much of the economy, particularly in manufacturing. Scotland's R&D and innovation have apparently improved recently, but Scottish performance is still relatively weak (particularly in smaller establishments of 10–29 employees), and below that of much of the remainder of the UK, Ireland, and such key German regions as Bavaria and Baden-Wurtemburg. Perhaps even more important, the dissemination and adoption of new technology tends to be slow, especially in locally owned firms, as compared with other economies.

It is arguable that low or weak *capabilities* play a role in the low Scottish R&D and innovation rates, and stem partly from the structure of Scottish industry, in which much of the corporate sector has its headquarters outside Scotland either as a result of an earlier takeover process or because of local decisions to locate the headquarters nearer to competitors, key suppliers and government in London. While Scotland should not be characterized as a 'branch plant economy,' the paucity of headquarters probably does restrict R&D in Scotland. A key issue here is the skill of domestic Scottish management, who, notwithstanding the competitive environment in which such companies must trade, do not seem to take innovation sufficiently seriously. This certainly handicaps policy that is intended to encourage R&D in such firms in Scotland, but need not impede efforts to speed the adoption of changing technology, perhaps by encouraging the Scottish divisions of such firms to remain sufficiently product and price competitive so that new products generated elsewhere within the group and much of their value added are rapidly introduced in Scotland. Financial incentives for investment in technical change in Scottish plants are also worth considering.

Scottish manufacturing firms are also less likely than firms in other advanced economies to form research collaborations with other firms and organizations (Fraser of Allander Institute 2001). According to Ashcroft (2002), much of 'traditional' manufacturing in Scotland focuses competitive efforts on price rather than on product differentiation and innovation. The result is that these firms avoid the innovative arms race, in which newer products and processes that are competitive with the evolving standards of rival enterprises become a matter of life and death for the firm. It appears that while average sectoral productivity rates are bolstered by the presence of a significant number of foreign-owned firms, the locally owned and managed firms tend to underperform.

POLICIES TO PROMOTE GROWTH AND INNOVATION IN THE SCOTTISH ECONOMY

Let me turn, finally, to possible policy approaches. Writing as an outsider, the determination of appropriateness must be left to others. In addition, it should be recognized that some of the recommendations refer to matters (such as patent rules and competition policy) reserved to the UK Parliament or the European Union. Nevertheless, it is important to recognize their importance for growth in Scotland.

The Stimulation of Entrepreneurship and the Creative Role of Small Business

For clarity, it must be emphasized that many economists have used the word 'entrepreneur' to refer to anyone who creates a new firm, whether that firm is the embodiment of a novel idea or merely replicates a host of older establishments. In contrast, Schumpeter (1947) used the term to describe an *innovator*: someone who invents or who recognizes the promise of some invention and organizes the steps needed to bring that invention to use *and to market*. Moreover, he used the term 'innovation' to refer not only to new machines, production processes and new products, but also to describe novel forms of economic organization (e.g. the joint-stock company or the patent pool). A Schumpeterian act of innovation is never the mere generation of the new idea alone but must also include the further step of design, to make the invention effectively usable, as well as undertaking the activities needed to ensure that it is rapidly and widely put to effective use. The difference is important, as is illustrated by the example of the Soviet Union. The record of invention by the Soviet Union's very capable scientists and engineers was impressive. They did not lack for *invention*, but what was absent from their economies was an effective mechanism for the stimulation of the other components of *innovation*: of dissemination and widespread adoption of the novel techniques and products.

This is also a key problem that has for so long affected Scotland: failure to commercialize and develop *within* Scotland a stream of world-renowned inventions from Scottish universities and individual Scottish inventors. Many of these valuable inventions, while generated in Scotland, have subsequently been taken up—commercialized—by others in other countries, with the subsequent added economic value and the associated new firms and industries created abroad. This has certainly bedevilled Scotland, and even the UK to an extent. There has been much policy effort to assist the commercialization element of the innovation process, as, for example, in the Proof of Concept Fund initiated by Scottish Enterprise. Currently, this particularly concerns the Scottish universities, whose research constitutes a significant science base with high academic publication ratings, but which has a relatively poor record in generating new patents, spinning out new firms and, more generally, in commercializing its research.

The importance of the dissemination element of innovation and its distinction from invention itself should be clear. But earlier we also emphasized the difference between the two connotations of entrepreneurship: (1) as founders of new firms of any variety, and (2) as contributors to the innovation process. This difference is also critical. A careful survey of firm-creating activity in 29 countries on five continents suggests that there may be little systematic relation between creation of new firms and economic growth (Reynolds et al. 2001, p. 12, Table 3). When the surveyed entrepreneurs are divided into two groups—the 'opportunity entrepreneurs', who form a business venture because they feel they have discovered a profitable opportunity, and the 'necessity entrepreneurs', who create a firm because they have no other viable options—it is, perhaps surprisingly, only the number of necessity entrepreneurs in the different countries that is significantly correlated with their country's real GDP growth rate. Opportunity entrepreneurship and economic expansion seem to have little systematic association, according to the data. The contrasting non-negligible correlation of growth with necessity entrepreneurship invites the conjecture that the primary relationship is one in which rapid growth leads to creation of new firms rather than the other way round, i.e. that firm creation per se does relatively little to stimulate growth.

But this does not mean that entrepreneurship, *in either sense*, is irrelevant for innovation and growth. On the contrary, the astonishing record of breakthrough innovations coming from entrepreneurial firms suggests that we cannot do without them if we want to stimulate growth effectively. What is apparently important is not the *number* of new firms that entrepreneurial activity provides, but the means by which those firms can hope to succeed—by competing with the aid of innovative products or processes. There are some specific steps that can be taken to encourage and facilitate entrepreneurial activity of this sort.

Financing. The Reynolds et al. (2001) report (pp. 24–28) emphasizes the role of financing in creating new firms: 'There are strong significant correlations between venture capital investments and ... entrepreneurial opportunity, entrepreneurial capacity and motivation. It also strongly correlates with high-growth start-ups, or the proportion of start-ups expected to create at least 15 jobs within the first five years' (p. 26). Financing from private and informal sources also plays a critical role in the formation of new firms. There are surely areas—geographic, in types of activity, and in the identity of the applicants—where government assistance of funding may be useful. An attractive form of assistance is the public-sector loan guarantee, which can also help to determine the directions in which funding will flow. In particular, the choice of ventures to which funding is provided with governmental guarantees to the supplier of funds can be slanted *to favour innovative enterprises, including firms that promise to introduce foreign technology into the domestic economy.* In such an arrangement, it would be part of the applicant's burden to demonstrate the novel features of the enterprise, as well as providing evidence of its likelihood of success. The fact that governments can be reasonably effective in evaluating claims to innovation is demonstrated by the record of the patent system, with its at least moderate effectiveness in weeding out patent applications whose required claim not to be replicating 'prior art' does not stand up to scrutiny. By adopting some variant of this approach, the government can ensure that its efforts encourage not mere firm formation, but the expansion of innovative entrepreneurship.

Encouragement of Participant Venture Capitalist Activity. Venture capital—that is, the supply of funding by private organizations that specialize in the supply of financial resources to new and innovative firms—is far more common in the US than anywhere in Europe, presumably including Scotland in the latter group, though there seems to be evidence suggesting that Scotland and the UK are generally in an intermediate position between the US and the remainder of Europe. The venture capitalists characteristically accept as part of their compensation a substantial share of the firm's equity capital. The firms are reportedly benefited indirectly but significantly because the venture capitalists are thereby induced to take an interest in their operations, offering the enterprises advice based on extensive knowledge and experience. In Gunnar Eliasson's opinion[9], the characteristic absence of this sort of participation in Europe is a major handicap to formation and success of new enterprises and a major advantage to the US economy (Eliasson 2002).

Training and Provision of Critical Information. There are two types of knowledge that are particularly critical for successful and innovative firms. First, they require personnel with the appropriate training in the relevant fields, including science, engineering and marketing. The second type of information pertains to the details of operation of new firms, including pitfalls stemming from the tax system, safety requirements to protect the labour force and environmental regulations. The formation of small businesses requires relatively limited academic training and entails only limited use of trained scientists and engineers. From carpenter John Harrison (the inventor of the ship's chronometer) to Thomas Edison and beyond, the contributors of breakthrough invention are not noted for their advanced education.[10] It is, rather, in the corporate R&D divisions that the employment of highly educated scientists and engineers is nearly universal. Yet entrepreneurs, in either sense of the

---

[9]The report is based on a substantial number of interviews with Swedish, European, US and Taiwanese small firms and venture capitalists.

[10]Reynolds et al. (2001) offer some empirical evidence on participation in entrepreneurial activity: '...for men...there is a reduced participation among those who go beyond secondary education, with the lowest levels among those with the most (i.e. graduate experience) or least (i.e. no secondary degree) education. But [among entrepreneurs who are not driven to start firms out of necessity] the patterns are quite different. Among those pursuing opportunities, there is no difference among men who have completed secondary school and [those who] received additional education at any level.' (p. 16).

word, do need information. Inventors need guidance through the morass of patent laws. The founders of new enterprises need help in dealing with regulations, from the tax laws to the fire regulations, in the requirements of record keeping, and so on. Government can obviously help here by providing an information office to which inexperienced entrepreneurs can turn for guidance. Brief training courses may also prove helpful.

Removal or Reduction of Impediments to Firm Formation.   Most economies have, over the years, adopted a number of legal provisions that, however well-intentioned, constitute impediments to the formation of new firms. For example, labour laws sometimes grant job tenure to employees after a very brief trial period. This can, of course, add materially to the risks entailed in starting a firm. Cost-causing and disincentive-creating rules of these sorts, ranging from onerous construction standards to rental obligations, can be phased in rather than imposed immediately after the opening of the enterprise. The handicapping rules need not be eliminated altogether, but can be phased in over, say, a 10-year period.

Reduction in Rent-Seeking Opportunities.   One of the historically significant impediments to the exercise of productive entrepreneurship is the availability of alternative outlets for entrepreneurial talent which provide little social benefit or are even damaging to the general welfare. The enterprising robber barons of the European Middle Ages or the warlords of early twentieth-century China are extreme examples. More pertinent to the modern industrial economy is the availability of lucrative positions in the government bureaucracy or opportunities for material gain through enterprising litigation in the nation's courts. Such activities, which economists label 'rent seeking', attract many individuals with entrepreneurial talent. There are ways to narrow such opportunities, such as limitation of lawyers' fees, reduction in the number of government positions, etc. The desirability of such steps may be obvious in itself, but their ability to serve as incentives for productive entrepreneurial activities is less widely recognized.[11]

Improved Incentives for Larger Innovating Enterprises

In Scotland, large firms are less prevalent that in the US and may well play a correspondingly more limited role in the innovation process. Moreover, one may understandably expect less willingness on the part of government to provide direct help to the large firms on the presumption that they are generally in a position to take care of their own needs. In addition, under EU rules, public-sector assistance to larger firms is severely circumscribed.

Still, there are several things it is appropriate for government to contribute to the innovative activity of this sector. The first and most obvious is *basic research*, that is, pure research, not undertaken for any concrete and immediate material objective, but

---

[11] This may be especially relevant in Scotland, where a high proportion of employment is in the public sector. Thus, for example, as emphasized in a recent *Economist* article ('Denationalising Pay', 21 June 2003), it is rational for job seekers to prefer a public-sector job in Scotland because national wage-setting has led the relative real pay to be high.

driven primarily by what Thorstein Veblen once described as 'idle curiosity'. Outlays on basic research are not, for obvious reasons, attractive to the typical established firm. The appropriate role for government and the universities in this area will be discussed below. A second role for government that is related to big business entails incentives for rapid dissemination of technological developments, a subject whose significance has already been noted. A last type of interaction between government and large firms to be discussed here relates to the public sector's efforts to curb the creation and exercise of monopoly power.

Patent Rules and Technology Dissemination Incentives. Rapid and effective dissemination of innovations can contribute to growth, so patent laws can make a substantial difference in the power of the incentives for a private firm voluntarily to make its proprietary technology available to others. This is one way in which large firms can be induced to share their innovations with others, with suitable compensation arrangements. For example, in the US and Canada, a patent is awarded to the party that provides evidence that it was the *first to invent* the item in question. In Japan and most other countries (including the UK), in contrast, the patent goes to the party that is *first to file* its application. This encourages early filing, making the technical information available sooner, and giving rivals an earlier opportunity to profit in their own innovative efforts. This can pressure the parties to arrive at a settlement, with the successful patent applicant precommitted to provide licences to rivals in exchange for agreement by the latter not to challenge the application.[12]

Other aspects of Japanese patent rules encouraging dissemination include public disclosure of technical details as soon as an application is filed; scope to challenge patents before they are granted rather than afterwards, which seems to encourage early licencing; and the ability to patent minor modifications, as the coverage of a patent is generally very narrow and rivals can create their own variations on the original invention.

All these patent provisions contribute strong pressure on Japanese innovators to enter into cross-licencing arrangements with rivals. In Ordover's words, 'the Japanese patent system subordinates the short-term interests of the innovator in the creation of exclusionary rights to the broader policy goals of diffusion of technology' (Ordover 1991, p. 48).

Anti-monopoly Rules and Cooperative Innovative Activity. Anti-monopoly statutes should take account of the possible benefits of *cooperation* in technology production. Research joint ventures, research consortia and even mergers in high-technology industries are frequently a socially optimal response to market failures that beset the production and dissemination of knowledge. Consequently, a relaxed rule-of-reason approach[13] to inter-firm coordination may well prove to be the best

---

[12]Most of content of the following paragraphs is a summary of materials in an extremely illuminating paper by Janusz Ordover (1991), which describes the pertinent Japanese arrangements and analyses their consequences.

[13]This is the broad UK approach in cases where the parties to an agreement control less than 25% of the market. In the case of mergers, such an agreement would be subject to the usual test: whether it resulted in a substantial lessening of competition, including the potential benefits from sharing of technology.

way to deal with the legitimate concerns apt to be raised by such coordination. In this process, consortia, joint ventures, information exchange and even mergers of firms with substantial current market shares in high-technology industries can be conducive to long-run efficiency—more so than in industries that are less technologically driven. In particular, anti-monopoly policy should avoid inhibiting the dissemination of information. Licensing schemes employed by patent holders must not be subject to more stringent anti-monopoly constraints than those affecting exploitation of other property rights. More generally, restraints on the use of the anti-monopoly laws to inhibit cooperation in invention and dissemination should be made as explicit and unambiguous as possible, although this can be more difficult to put into practice under the rule-of-reason approach. A parliamentary measure explicitly exempting from the anti-monopoly laws coordinated action by firms for the acquisition of technology abroad could encourage and facilitate such efforts.

On Governmental Promotion of Innovation and Growth

As already noted, the universities and government agencies have made major contributions to technological progress. But the contributions of these institutions have also tended to be rather specialized and differ from those of private industry.

Funding and Execution of Basic Research.　It is to the public sector and universities that we must look primarily for the results provided by basic research as distinguished from applied research. What is clearly called for is governmental funding of basic research, to be carried out by its own agencies or some appropriate outside agencies, most notably the universities. So far as grants for university research are concerned, if the primary purpose is to facilitate innovation rather than promotion of general education, perhaps the most effective grant allocation procedure is funding of particular proposed projects on the basis of formal project submissions by faculty members.

The Role of Government in Acquisition of Foreign Technology.　Economists generally agree that private enterprises lack the incentive to supply optimal quantities of socially valuable goods and services. The encouragement of technology transfer from abroad is a significant case in point. A small economy should recognize the contribution to its growth offered by rapid acquisition and absorption of technological information from elsewhere. But the transfer process invites a role for the public sector. For example, the work of monitoring foreign technical journals and of providing English translations of pertinent articles can be carried out nearly as cheaply for many UK firms, or even of industries, as it can on behalf of any single business. Countries appear to have differed substantially in the quantity of resources they devote to this purpose. Edwin Mansfield (1990, p. 343) reports, on the basis of a survey of 100 American firms in 13 industries, that these respondents believed only 29% of US firms spend as large a percentage of their sales on the monitoring of foreign technology as the average amount spent by the Japanese, only 47% as much as the Germans do, only 51% as much as the French do, and only 70% spend as much as the average British enterprises in the corresponding industries. There may well be an opportunity for Scotland to seek to gain a differential advantage in its monitoring and adoption of foreign technology. For example, it may prove to be profitable socially for the government to establish a special Office of Technology Transfer.

The Scottish Executive could establish scholarships for the study of engineering and other pertinent subjects by Scottish students studying in the US, Japan, Germany or other innovative countries. The students could be obliged, upon completion of their courses, to take suitable jobs at home for a period of (say) five years after completion of their studies. A fund could be established to provide subsidies for the immigration, permanent or temporary, of foreign scientists, engineers and technicians. It may be desirable to require such a prospective immigrant to be sponsored by a Scottish firm, university or government agency, with the sponsor obliged to provide employment to the immigrant. Specialist observer posts could be created in certain UK embassies to monitor technological developments. These specialists could also help to facilitate technology transfer agreements between those firms and Scottish enterprises.

It should be emphasized that steps to facilitate technology transfer promise to be beneficial not only to Scotland but to the economies of the other industrial nations. Rapid replacement of the obsolete can be beneficial to all, and recognition of its benefits can be used to promote a universally advantageous increase in openness of ideas.

University Contributions to Research

Finally, only a little need be said about encouragement of contributions to innovation from the universities. Clearly, provision of facilities such as laboratories and grants for use by researchers both among the faculties and the advanced students can be very helpful. Recognition of successful contributions to invention in student grants and faculty salaries and promotions are also clearly appropriate.

There is an additional step that merits consideration, though it has proved to be controversial in the US, where it seems increasingly to be employed. This entails patenting by a university of inventions created under its umbrella, with licencing of their use outside the university, for fees that add to the university's financial resources. Those fees can, of course, be shared with the inventors. The incentives for innovation that this process entails are clear. However, it has also brought the complaint that there is a resulting risk of unhealthy commercialization of academic activities.

The preceding list of programmes is meant merely to be illustrative and to stimulate ideas that are perhaps better adapted to Scotland's needs and circumstances. The one lesson that does follow from the discussion is that the future prosperity of any economy, and that of Scotland in particular, depends to a considerable extent on the its success in promoting entrepreneurship, innovation and the effective and prompt importation of technological advance from abroad. It also follows that the incentives for these developments should not be left exclusively to chance and the natural spirit of enterprise to be found within the population. There are measures that can be adopted to stimulate and facilitate them.

SOME FINAL OBSERVATIONS

While the evidence suggests that Scotland's performance in growth and innovation does not place it in the forefront among the industrial economies of the world, it is hardly negligible. Still, Scotland's distinguished history of innovative contribution, and the comparative performance of the Irish Republic, imply that more can be hoped for.

Of course, much of the incentive for improvement, it can be argued, will be provided automatically by the market mechanism. Failure by Scottish firms to innovate sufficiently will lead the market to favour more innovative firms, with the less-innovative firms growing less quickly, declining and even going out of business. The problem for Scotland is that such a process would be likely to be associated with relocation of the more innovative new and expanding firms to countries and regions outside Scotland.

This leaves Scotland with several disturbing challenges. When it comes to the links between universities and business, should there be further strengthening of the outstanding *capabilities* of universities in basic research, idea generation and invention; or instead a focus on the *incentive* regime for application of university research results? In the domestic corporate sector, on the other hand, *capabilities* appear to constitute more of the problem, since the *incentives* are broadly comparable among the regions of the UK and yet business R&D and innovation tend to be lower than average in Scotland.

This chapter has sought to indicate where the sources of outstanding performance in the pertinent arenas are to be sought. Incentives for increased R&D spending by firms and larger outlays for the purpose by government are promising and perhaps even critical steps. Government assistance for more rapid transfer of technology from abroad and incentives for the activities of venture capitalists may well be worth considering.

REFERENCES

American Philosophical Society. 2003. Biomedical advances, experienced and projected, during one surgeon's seven-decade career: in honor of Jonathan E. Rhoades, M.D., D.Sc. (1907–2002; APS 1958). (Session by R. M. Satava.) *APS Proceedings* 147, 3 September 2003. (Available at http://www.amphilsoc.org.)

Ashcroft, B. 1997. Scotland's economic problem: too few entrepreneurs, too little enterprise? Department of Economics, Fraser of Allander Institute, University of Strathclyde.

———. 2002. *Scotland in a global economy: the 2020 vision* (ed. N. Hood, J. Peat, E. Peters and S. Young), Chapter 1. Palgrave Macmillan.

Ashcroft, B., D. Bell and D. McRae. 1999. The growth agenda. University of Stirling Working Paper. (Available at *EconPapers*, http://econpapers.hhs.se.)

Ashcroft, B., S. Dunlop and J. H. Love. 2000. Industry and location effects on UK plants' innovation efficiency. *Annals of Regional Science* 34:489–502.

Baumol, W. J. 2002. *The free-market innovation machine: analyzing the growth miracle of capitalism.* Princeton University Press.

Curtis, J. 2003. A futurist's view: an interview with Richard M. Satava, M.D. *Yale Medicine* (Winter). (Available at http://www.med.yale.edu/external/pubs/ym_wi03/future.html.)

Detkin, P. N. 2002. Statement of Peter N. Detkin, Session on 'Business perspectives on patents: hardware and semiconductors'. Federal Trade Commission hearings on 'Competition and intellectual property law and policy in a knowledge-based economy'. (Available at http://www.ftc.gov/opp/intellect.)

Eliasson, G. 2002. The venture capitalist as a competent outsider. Department of Industrial Economics and Management, The Royal Institute of Technology, Stockholm.

Fraser of Allander Institute. 2001. Tracking the bigger picture (database on Scotland's economic performance), Fraser of Allander Institute, University of Strathclyde, Glasgow. (Available at www.fraser.strath.ac.uk/BiggerPicture.html.)

Fraser of Allander Institute. 2003. *Smart, Successful Scotland*, Draft Report (4), March 2003, Fraser of Allander Institute for Research on the Scottish Economy, University of Strathclyde, Glasgow. (Available at www.fraser.strath.ac.uk.)

Levie, J., W. Brown and L. Galloway. 2002. Global entrepreneurship monitor, Scotland 2002. University of Strathclyde, Hunter Center for Entrepreneurship.

Maddison, A. 2001. *The world economy: a millennial perspective*. Paris: OECD.

Mansfield, E. 1990. Comment. In *Productivity growth in Japan and the United States* (ed. C. R. Hulten), pp. 341–346. Chicago University Press.

MacRae, D. J. R. 2002. Scotland—the next Celtic Tiger? Inaugural Lecture, University of Abertay Dundee Business School, 19 November 2002. (Available at www.abertay-dundee.ac.uk.)

Markoff, J. 2003. Technology: is there life after Silicon Valley's fast lane? *New York Times* (Business/Financial Desk, Section C), 9 April, p. 1.

Marx, K. and F. Engels. 1848. *Manifesto of the Communist Party*. (Reprinted by Lawrence & Wishart.)

National Science Board. 2000. *Science and engineering indicators—2000*. Arlington, VA: National Science Foundation.

——. 2002. *Science and engineering indicators—2002*. Arlington, VA: National Science Foundation.

OECD. 2003. *The sources of economic growth in the OECD countries*. Paris: OECD. (Available at www.sourceoecd.org.)

Ordover, J. A. 1991. A patent system for both diffusion and exclusion. *Journal of Economic Perspectives* 5(Winter):43–60.

Patent Office (UK). 2001. *The Patent Office annual facts and figures 2000–2001*. (Available at www.patent.gov.uk.)

Reynolds, P. D., S. M. Camp, W. D. Bygrave, E. Autio and M. Hay. 2001. *Global entrepreneurship monitor: 2001 executive report*. Wellesley, MA, Kansas City, MO, and London, UK: Babson College, Kauffman Center for Industrial Leadership and London Business School.

Schumpeter, J. A. 1947. *Capitalism, Socialism and Democracy*, 2nd edn. New York: Harper.

Scottish Executive. 2001. Scottish Economic Report, June 2001, Chapter 4, p. 1. Selected Economic Issues, Section B, Productivity in Scotland.

——. 2003a. Scottish economic report: January 2000. (Available at www.scotland.gov.uk.)

——. 2003b. Scottish economic report: February 2003. (Available at www.scotland.gov.uk.)

——. 2003c. Business enterprise research and development in Scotland 2001: size and ownership of firms performing R&D in Scotland.

Smailes, B. 2002. Exploitation efficiency: US vs Scottish universities, Edinburgh research and innovation. University of Edinburgh, September. (Available at www.research-innovation.ed.ac.uk.)

US Small Business Administration. 2001. *The state of small business: a report of the President, 1999–2000*. Washington, DC: US Government Printing Office.

US Small Business Administration. 2003. Small serial innovators: the small firm contribution to technical change. Small Business Research Summary no. 225, February 2003. CHI Research Inc., Haddon Heights, NJ. (Under contract no. SBAHQ-01-C0149 for SBA Office of Advocacy.)

Four Challenges for Scotland's Cities

By Edward L. Glaeser

INTRODUCTION

One-half of Scotland's population lives in Glasgow or Edinburgh or in one of the council areas that directly abuts those cities; more than one-half of Scotland's gross domestic product is made in those areas. These 12 council areas are sufficiently close to one another, and sufficiently interconnected, that it is reasonable to treat them as a single metropolitan region. Moreover, this region is so important to Scotland that it is reasonable to believe that Scotland's future depends on the success of its urban core. The success of the metropolitan region in turn depends on its ability to address a series of challenges, which are facing all of the world's major cities.

Over the past 50 years, the history of urban Scotland has to a great extent been dominated by the decline of Glasgow. That city once had more than 1.1 million inhabitants and stood as the second city of the British Empire. Over the past 40 years, Glasgow's population declined by 10% per decade and today Glasgow's population is 577 000. The magnitude of Glasgow's decline is well illustrated by the fact that some people heralded its more modest population loss in the 1990s as an urban renaissance.

This decline is not surprising; it was inevitable. Glasgow was a manufacturing city located in a cold, Atlantic port. Every city that fits that description has declined. The US is littered with one-time urban giants which are now shadows of their former selves. These places, like Glasgow, once existed because of the tremendous cost savings involved in producing manufactured goods near the port. As transportation costs plummeted, there was no reason to manufacture goods in these towns any more. Instead, industry moved to warmer climes, and places with cheaper labour and friendly, pro-business regulations. Boston, New Haven, Baltimore and Philadelphia, like Glasgow, all declined as manufacturing fled.

As firms left and productivity fell, Glasgow and many of the neighbouring regions acquired concentrations of poverty and social distress. The great social problems of Scotland's urban corridor are in many ways the residue of the manufacturing exodus.

But despite this exodus, and despite the hard times over much of the past 40 years, I believe that Scotland's urban centre is ultimately resilient and at this point impressively productive. In part, this productivity is the result of Edinburgh, which has evolved into a banking centre thriving in the information age. Edinburgh's universities and its remarkable beauty serve to attract the skilled, who in turn provide the basis for urban success. Indeed, just as Glasgow's decline between 1960 and 2000 seemed unavoidable, Edinburgh fits the pattern of urban success. Cities that are high in skills and loaded with consumer amenities have done extremely well in the information age.

Moreover, Glasgow itself has done a remarkably good job of restructuring its economy. Glasgow has less banking than Edinburgh, but it is still almost completely a service economy. Glasgow's GDP per capita is close to that of Edinburgh, and higher than any other area in Scotland. Glasgow's unemployment rate has fallen by 50% since 1997. Glasgow starts with a much lower skill base than Edinburgh, so we would be surprised if the city flew as high; but given where Glasgow was in 1980, in 2001 the city looks spectacular.

Nonetheless, Scotland's urban core faces a series of challenges if it is to continue its success in the twenty-first century. First and most important, the area must continue to attract firms and to create new entrepreneurs. In the past, cities like Glasgow could attract firms because of their favourable geography, but geography has little remaining relevance. Instead, the available evidence suggests that the important determinant of firm location is the presence of skilled workers. If Glasgow and Edinburgh want to attract employers, they need to create, attract and maintain a skilled workforce. This requires education, both at the lower and upper levels, and amenities that attract the skilled. Moreover, government policies cannot be too oriented towards the poorest residents, otherwise the rich will flee to communities outside the cities that cater to their own needs.

Yet while the city needs to keep its skilled residents, Glasgow and Edinburgh obviously also face a challenge caring for their socially isolated, poorer residents. While America's cities offer abundant examples of economic success, they offer far fewer examples of solving inner city poverty. Segregation appears to be very damaging, but forced integration is explosive. Badly performing schools are a disaster, but increasing school spending is no guarantee of success. Targeting spending at the poorest neighbourhoods has the perverse effect of inducing the poor to stay in poor places. If anything, American urban policy has been most effective at solving the crime problem, which is a benefit for the poor. Scotland's cities face a tremendous social challenge, but without national help it is hard to see how they can meet this challenge effectively.

The third challenge faced by these cities is housing. A city's population is, in a sense, determined by its housing stock, and wages must always be high enough to compensate workers for high housing prices. Historically, the great housing challenge was to supply the poorest people with adequate housing. Today, the great housing challenge is allowing middle-income people to afford homes in cities that are increasingly being priced out of their reach. High housing prices are actually easy to handle, if governments have the will to reform construction regulation. High housing prices are almost always due to limits on new construction, which are usually the result of government regulation. If Edinburgh or Glasgow were to radically reform their planning procedures to make it easy to build large apartment buildings or large housing developments, prices would quickly fall.

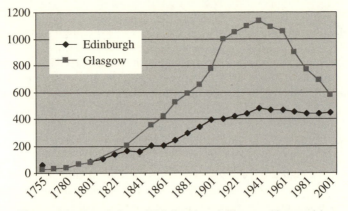

Figure 4.1. Population of Edinburgh and Glasgow (thousands).

Finally, the fourth challenge faced by Scotland's urban core is transportation. The move to car-based living is inevitable and not a particularly bad thing. After all, cars are so popular because they do confer real advantages, especially saving significant amounts of time. Nonetheless, driving involves far greater congestion problems than any older technology. One primary reason for this is that cars require much more space to drive and park per traveller than other modes of transportation. It can be useful to subsidize buses as an alternative (although this seems more than a little quixotic) but trains are generally horribly wasteful financially (buses are always more efficient). It makes sense to build more roads, but these roads will themselves shortly congest without better taxation of roads and drivers. Ideally, congestion charges can become more sophisticated over time and eventually be used to charge people different amounts for driving at different times of day.

THE ECONOMICS OF CITIES

Economists define cities as the absence of physical space between people and firms. The essence of urban life is proximity. This simple fact guides all of our understanding of why cities exist and what determines their success and failure: cities ultimately exist to eliminate transportation costs for goods, for people and for ideas. Cities that succeed are those which offer proximity to something valuable. Historically, that was proximity to a port, or a coal mine, or the government. Today, cities succeed by offering proximity to people and their ideas. As such, urban success depends on attracting skilled residents.

The oldest cities were commercial and political. Residents came to them for access to the government, as in the cases of Jerusalem, Babylon or Rome, or because of access to a trading route, like the German cities of the Rhine. Commercial cities were invariably ports because of the vast cost savings of water-borne transportation. During the Roman Empire it cost more to ship goods 75 miles over land than from one edge of the Mediterranean to the other.

Certainly, Edinburgh and Glasgow both had plenty of politics and trade, but Edinburgh's history is ultimately centred on its role as Scotland's capital while

Glasgow's fame rests on its mercantile and manufacturing tradition. Figure 4.1 shows estimates of the populations of the cities of Edinburgh and Glasgow over the past 250 years. Edinburgh was a much larger city than Glasgow until the late eighteenth century, its size related to the Scottish government. Glasgow's importance stemmed from its status as an Atlantic port. Glasgow, like every major American city in the early nineteenth century, grew because it was located where a big river hit the sea. Indeed, Glasgow's rise seems geographically preordained: the Clyde is Scotland's only major inland waterway flowing into the Atlantic.

Glasgow's development followed the same pattern as that of other Atlantic seaboard ports such as New York, Boston and Liverpool (Glaeser 2003). The city first expanded in the eighteenth century as a centre for transatlantic trade. The dominant product was tobacco and the dominant source was the West Indies. Naturally, over the nineteenth century Glaswegian ships acquired a global range and the products handled broadened considerably. But it was manufacturing, not trade, that made Glasgow the second city of the British Empire. Manufacturing came to dominate all these port cities and the goods were generally shipped by boat. Manufacturers agglomerated around the ports to save on transportation costs. After all, in an era when shipping by land remained enormously expensive, if you wanted your goods to be sold outside of your home market, you needed access to boats.

Glasgow initially specialized in processing the cotton which the city's ships brought back from the New World. Workers then came for the jobs. For some subsidiary industries, the important factor was proximity to other industries that were involved in exporting. Taverns locate in ports, not because they are shipping their ale abroad for sale, but rather to gain proximity to the sailors who are manning the ships. This example is typical of the increasing returns to economic activity in cities. Once a critical mass of firms exists, other producers join that mass to save on the costs of buying from and selling to those firms.

But the twentieth century was not kind to these cities based on transportation costs for goods. Over the century, the costs of moving goods plummeted (Glaeser and Kohlhase 2004). For example, the real costs of rail transport in the US fell by 95%. New technologies, such as trucking, also reduced the costs of moving goods, and freed firms from the need to cram in close to a port or rail yard. Instead, manufacturing firms could disperse throughout the countryside in search of cheaper land and lower wages. Manufacturing decentralized within cities, fled cities for less urban places, and in many cases left the developed world altogether.

The decline in transportation costs and the consequent decline in urban manufacturing wrought havoc on cities everywhere, and Glasgow was no exception. Since World War II, Glasgow appears to have lost 500 000 residents or 45% of its population. The extremity of this decline is such that many people have described the 1990s as a remarkable comeback, although Glasgow lost 10% of its population during those years.

Glasgow's decline is large, but not unusual. Many of America's large cities experienced similar declines and for similar reasons. In 1950, America had 10 cities with more than 800 000 inhabitants. Eight of those cities have lost 20% of their population or more. Four of those cities lost more than 500 000 people (Chicago, Detroit,

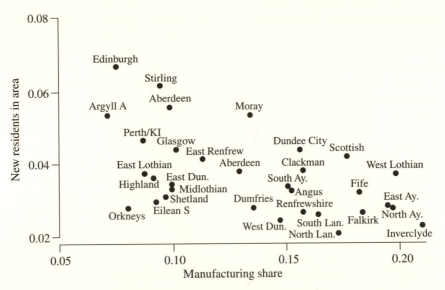

Figure 4.2. New residents and manufacturing.

Philadelphia and St. Louis) and three of those cities have lost more than 45% of their 1950 populations (Cleveland, Detroit and St. Louis).

Glasgow simply got hit by the same forces that made manufacturing cities throughout the US and UK suffer. In the US the raw correlation between metropolitan area growth between 1980 and 2000 (measured as a percentage of the 1980 population) and share of the labour force in manufacturing is −48%. Figure 4.2 shows this pattern for Scottish council areas using one measure of growth: the proportion of residents in a council area in 2001 who had lived elsewhere one year earlier. This variable is strongly related to concentration in manufacturing; the raw correlation of these variables is −54%. There is a much weaker relationship between population growth between 1981 and 2001 and manufacturing in 2001, primarily because of Glasgow (which declined heavily and has little manufacturing left) and Eilean Siar (Western Isles). Without those two observations, the correlation between dependence on manufacturing in 2001 and population change over the previous two decades is −28%.

The lack of importance of transportation costs for goods shows up in the locations of manufacturing plants within the US. Dumais et al. (1997) find that manufacturing establishments no longer locate near their suppliers or customers. Instead, manufacturing plants locate near other plants that use the same type of worker. Kolko (2000) finds that services still locate near their customers and suppliers.

Why do manufacturing plants care only about proximity to their workers, but services care about proximity to clients? The essence of services is that they involve personal interactions. Overwhelmingly, to deliver a service the supplier needs to be in the same place as the client. As such, for services it is the transport costs for people, not for goods, that matter. The twentieth century drove the costs of moving goods down tremendously, but the transportation costs for people are still quite significant.

After all, the primary element of the costs of moving people is their time, and time has become very much more valuable over the twentieth century. Even with the automobile and air travel, moving people around is expensive and likely to remain expensive as time continues to become more valuable. In general, the question of whether transport costs for people will rise or fall in the future depends on whether travel speeds increase more quickly than the value of time.

As such, now that goods are cheap to transport, cities should be understood primarily as social organizations meant to create proximity between people. I have already mentioned the role of proximity in facilitating the delivery of services. Urban proximity has several other important effects. As big cities bring people closer to multiple employers, this enables people to move between firms more readily, which in turn facilitates responses to business downturns. In a one-firm town, the labour force can be badly hurt if that firm goes bankrupt. In large, multi-firm cities, those workers can generally find other employers. Furthermore, the presence of multiple employers ensures that young workers can hop from firm to firm to learn which occupation best matches their own skills.

Proximity is therefore important to the functioning of labour markets, but it may be just as important in creating social connections. Accounts of rural–urban migration, such as Dreiser's *Sister Carrie*, often emphasize the social benefits of city-living above the higher wages. While radio and television have done much to alleviate the social isolation of low-density areas, young, single people still flock to urban areas in order to meet other young, single people. Thus 21.3% of the residents of Edinburgh are single people between the ages of 20 and 34; 11.6% of the population of the Highlands consists of single people of those same ages. Some authors have even described cities as 'marriage markets'.

So the increasing importance of people, relative to goods, has driven a major transformation of the urban landscape. Firms are increasingly moving towards places where people want to live and this has created the rise of the 'consumer city'.

This phenomenon can be particularly seen in the rise of warm, dry places within the United States. Somewhat unfortunately for Scotland, people appear to prefer warmth. Because of this preference, as productivity differences between north and south declined within the US, people flocked to the warmer climes. There is no better predictor of urban growth over the last 80 years than warmth. Half of US metropolitan area population growth between 1980 and 2000 is accounted for by the average January temperature within the metropolitan area (the correlation coefficient is 50%).

The power of warmth is only the most obvious piece of evidence suggesting the increasing importance of consumer preferences. Glaeser et al. (2001) provide evidence showing a link between many measures of consumer amenities and city growth, in the US and elsewhere. Tourist destinations have grown. Places with museums have grown. Cities that have high housing prices, relative to their wages, have grown more quickly. This finding may seem somewhat surprising—after all, you might expect people to flee cities that are expensive—but urban economists believe that high housing prices reflect either high wages or popular places. Indeed, we find that within the US all of the places with high housing values relative to wages are in California or Hawaii. As such, this measure of excess housing prices serves as a proxy for consumer amenities and this proxy also predicts growth.

While reducing the transportation costs for people is a primary reason that cities continue to exist, changes in transportation technology continue to change the shape of urban areas. In America, and increasingly elsewhere, the automobile has reshaped the urban form. In the eighteenth century, cities were built to accommodate walking. In the nineteenth century, cities spread out and took advantage of the omnibus, the trolley, the subway and eventually the bus. But all of these still required enough density that people could walk to the subway or trolley stop. The car has had the biggest impact of all, because automobiles eliminate the need for walking altogether. Moreover, cars themselves require much more space for driving and parking.

For these reasons, the automobile has created a total revolution in urban form. The American urban frontier is built at extremely low densities. Both firms and residences are widely dispersed throughout endless miles of suburban highway. Many urban critics find these edge cities horrific, but the fact is that they provide undeniable benefits for their residents. Car-based travel is generally far faster than using public transportation. The average commute by car is 23 minutes in the US. The average commute using public transportation is 47 minutes. Edge cities also allow firms and people to live in big homes with large lots. Consumer goods are also cheaper because retail trade can be dominated by 'big box' stores that minimize the need for personnel. Those of us with an elitist taste for traditional cities may sniff at the endless suburban developments, but they have grown for a reason: they deliver speed and space and comfort to tens of millions of Americans.

Proximity facilitates social interactions and eases service provision, but it also speeds the flow of ideas. Even today, the record of scientific citations shows that people, even scientists, are much more likely to learn ideas from people who are physically close to them (Jaffe et al. 1993). As economic growth depends on knowledge creation, the urban edge in information transmission remains critical. Some cities can survive on the basis of warmth and beauty, but for the rest of the urban world, success depends on providing the great modern commodity: information. If Glasgow and Edinburgh are going to remain important in the twenty-first century, they must provide their residents with knowledge.

The transmission of ideas is important to urban success in many different ways. For firms that hope to innovate, being at the heart of an innovative cluster can ensure access to the latest ideas. Firms in Silicon Valley find it easier to stay abreast of developments in computer technology. For industries, like finance or journalism, where success requires up-to-date information, dense urban cores provide access to the latest rumours. Finally, as the great economist Alfred Marshall emphasized a century ago, for young workers, proximity to older workers in dense agglomerations, provides the young with an opportunity to learn skills and improve in their trades. And cities act as forges of human capital: as skills have become more important, young workers have increasingly come to big cities to learn.

Some people believe that information technology will ultimately make space obsolete, by eliminating the need for face-to-face interactions. According to these theorists, email, faxes and videoconferencing will speed the flow of information with no need to be around people. Certainly, some interactions which used to be face-to-face are now done at long distances electronically. However, while technology eliminates the need for some face-to-face interactions, it does not follow that face-to-face interactions are actually being phased out. We live in an increasingly interactive economy with an increasing demand for knowledge.

As such, the future demand for density depends on a horse race. Will the demand for face-to-face interactions decline because of competition from electronic substitutes or will the overall increase in demand for interaction cause both face-to-face and electronic interactions to become more important? In principle, the next 50 years could see either a decline in the need for urban density or an increasing concentration in mega-cities. I believe the available evidence suggests that information technology is actually increasing the demand for face-to-face interactions and ultimately cities.

There are several pieces of evidence that support this view. First, and most obviously, urbanization has not been declining over the past 20 years and in many ways, these have terrific decades for cities, like London and New York, which specialize in knowledge transmission. Secondly, while faxes and email were supposed to eliminate the need for business travel, since 1985, business travel has soared as the entire world economy has become far more interactive. Gaspar and Glaeser (1998) find that this timing suggests the impact on travel of increased demand for interactions has been greater than that of falling air travel prices due to deregulation.

Evidence from the original high-tech communication device, the telephone, also supports the view that improvements in communications technology are not bad for cities. A hundred years ago, seers were predicting that telephones would eliminate the need for cities. Obviously, this didn't happen. In general, telephone usage has more often been a complement to face-to-face interactions than a substitute. Unsurprisingly, phone calls occur much more often between people who are physically close and see each other more often. It is also true that across time and across countries, telephones and cities have tended to go together, even controlling for country wealth.

Perhaps the most striking piece of evidence suggesting that technology doesn't eliminate the need to be physically close is that the most famous physical agglomeration of the modern age, Silicon Valley, is in the industry with the best access to information technology. Indeed, as Saxenian (1994) details, face-to-face transmission of ideas was crucial for the growth of the valley. Silicon Valley is not unique, as industries that specialize in knowledge (as measured by having highly educated workers) tend to be far more urbanized than other industries (Glaeser and Kahn 2001).

The rising importance of information, and the continuing costs of moving people across space, together imply that successful cities should be skilled cities. If knowledge has become more important, then proximity to people with knowledge should have grown more valuable too, and, indeed, there should be a connection between a city's initial and current level of skills. Following Glaeser (1994) and Nardinelli and Simon (1996), there have been a large number of papers documenting the powerful connection between skills and city growth. Initial skills are correlated with subsequent population growth, housing price growth and wage growth (Glaeser and Saiz

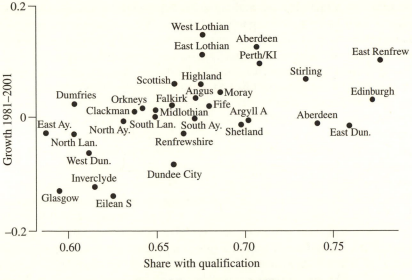

Figure 4.3. Growth and skills.

2004). This connection occurs in the US, the UK and elsewhere. Moreover, while skills predict growth throughout the twentieth century, their importance has risen over the postwar period.

In the US the raw correlation between city growth between 1980 and 2000 and the share of the adult population with college degrees in 1980 (including all US cities with more than 250 000 residents in 1980) is 53%. While I do not have data on skill levels in 1981 across Scottish council areas, I can correlate skill in 2001 with growth over the 1981–2001 period. I use the share of the population with some form of educational qualification (i.e. O-levels or GSCE A–C grades, or higher) as the measure of skill. The connection between skills and growth is shown in Figure 4.3. The correlation coefficient of the two variables is 50% across Scottish council areas, just as it is across larger American cities.

The correlation for American cities becomes much stronger if we look at the Northeastern and the Midwestern regions. For cities in these regions, the skills-growth correlation for cities in the Northeast and the Midwest rises to over 70%. But in the west, the correlation is actually negative. The natural interpretation of this fact is that the places within the US that were endowed with good climates did not need skills to thrive. People just came to California looking for the good life. However, the places that were cold, former manufacturing towns only survived when they had skilled residents. These skilled residents helped the successful cities find new industries and reinvent themselves (Glaeser 2003).

While I believe that cities will continue to thrive over the next century, it is important to stress that urban form has changed and will continue to change. It is very difficult to fight the power of the automobile, at least without massive taxation of gasoline. The car is just too effective a means of getting around. Glaeser et al. (2000) estimate that each public transportation trip involves on average an 18 minute fixed time cost, which requires walking to the bus stop or train station, waiting for the bus or train, and then walking to your final destination from the end stop. When the average car commute in modern car-based cities is rarely more than 20 minutes, it is easy to see why people and firms have been flocking to the urban edge.

The cost advantages mean that cities of the future everywhere are likely to be built around the automobile, just like American cities over the past 30 years. These cities have not lost the ability to connect people and ideas. After all, travel times are quite often shorter in these places. Silicon Valley is a car city—not a public transportation city. Not all of this switch to the automobile is good, and it certainly needs managing. But given that Scotland's car ownership has risen by 200% over the last four decades, it seems obvious that Scotland is heading in the same direction as the US towards car-based living and car-based cities.

The changes in transportation technology have created challenges for Scotland's cities. Despite claims of a Glasgow renaissance, the data suggest that this rebirth is far from complete. It does not seem too clear whether Glasgow is ultimately going to follow the pattern of St. Louis (unrelenting decline) or Boston (a complete turnaround). Edinburgh is clearly doing much better. In addition, both cities have extremes of wealth and poverty and a certain amount of social segregation. Furthermore, the car has problems—pollution and congestion—which need to be managed. Finally, recent increases in housing prices (which is after all a fundamentally good sign) present the challenge of providing affordable housing for Scotland's urban residents.

The Productivity Challenge

Beautiful but unproductive small towns can survive, but cities cannot continue to attract or keep residents without well-paying jobs. American cities with high-income residents grow; cities with low-income residents shrink. It goes without saying that the first and most important challenge of the Edinburgh–Glasgow urban corridor is to ensure that firms come to and stay in the area. Without jobs, housing and transportation do not mean much.

Some authors are tempted to focus on the supposed differences between Edinburgh and Glasgow, whereby Edinburgh is depicted as a booming capital of the information age and Glasgow as an industrial relic. The figures show that this caricature is deeply misleading. Productivity per capita is high relative to the rest of Scotland, or indeed the rest of the United Kingdom, in both places. Of course, differences in GDP across space reveal differences in productivity, not well-being. These statistics are corrected for national, not local prices, and places that are productive are also more expensive. Still, if we are interested in productivity we want to consider output per capita without adjusting for local housing costs.

Scottish Economic Statistics 2002 reveals that Edinburgh and Glasgow are by far the most productive areas in Scotland; indeed, they are two of the four areas in Scotland which are more productive than the UK as a whole (Edinburgh, Glasgow, Northeastern Scotland including Aberdeen, Aberdeenshire and North East Moray, and the Shetlands). Table 4.1 lists the five most and five least productive areas in

Table 4.1. Five most (left) and five least (right) productive areas in
Scotland with their GDP per capita (pounds per annum).

Edinburgh	18 417	East Lothian and Midlothian	7503
Glasgow	16 495	East Ayrshire	8191
Shetland	15 107	Caithness	8467
Falkirk	12 227	Dunbartonshire	8489
Perth, Kinross, Stirling	12 203	Lochaber	8630

Source: Scottish Economic Statistics 2002 (Table 6.1). Area definitions are Nomenclature of Territorial
Statistics level 3 areas.

Scotland according to 2002 GDP figures. Strikingly, the composite region of East
Lothian and Midlothian (between Edinburgh and Glasgow) is the least productive
area in Scotland, with GDP per head less than 50% of GDP per head in Edinburgh.
So while there are important differences between Glasgow and Edinburgh, the more
striking difference is the contrast between either city and the corridor in between
them.

The fact that firms in Edinburgh are able to be twice as productive, on average,
than their neighbouring Midlothian rivals reflects in no small part higher levels of
human capital in Edinburgh: just 15% of the residents of East Lothian have a top
qualification; 32% of Edinburgh residents have those same qualifications. Edinburgh
is the best-educated city in Scotland; the Lothians are less educated.

But the available evidence suggests that Edinburgh earnings are higher than its
level of skills would lead you to expect. In Edinburgh average weekly earnings for
full-time residents are high, even controlling for the high share of its residents with
higher qualifications. Indeed, while Glasgow's earnings are lower on average than
those of Edinburgh, controlling for skill, Glasgow is actually richer. Both of these
cities are wealthier than their skills alone should warrant.

High earnings in Edinburgh and Glasgow are part of a pervasive pattern: dense
areas are more productive. Figure 4.4 shows the relationship between the logarithm
of council area density and the average unexplained earnings in the council area.
I have labelled this measure 'unexplained earnings' because I first controlled for a
set of council area level schooling indicators, so in principle this measure attempts
to control for the skill level of the community. The graph shows the significant
positive relationship between population density and earnings. As density doubles,
earnings rise by five pounds per week. Indeed, density does a good job of explaining
earnings, except for Dundee and its surrounding areas (which are unusually poor)
and Aberdeen (which is unusually rich).

The connection between density and earnings tells us that urban areas are still
more productive and there is still an edge to eliminating the transport costs for goods,
people and ideas within urban areas. Indeed, my previous discussion of the role that
cities now play in eliminating transport costs for people and ideas, but not for goods,
is well illustrated by the current industrial mix of Glasgow and Edinburgh. Neither
city is oriented towards manufacturing any more. In Glasgow 7% of employment
is in manufacturing, in Edinburgh 6%. Today, the areas that are heavily oriented

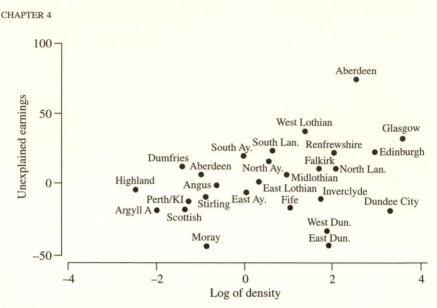

Figure 4.4. Unexplained earnings and density.

Table 4.2. Share of employment (%) by industry in Edinburgh and Glasgow.

Name	Edinburgh	Glasgow
Energy and water	1	1
Manufacturing	6	7
Construction	3	4
Retail, wholesale, hotels	21	22
Transport, communications	5	6
Finance and business	33	23
Public	32	36

Source: Scottish Executive, Analytical Service Division, city briefings.

towards manufacturing are on the urban edges: Inverclyde, West Lothian, North Ayrshire and East Ayrshire.

Edinburgh's stronger human capital base has helped it to be more firmly oriented towards business and finance: 33% of its employment is in these areas (23% for Glasgow). Glasgow has more people in the public sector (36%) than Edinburgh (32%). But apart from Edinburgh's greater strength in finance, the industrial structure (and average earnings) in the two cities looks quite similar (see Table 4.2). They are both high-wage service cities.

It is unquestionable that Glasgow has more economic distress than Edinburgh. The unemployment rates in December 2003 in Glasgow and Edinburgh were 5.6% and 3.4%, respectively. Unemployment understates the true extent of dependence on social services. In May 2001, 29% of working-age Glaswegians were claiming some key benefit (unemployment, disability or single parent) compared with only 13% of Edinburgh residents (*Scottish Economic Statistics 2002*). The most striking

Table 4.3. Economic changes 1995–2003.

Area	Unemployment 1997	2003	Change in jobs since 1995 (manufacturing)	(service)
Glasgow	10%	5.6%	−7100	+60 000
Edinburgh	6.0%	3.4%	−7000	+48 100
North Lanarkshire	6.8%	4.0%	−8400	+22 000
South Lanarkshire	5.8%	3.3%	−4100	+10 800
East Renfrewshire	4%	2.3%	−400	+2 200
Midlothian	3.9%	2.1%	−700	+5 000
West Lothian	4.5%	3.1%	−1500	+14 500

fact is that 19% of Glasgow residents were receiving disability benefits. This is the highest rate in Scotland.

Many of the council areas surrounding Glasgow have similar levels of economic distress. 23% of the residents of North Lanarkshire are receiving some kind of key social benefit, 21% of the residents of East Ayrshire. Moreover, the GDP per capita in these regions is much lower than in Glasgow or Edinburgh. While Glasgow is clearly a city with both tremendous wealth and deep poverty, many of the surrounding areas have the poverty without the wealth.

It seems clear, however, that the past 10 years have been relatively good for both cities, as for pretty much every other area. Table 4.3 looks at seven council areas and shows the unemployment rates in 1997 and 2003 and the changes in manufacturing and service employment over the same period. The fundamental message from this table is that, everywhere, the economy of this corridor is improving. Unemployment is down in all of these areas. In some cases, such as Edinburgh, unemployment has declined from low to lower. In other cases, such as Glasgow, the unemployment rate has fallen from a very high level to a much more moderate level.

Employment changes tend to show a pervasive pattern. Every region is tending to lose manufacturing jobs and gain service jobs. Moreover, everywhere the gain in the service sector is more than overwhelming the loss in manufacturing. The growth of the service sectors is more than offsetting the continuing decline of manufacturing. Economic deprivation remains, but this is not the result of a weak economy overall. Instead, lack of skills and social isolation lie behind the poverty that remains in the Edinburgh–Glasgow corridor. I will turn to these problems in the next section. Now I will focus on the future of the area and appropriate policies.

The Future of the Economies of Edinburgh and Glasgow

Peering into a crystal ball is perilous work, but we can base our predictions on two relatively reliable trends. First, economic growth will continue and it will continue to favour human intellect over muscle. This trend implies that human capital will continue to dominate urban success. The single most important thing to ensure that a city will do well is to attract skilled residents. The trend also implies that people will increasingly demand pleasant urban amenities. After all, when people become richer they want to consume nicer things. A pleasant urban environment is one of the things on which they want to spend money. The second trend is that transportation technologies will continue to improve. The implication of this is that manufacturing will continue to flee Scotland and that people will move more and more to car-based living.

Together these forces spell three things for the economic future of the Edinburgh–Glasgow area. First, the city centres of Edinburgh and Glasgow will surely continue to succeed on the basis of their human capital levels and their amenities. Edinburgh, in particular, has a powerful combination of skills and scenic beauty. In combination with the city's other amenities, this will continue to ensure that Edinburgh has a strong skill base and will continue to succeed. Glasgow is somewhat weaker, but its core still has both skills and urban amenities.

Second, some suburban areas will continue to really thrive, as employment increasingly decentralizes. The fastest-growing cities in the US in the 1990s were Las Vegas, Nevada and Plano, Texas, which grew spectacularly as employment built up in endless office parks and development. Some of this is already occurring in the Edinburgh–Glasgow corridor and much more is to come. Past experience suggests that this growth will tend to come in the areas of the metropolitan region with high levels of human capital and relatively low density levels.

Third, the low-income suburbs that were built at higher densities around public transportation are likely to continue to have problems. These areas have neither the excitement of downtown, which attracts young skilled workers, nor the advantages of lower-density, car-based cities. They once provided cheap housing with access to public transportation for low-income manufacturing workers. At one point this served a tremendous social function, but now such areas are likely to continue to decline. Either the homes will be torn down and replaced with lower-density housing for richer people, or they will increasingly sink into social distress.

What is to be done? Policy Approaches to Productivity

Economic research into urban productivity tells us that there are no magic bullets and that central economic planning tends to be disastrous. The most important ingredient in keeping firms in a region is to make sure that it has plenty of skilled workers. The second most important ingredient is to provide basic infrastructure and relatively low taxes. All of us may agree that society needs higher taxes to take care of the less fortunate, but if this kind of redistribution is tried at the local level, then the rich just flee to other localities and leave the poor in unaided isolation.

These facts suggest that urban policy should worry about attracting *people* at least as much as attracting firms. This means good schools for children and amenities that are attractive to skilled, often younger, workers. Safe streets are particularly important. New York's renaissance in the 1990s was built in part on its increasingly safe urban environment. Catering to the less fortunate may be morally preferable, but at the city-level, it means that a city will attract the poor, rather than the rich.

An increasing body of evidence (e.g. Haughwout et al. 2003; Holmes 1998) shows how high taxes and regulation influence firms' location decisions. It is not easy to ensure that firms will come to a region, but high taxes and aggressive regulation can ensure that they stay away. This may sound just like another economist's laissez faire prescription, but the ability of firms to relocate effectively ties the government's hands at the local level. Unless big government intervention is uniform everywhere, then a city just hurts itself by trying independently to increase the size of its welfare state.

What should *not* be done? First, it is not obvious that national well-being is well served by place-specific policies. The government has an obligation to every person, but not to every spot of ground. Some regions are no longer very productive, and as a result people should not live there anymore. We are better off allowing the market to work, and allowing or helping people to leave declining regions, than we are fighting to keep people in declining regions. There may well be a case for support for the residents of these areas, at least in the short term, but there is no case for using government policies to induce people to stay in poor places. Most place-based financial aid does exactly that and as such may do more harm than good.

Second, it is also clear that governments are not very good at picking industries or subsidizing particular firms. Attempts to micro-manage urban growth frequently become mired in political patronage or outright corruption. As such, cities should work on creating a good business environment, not on helping individual businesses or industries. The history of Boston suggests repeated reinvention.[1] The history of Scotland does too. This reinvention is *always* bottom up as entrepreneurs figure out how to better use existing urban resources. If the government attempts to push those resources in particular directions, then the reinvention process will surely be stymied.

The economy of the Edinburgh–Glasgow corridor is currently doing well. These core cities and some suburbs are likely to do well in the future. Many of the higher density suburbs will continue to have problems. The best thing that can be done for those areas is to spend on educating their children. After that, permitting business development with low taxes and light regulation is surely also helpful. Specific place-based policies or industrial planning are surely mistakes.

THE SOCIAL CHALLENGE

If there is one force that presents the greatest challenge to the Edinburgh–Glasgow corridor becoming a high-human-capital centre of idea creation, it is the legacy of poverty created by the decline of manufacturing. Both Glasgow and the surrounding areas have massive amounts of concentrated poverty and the social problems that always surround such poverty. Among American industrial cities, the problems of poverty generally stand as the greatest barrier to an information-age rebirth. The Scottish concentrations of poverty are both troubling in themselves and likely to deter further growth of the region, primarily because the skilled fear living among the poor.

---

[1] Boston has reinvented itself three times: in the early nineteenth century as the provider of seafaring human capital for a far-flung maritime trading and fishing empire; in the late nineteenth century as a factory town built on immigrant labour and Brahmin capital; and finally in the late twentieth century as a centre of the information economy. In all three instances, human capital—admittedly of radically different forms—provided the secret to Boston's rebirth.

I have already shown that population density is generally associated with higher levels of productivity. It is also related to higher levels of unemployment. Paradoxically, dense cities are related to both high output and to people being out of work. This paradox has two resolutions. The first is historical. While Glasgow is still highly productive, it was more productive in the past and as this productivity has declined, people have become unemployed.

The second reason why density is related to unemployment, or poverty more generally, stems from transportation costs. Low-density living requires automobiles, which are expensive. As a result, the poor and the unemployed tend to stay in high-density areas to save on transportation costs. Within the US, Glaeser et al. (2000) find that poor people crowd around public transportation and that the tendency of the poor to live near city centres can be explained by greater access to buses and subways. This argument suggests that the tendency of the poor to live in and around Glasgow is not temporary, but rather a permanent feature of the urban landscape.

Data on absolute unemployment levels hide the true extent of concentrated poverty in Glasgow. *Scottish Economic Statistics 2002* shows that Glasgow has a remarkable number of the highest poverty wards in all of Scotland. Not only do the poor live in Glasgow, but they crowd together in segregated communities within the city. An increasingly large body of research is coming to document that these segregated centres of poverty have deleterious effects on the residents of these areas and on their children. In past work, I have found that segregation is connected to low educational outcomes, childbearing outside marriage and youth unemployment.

Moreover, crime is regularly a companion of poverty. Because the poor have a lower opportunity cost of crime, and because police often fail to enforce the law in poorer communities, concentrated poverty often creates disorder. This then creates a vicious circle as firms avoid poorer areas because they fear crime. In the 1990s, Glasgow had a murder rate of 58.7 per million per year, almost four times the rate for Edinburgh (15.6 per million per year) and almost three times the rate for Scotland as a whole.

What can be done about concentrations of poverty? Broadly speaking, there have been three main policy approaches. First, in some cases place-based employment policies have tried to create jobs to employ the poor. In the US, these policies have taken the form of Empowerment or Enterprise Zones and have operated by giving tax breaks to firms that operate in disadvantaged areas. In some cases, public firms have themselves operated in these areas.

These policies have had very modest success. A typical pattern is that firms will open in these areas and then employ high human capital workers from elsewhere. The net result is that property values and rents rise in the disadvantaged area (disadvantaging the poor even further) while employing only outsiders. Moreover, on conceptual grounds these policies are often faulted as attempts to 'gild the ghetto'. Many people, including myself, believe that the poor should be encouraged to leave these segregated communities. Place-based policies, even if they work, stop this tendency and keep the poor in their communities.

The second major policy approach has been forced integration. In the US, busing of schoolchildren was the most aggressive form of forced integration. The evidence suggests that the bused children often experienced real gains, but at a considerable cost. The children had long commutes and the outside communities fought this integration bitterly. Many American cities still bear the scars of the political battles fought over busing.

The Moving-To-Opportunity programme was a more recent, and much more modest, attempt at integration. This programme gave housing vouchers to poor parents and some of these vouchers required the parents to move to low poverty neighbourhoods. In fact, even the housing vouchers that did not require the poor to move led to them doing so anyway. These disadvantaged parents used the housing money to buy a better neighbourhood for their children. Analysis of these programmes is ongoing, but the evidence to date suggests that female children do much better when they leave the ghetto, but that male children often do worse. Indeed, sometimes leaving the ghetto appears to increase the number of criminal arrests of poor children.

Still this sort of programme offers some hope, certainly relative to public housing. Public housing has had the unfortunate effect of concentrating the poor in a small geographic area. Vouchers enable the poor to spread. As such, it makes sense to structure housing assistance to the poor in the form of vouchers. Furthermore, since part of the objective is to ensure that children grow up outside ghettos, these vouchers should be targeted towards parents.

A third policy approach to concentrated poverty is to improve public goods, like schools and safety, in those areas. These public goods may have the advantage of improving the skills and reducing the poverty of the next generation. Unfortunately, there is little evidence that increased spending on city schools achieves much. There is some evidence that increased school choice is helpful (see Chapter 8), but there remains a great deal of debate on this question as well.

The evidence on safety is more hopeful. Improvements in police technology in the 1990s appear to have significantly reduced crime in a large number of American cities. Community policing and the use of information technology can significantly improve arrest rates, which in turn leads to better protection of the poor. At the very least, guaranteeing safe streets for the poor and their middle-income neighbours appears to be one road to urban renewal. Certainly, the success of New York in the 1990s owes much to improved public safety.

The Housing Challenge

The traditional challenge of housing policy was to provide better housing for the most disadvantaged citizens. Over the twentieth century, governments used policies such as public housing, rent regulation and even vouchers to try and improve the housing quality of the poor. Indeed, because of government policy, rising incomes and decreasing construction costs, housing quality has soared. We began the century with families crowded into one-room tenements, and frequently lacking running water. In the 2001 census, the average Scot has 2.09 rooms and only 11% of the population is classified as having too little space; 93% of the population has both central heating and their own shower or bath.

Table 4.4. The rise in housing prices between 1997 and 2003.

Area	Average price 1997 (first quarter)	Average price 2003 (last quarter)
Greater London	114 248	247 834
Lothian	73 516	149 784
Strathclyde	61 452	100 330
Tayside	61 702	108 108

Source: Halifax historical housing data. (Available at http://www.hbosplc.com/ economy/HistoricalDataSpreadsheet.asp.)

There are certainly remaining problems, but the progress has been staggering. By and large, the remaining housing problems are tightly linked with urban poverty. For example, 17% of the houses in Glasgow are without central heating. Still, we are at the point where the fundamental nature of the problem has changed. Once, the housing problem was substandard housing for the poor. Now the housing problem is extremely expensive housing for everyone.

Rising prices over the past 20 years in the Edinburgh–Glasgow region have meant that housing is an increasingly large burden for much of the population. These high housing prices reflect an increased desire to live in Edinburgh and Glasgow, but the great housing challenge is how to continue making the Edinburgh–Glasgow corridor grow without causing housing prices to continue ballooning.

Table 4.4 shows the path of house prices since 1997 for Greater London and three regions in Scotland: Lothian (including Edinburgh), Strathclyde (including Glasgow) and Tayside. Over the almost seven-year period, housing prices in London have more than doubled, making it one of the most expensive places to live in the world. London is more than 50% more expensive than Lothian or Strathclyde, but these areas have also increasingly become costly. Lothian housing prices have more than doubled since 1997. Strathclyde prices have risen by more than 60%. Certainly, Edinburgh has the worst house price problem in Scotland, but the striking thing is that housing prices have risen remarkably everywhere.

Why have housing prices risen so quickly in the UK? Like any other market, housing prices are driven by supply and demand. Housing demand is a critical reflection of urban success in the Edinburgh–Glasgow corridor.

However, rising demand for a region does not necessarily mean increasing prices. If rising demand is met with elastic supply, then new demand will just increase the quantity produced, not the cost of housing. This fact is necessary to understand why the fastest-growing cities within the US generally have only modest increases in housing prices. In growing regions, with new construction like the west and the south, house price growth has been modest. In regions with no new construction, like the northeast, housing prices have risen dramatically. In fact, it is quite plausible that the places with the highest increases in demand, like Florida, have had some of the lowest price increases because supply in those regions has been so flexible.

What about the supply of housing in Scotland? Over the past 10 years, Scotland has built around 22 000 new units per year. In the third quarter of 2003, which is the most recently available quarter, 544 housing units were started in Edinburgh and 458 units were completed. In the same quarter, 327 housing units were started in Glasgow and 567 were completed. In both places, the private sector dominates construction. There are 204 000 housing units in Edinburgh and 271 000 housing units in Glasgow. Thus, new construction is providing for about a 1% increase in the housing stock annually in Edinburgh and less than that in Glasgow. Over a decade, at this rate, we might expect to see a 10% increase in the number of Edinburgh's housing units.

Consider two American cities, both of which have fewer housing units than either Edinburgh or Glasgow: Atlanta, Georgia and Las Vegas, Nevada. Las Vegas built more than 5500 new units in 2002 and Atlanta built more than 6500 new units in the same period. These places have adjusted to increases in demand by building many new homes. As a result, housing prices have risen only slightly. In general, sufficient construction keeps housing prices close to the price of construction, which is rarely more than 80 dollars per square foot in the US.

Why isn't housing supply increasing in Edinburgh, Glasgow or London? There are two prevailing theories about the limits on housing supply. One theory emphasizes the natural limits due to land shortages. If this is correct, then there is little the government can do to reduce housing prices, because there is a real commodity (land) that is fundamentally in short supply.

The alternative theory argues that it is government regulation, not the scarcity of land, that keeps housing expensive. A lengthy warranting or permitting process creates tremendous delay and uncertainty that prevents new construction. Neighbours are able to limit new construction. Rules concerning building height or historic districts also act to reduce the amount of new building. Together, these forces restrict supply, but this restriction is fundamentally artificial and can be altered readily through revising government regulations.

In the US, I believe that work I have done with my co-author Joseph Gyourko has made a reasonably compelling case for the view that government regulations, not land shortages, are responsible for the lack of supply in high-cost areas. It is beyond the scope of this chapter to do something comparable for Scotland. Nonetheless, Figure 4.5 does introduce a provocative fact: there is no correlation between current density levels and the rate of new construction (i.e. new housing starts divided by the current housing stock). If the lack of land was so important, then we should expect to see building in low-density places but not in high-density places. In fact, we see no correlation whatsoever. This hardly makes the case for the role of government regulation, but it does at least suggest that density does not determine the level of new development.

Another piece of evidence helpful for deciding between the two hypotheses is to look at the price of new apartments. In a free market, since the marginal cost of supplying an apartment is always the cost of the next floor, we would expect new apartments to cost roughly the same thing as building up higher within an existing structure. In Glaeser and Gyourko (2003), we found that apartments in Manhattan cost roughly three times the cost of building apartments up. We interpreted this as meaning that government regulation was stymieing new construction.

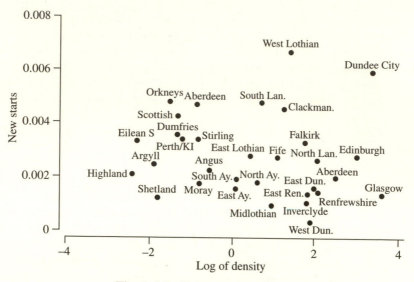

Figure 4.5. New starts and density.

I believe that limited housing supply is the cause of high housing prices in Edinburgh and Glasgow and I suspect that this limited housing supply has more to do with regulation constraints than with limited land. However, this does not mean that optimal government policy involves complete laissez faire in the construction market. Cities need to be planned and new buildings need to be monitored. The important point is that restricting new building has real consequences for the cost of living. If making Edinburgh affordable is a desirable goal, then making building easier will have much more of an effect than public housing.

THE TRANSPORTATION CHALLENGE

As I have attempted to argue throughout this chapter, the great transportation revolution is the automobile. Car ownership in Scotland has skyrocketed over the last 30 years. In 1962, Scotland had 775 000 licensed vehicles. In 2002, there were 2.3 million licensed vehicles. Forty years ago, cars were luxuries or used primarily in very low-density rural areas. Today, almost everywhere, the car is the most common means of transportation.

Given the strong relationship between automobile ownership and income, it is hard to doubt that Scotland is moving, like the US and England, towards a totally car-oriented society. We may bemoan this fact, as anti-car activists have for decades, but the growth in automobile usage continues unabated. I believe that given a reasonable value of time (say 15 dollars per hour), and given moderate traffic levels, the car is a more efficient means of transportation than the bus or the train. The car saves the 15–20 minute fixed time cost involved in public transportation. At 15 dollars per hour, this translates into a $2500 savings in time from reduced commuting costs alone (250 days times 0.66 hours per day). At higher wages, the car achieves even bigger advantages.

These time-saving advantages represent the great plus of the automobile, but it is offset by two major social costs. First, cars pollute. My belief is that the evidence suggests that technology is reducing these pollution costs significantly over time (see Glaeser and Kahn 2003). As long as sufficient regulatory pressure continues to be put on car manufacturers, we will continue to get cleaner cars and the pollution costs will continue to fall. Indeed, over the last 25 years, pollution levels in many American cities, such as Los Angeles, have fallen considerably. The one big uncertainty is global warming, and I cannot possibly make any reasonable estimations on such an uncertain topic.

The second major social cost of the automobile is congestion. Cars take up far more space per passenger than any other form of transportation. Moreover, while central planners can choose the timing of public transportation to mitigate congestion problems, the private nature of car commuting means that driving often bunches at peak times. Without massive road construction, it is inevitable the car usage will create congestion.

There are essentially three approaches to managing congestion. First, there are the advocates of non-car alternatives, such as buses and subways. As I have already discussed, I strongly doubt that these alternative modes will be able to compete effectively with the car. Certainly within central Glasgow and Edinburgh, public transportation will continue to thrive, but as the population and firms increasingly spread to the urban edges, public transportation will continue its 40-year decline in market share. The time delays involved will also become increasingly more frustrating as the value of people's time continues to increase.

If non-car alternatives continue to be pushed, then at least these alternatives should focus on buses, which are cheap and flexible, rather than rail, which is expensive and inflexible. There is nothing that can be done with intra-city rail that cannot be done with a bus and a dedicated lane or tunnel at a much lower cost. Certainly, bus travel provides one of the best ways of providing cheap transport to the less well-off.

The second approach to congestion is new infrastructure. In principle, enough roads can always eliminate delays. The big problem with this approach is that more roads tend to encourage more drivers. If the supply of car trips is sufficiently elastic, then a new lane will create enough new car trips to keep the average congestion level constant. I don't believe that this extreme is true, but I certainly do believe that it is extremely costly to try and handle congestion with infrastructure alone.

The third approach to congestion is better trip management, primarily through tolls and other user fees. In theory, this system offers the advantage of charging drivers for the social costs of their actions. User fees can be charged according to time of day and by highway so that drivers are encouraged to avoid peak times and crowded roads. The disadvantage of this approach is that the administration of the toll can be costly and occasionally the administration itself creates added traffic. For example, traditional tolls, where drivers wait in line to pay, are frequently traffic bottlenecks. More advanced systems like Singapore's cordon pricing which charges for driving in a small localized area can also create excess traffic in the roads directly surrounding this area.

Still, despite early cynicism about fees for driving, the London experiment offers great hope. Not only did a democratically elected government show great courage in pushing through a politically difficult congestion charge, but the charge also appears to have cut central city traffic by about 20%. The London system seems to be working well and provides a model for other cities such as Glasgow and Edinburgh, which may also want to introduce congestion charges of various forms. (It is currently under active consideration in the case of Edinburgh.)

In principle, charges could usefully be levied on a wide range of major arteries. Some of the biggest advantages can come from charges that vary sharply with time of day, so that drivers are encouraged to drive at off-peak hours. To avoid congestion at toll-booths, some form of registration and video monitoring seems particularly effective. The car is a useful technology, but it inevitably generates social costs. Drivers must be charged for those costs if the full advantages of car-based living are going to be realized.

CONCLUSION

Scotland's urban core could end up as one of the great centres of the information economy. It may continue to attract some of the world's most skilled and innovative people, as it has for centuries. However, to maintain this success, the Edinburgh–Glasgow corridor must successfully meet a series of challenges. Most importantly, it must continue to attract firms and this requires attracting skilled workers. Education, urban amenities and limited income redistribution by government are the keys to attracting the skilled.

Moreover, the urban core must also stop its social problems from overwhelming the city. Like all erstwhile manufacturing towns, Glasgow has a large population of concentrated poor. There is no easy solution. In principle, more spending on education can help their children and better policies can limit the costs of segregation. Still, the poverty of Glasgow and the poorer areas between the two cities stands as the greatest challenge.

Expensive housing is another challenge, but in this case the problems are created by the government and the solution is transparent. Expensive housing is the result of limits on housing supply. Without these limits, prices do not rise above construction costs. By eliminating the regulatory barriers to large-scale construction, Edinburgh and Glasgow's housing prices will moderate and the cost of living in these cities will fall.

Finally, since cars are the future, urban success requires regulating the car. To a small degree, this requires non-car alternatives, particularly buses. However, the advantages of the car mean that the biggest gains will come from making congestion less problematic. The most successful strategy against congestion will surely be to follow London's lead and adopt congestion charges.

REFERENCES

Dumais, G., G. Ellison and E. Glaeser. 1997. Geographic concentration as a dynamic process. NBER Working Paper 6270.

Gaspar, J. and E. Glaeser. 1998. Information technology and the future of cities. *Journal of Urban Economics* 43:136–156.

Glaeser, E. 1994. *Cities, information and economic growth*. Cityscape.

———. 2003. Reinventing Boston. NBER Working Paper.

Glaeser, E. and J. Gyourko. 2003. Why is Manhattan so expensive? NBER Working Paper.

Glaeser, E. and M. Kahn. 2001. Decentralized employment and the transformation of the American city. Brookings-Wharton Papers on Urban Affairs.

Glaeser, E. and M. Kahn. 2003. Sprawl and urban growth. HIER Discussion Paper 2004.

Glaeser, E. and J. Kohlhase. 2004. Cities, regions and the decline in transport costs. *Papers in Regional Science* 83(1):197–228.

Glaeser, E. and A. Saiz. 2004. The rise of the skilled city. Brookings-Wharton Papers on Urban Affairs.

Glaeser, E., M. Kahn and J. Rappaport. 2000. Why do the poor live in cities? NBER Working Paper 7636.

Glaeser, E., J. Kolko and A. Saiz. 2001. Consumer city. *Journal of Economic Geography* 1(1):27–50.

Haughwout, A., R. Inman, S. Craig and T. Luce. 2003. Local revenue hills: evidence from four US cities. NBER Working Paper 9686.

Holmes, T. 1998. The effects of state policies on the location of industry: evidence from state borders. *Journal of Political Economy* 106:667–705.

Jaffe, A., M. Trajtenberg and R. Henderson. 1993. Geographic localization of knowledge spillovers as evidenced by patent citations. *Quarterly Journal of Economics* 63:577–598.

Kolko, J. 2000. Services in the city. PhD dissertation, Harvard University.

Nardinelli, C. and C. J. Simon. 1996. The talk of the town: human capital, information, and the growth of English cities, 1861–1961. *Explorations in Economic History* 33:384–413.

Saxenian, A. 1994. *Regional advantage*. Harvard University Press.

The Economic Case for Fiscal Federalism

By Paul Hallwood and Ronald MacDonald[1]

In this chapter we try to move the debate about fiscal federalism away from the contentious link between fiscal federalism and political independence for Scotland towards an economic analysis of the issues.[2] These issues are not unique to Scotland but apply in any country whose government is not entirely centralized. We take the existing constitutional settlement in the UK as given and set out arguments based on economic theory and evidence relating to the devolution of economic powers from Westminster to Edinburgh.[3]

For any devolved or federal system to function effectively it must do the following: assign expenditure responsibilities between the respective levels of government; define how those expenditures are financed in terms of tax and revenue raising by the different levels of government; specify the nature of transfers between the different levels of government; and address the ability of subnational governments to borrow.

The first of these issues was essentially settled with the establishment of the Scottish Parliament, which represents a significant step towards fiscal federalism. However, the other issues have not so far been properly addressed in the Scottish context. At present the Scottish Executive has the power to change personal income taxes by plus or minus three pence in the pound, the so-called tartan tax, and to set and raise non-domestic rates (property taxes), the proceeds of which accrue to local government. In addition, it can set a range of user charges, such as student tuition fees. However, these are limited powers, in terms of both likely revenue and effects on incentives.

The phenomenon of central government having greater power to obtain income than it actually needs for the exercise of its authority, while the sub-central level has less power to raise income than it needs, is referred to in the fiscal federalism literature as *vertical imbalance* or *fiscal mismatch*. An imbalance should be addressed if the sub-central level of government is to operate properly. However, an exclusive focus on vertical imbalances could result in *horizontal imbalance* if transfers

---

[1]The authors are grateful to Wendy Alexander, Jo Armstrong, Brian Ashcroft, Tam Bayoumi, Diane Coyle, Dhammika Dharmapala, David Heald, John McLaren and Arthur Midwinter for their very helpful comments on an earlier version of this chapter. The usual disclaimer applies: we are responsible for any remaining errors of omission or commission and for the views expressed here.

[2]Previous papers focusing on the economics of fiscal federalism for Scotland include Bell and Christie (2002) and Darby et al. (2002).

[3]In particular, we use the 'traditional' and 'new' fiscal federalism literatures, the optimum currency area literature, and draw on time consistency issues from the macroeconomic literature.

from the centre are inadequate for the equalization of resources based on needs at the regional or local level. Needs equalization exists in all fiscal systems; some is inevitable to finance common services. The question is the extent to which it occurs. This equalization mechanism may be directed to a specific service, such as health, education or social security—or, as in the case of Scotland, the overall block grant.

The challenge facing Scotland, like all regional economies, is finding the most satisfactory trade-off between equity and efficiency objectives. Scotland's current financing system is characterized by a high level of equalization and a high level of vertical imbalance. Hence the choice is, how much horizontal balance and, therefore, needs equalization with the rest of the UK, is Scotland willing to give up in exchange for more autonomy in raising finance, and so a reduction in vertical imbalance? The choice should be informed by theory and evidence on three key economic roles of government, namely: promotion of allocative or economic efficiency; equity between individuals; and macroeconomic stabilization.

In designing a fiscal system there is inevitably a trade-off between these three functions. As we shall see, in any regional economy there is little scope for the devolution of a macroeconomic stabilization role for fiscal policy. Our analysis of trade-offs will therefore focus mainly on allocative efficiency and equity considerations.

At the moment the allocation of additional revenues to Scotland is based on an unconditional grant (the *Barnett formula*, discussed in more detail below). This formula is widely regarded as favouring Scotland because Scotland has higher per capita expenditure than the rest of the UK. The argument that Scotland requires higher per capita spending relative to the rest of the UK is based on the perceived greater needs in Scotland due to, for example, its poorer health record and the sparsity of its population.[4] In essence the current arrangements for financing the Scottish Parliament trade off efficiency in favour of equity. Moving to a fiscal federalist structure in Scotland would mean moving the trade-off in the opposite direction: sacrificing some equity in favour of potentially greater efficiency. This could produce an improved allocation of resources in the longer run and thus incentivize growth and ultimately generate additional revenues.

There are separate arguments for fiscal federalism in Scotland which, although related to the economic analysis, are more to do with political accountability. David Heald (1990) eloquently expressed one aspect of the accountability view:

> Such an arrangement [a fiscal federalist arrangement] is essential for the constitutional accountability of a Parliament which would possess extensive legislative responsibilities and expenditure programmes. Moreover, there would be much stronger incentives to fiscal responsibility under a financial arrangement whereby a Scottish Executive must justify to a Scottish Parliament, electors and taxpayers, its chosen trade-off between services and taxes.

---

[4]The Barnett formula was first applied in 1978. In 1979 the Treasury conducted a needs assessment exercise which generally favoured Scotland (and Northern Ireland) and despite the fact that Barnett was supposed to act as a convergence formula (equalizing per capita spending across the regions in the UK) it has in fact simply enshrined the favourable differential that existed in 1979.

The last sentence of this argument is similar in spirit to the economic case for fiscal federalism that we make in this chapter.

A second political aspect relates to the constitutional settlement in the UK, in particular the possibility of a political party of one colour being in office in Westminster and a different party in Edinburgh. Since under the current settlement, funding for the Scottish Parliament is essentially at the behest of the political party in office at Westminster, a constitutional crisis could arise if there were disagreement between the two parties over the block grant allocation. We believe that these arguments are in themselves powerful ones in favour of some form of fiscal federalist solution for Scotland. However, the main focus here is the economic trade-off between equity and efficiency.

THE THEORY OF FISCAL FEDERALISM

The 'traditional' case for fiscal federalism considers the provision of goods financed by taxes and the appropriate revenue collection system at the regional level (see Tiebout 1956). We will sometimes also use 'sub-central government' (SCG) for level(s) of government below that of 'central government' (CG). The economic case for fiscal federalism involves several considerations:

- how best to provide public goods and services at the regional or federal level;
- hard and soft budget constraints;
- needs equalization;
- the role of fiscal federalism in stimulating economic growth;
- the link between fiscal federalism and the national monetary union.

Public Goods and Services at the Regional or Federal Level

The basic principle in the traditional theory of fiscal federalism is that SCG should have the ability to provide goods and services that match the particular preferences and circumstances of its constituents. The key presumption is that the provision of public services should be located at the lowest level of government encompassing geographically the relevant costs and benefits. In that way efficiency and economic welfare can be increased above that generated by a more uniform allocation mechanism.

This 'benefit rule' is a standard result in public finance. Rational decisions are much more likely to be made when people in a 'benefit region' have to pay the costs as well as enjoying the benefits of public expenditure. Goods which are ideal candidates for centralized provision, because their benefits extend nationwide (or because there are economies of scale) are foreign affairs, defence and interregional infrastructure such as transport and telecommunications. But many other public goods have benefits that are locationally circumscribed—such as the local fire department, street infrastructure, and spending on health and education to name a few.

The functions of macroeconomic stabilization and income redistribution should also be left with central government. With high capital mobility, a fixed exchange rate and a unitary interest rate, fiscal expansion in a single region within a country would spill over into other regions. Redistribution at the local level is hampered by the mobility of households. For example, the provision of more generous social security in one region will likely lead to an influx of poor and an exodus of higher-income individuals who have to bear the tax burden.

Hard and Soft Budget Constraints

Below we discuss in detail the kind of taxes and grants that would be required to pay for public expenditure in Scotland. As we shall see, grants from the centre are needed in any fiscal federalist solution in order to ensure that the objective of needs equalization is satisfied. However, the principle of equalization, effected by a block grant, raises the 'moral hazard' issue caused by the lack of a hard budget constraint on public spending in Scotland. If a region knows that the size of the block grant it receives is related to the size of its needs, the incentive to reduce its fiscal imbalance is reduced: in effect it faces a soft budget constraint. Money received in the form of a block grant from the central fiscal authority will invariably be spent, rather than used for tax cuts, by the regional fiscal authority (Hines and Thaler 1995). Equally, a cut in the size of grants from the centre leads to lower expenditure at the devolved levels (Stine 1994).

This traditional view has been updated by the 'new fiscal federalism' (Oates 2004), which takes a public choice perspective. This contends that politicians and civil servants do not necessarily maximize the welfare of the electorate; rather they are concerned with their own utility—and, for reasons of personal satisfaction, having control over a large budget is better than a small budget. This public sector as a monolith (Leviathan) argument is now influential and implies that fiscal federalism will restrain the behaviour of a revenue-maximizing government (Buchanan and Brennan 1980). At issue is how to align more closely the decisions of politicians and officials (the agents) with those of the electorate (the principal).

From the electorate's perspective, horizontal tax competition between regions has the dual benefits of stimulating private enterprise and reducing the scope for wasteful government spending. Therefore, increased fiscal decentralization should limit the size of the public sector. Furthermore, increased tax competition between jurisdictions need not mean reduced provision of public goods because the tax base may grow. However, competition between regions in the UK is limited because only the Scottish Parliament currently has the ability to change personal income taxes and the English regions do not have elected assemblies. Besides, empirical studies testing the 'Leviathan' hypothesis have produced conflicting results (see, for example, Oates 1985; Grossman 1989; Ehdaie 1994).

In any case, the benefits of a harder budget constraint might be lost unless central government can credibly commit not to rescue an overspending SCG or distance itself from political pressures from SCG to raise spending limits. This is a so-called 'time inconsistency' issue. Ensuring time consistency is an important part of the institutional framework which ensures the credibility of a fiscal federalist system.

What might be compromised in a move to a harder budget constraint—the closer matching of spending and taxation in Scotland—is the insurance function played by central government. Regions affected by asymmetric economic shocks may be supported by transfers from CG, but this is likely to be more difficult when SCG spending and taxes are closely matched. Such asymmetric shocks could well occur if Scotland was, say, overly reliant on North Sea oil tax revenues, known to be quite variable over time.

Fiscal Federalism and Economic Growth

Although fiscal arrangements are not central to economic growth, there may nevertheless be an important link. The key economic argument in favour of fiscal federalism, that it improves efficiency in the use of resources ('allocative efficiency'), should also apply in a dynamic—economic growth—framework (Oates 1994). For example, the greater ability of local politicians to reflect local preferences on education, innovation and the infrastructure could have an important influence on growth. A second argument, and one we believe may be of considerable importance for Scotland, is that the current devolution settlement does not give local politicians an incentive to improve economic growth. At present the Scottish Parliament is given a lump sum, based on the Barnett formula, which is spent on public services and goods. Politicians have little incentive to spend much of the budget on goods and services which might raise economic growth since the benefits of improved growth, in terms of increased tax revenue, accrue to the exchequer in London. Another argument in the theoretical literature is that by lessening the concentration of political power and promoting some tax competition, fiscal federalism loosens the grip of vested interest groups on public policy, which promotes democracy and (longer-term) economic growth.[5]

Achieving allocative efficiency, and thereby contributing to improved growth, in practice has two dimensions: not only the incentivizing dimension, associated with greater revenue powers discussed above, but also improving productivity on the spending side. Many feel the potential of devolution to achieve more efficiency in public expenditure in Scotland has not been fully grasped. For fiscal federalism to work, the appropriate institutional framework has to include a willingness on the part of the local politicians to abide by the rules of a hard budget constraint (Tanzi 2001). But, as Nicholas Crafts shows in Chapter 8, there is some evidence to suggest that Scotland is more producer-orientated and resistant to competition, particularly in public services, so undermining the potential gains in allocative efficiency offered by the current degree of fiscal devolution.

There have been a few empirical studies of the growth-fiscal federalism link. Oates (1985), for example, showed in a study of 43 industrialized and developing countries that the average share of central government spending was 65% for the industrialized countries and 89% for the developing countries: industrialized countries therefore seem to have much more fiscal decentralization than developing countries. Therefore, countries with high per capita income have greater levels of fiscal decentralization than low growth/low per capita income countries. But the

---

[5]Various statistical studies support the notion that fiscal federalism promotes growth. These include Oates (1985), Bahl and Linn (1992), Thießen (2003) and Mankiw et al. Weil (1992.

key question is whether fiscal decentralization is a cause or consequence of growth. The evidence on causality is inconclusive (see, for example, Oates 1999; Bahl and Linn 1992). More recent studies, based on regression analyses (see, for example, Davoodi and Zou 1998; Xie et al. 1999; Zhang and Zou 1998; Thießen 2003) report that there is a statistically significant relationship but it is often negative: increased fiscal decentralization is associated with slower growth.[6] However, in general, these studies are unsophisticated in the way they treat causality, so this negative result might be spurious. At best, the empirical evidence on the fiscal federalism-growth link is ambiguous.

Recently, a number of researchers have argued that decentralization of fiscal policy, by bringing government closer to the people, may strengthen social capital, which in turn could boost growth. There are a number of reasons why the devolution of fiscal policy may improve social capital.[7] In particular, the decentralization of fiscal policy should lead to stronger links between the community in general and government and encourages community-wide participatory initiatives. De Mello (2000) seeks to test the link between fiscal federalism and social capital. He uses three social capital indicators: confidence in government, civic cooperation and associational activity for 29 market economies.[8] An indicator of vertical imbalances does show the expected relationship with respect to the different measures of social capital[9]; other indicators of fiscal decentralization prove to be statistically insignificant. The results suggest it may be possible that social capital can be boosted when local differences in needs and preferences are taken into account by policy makers.

Optimal Currency Area Issues and the Case for Fiscal Federalism

The economic literature on optimal currency areas also has implications for fiscal federalism, including macroeconomic risk-sharing within a monetary union. We believe that it is strongly in Scotland's interest to maintain a currency union with the rest of the UK, i.e. continue to use the pound sterling, or join the Euro if the UK does so. For if Scotland did not have the same currency as the rest of the UK it would face enormous strains on its trade and investment linkages with by far its largest trade partner, the rest of the UK.[10] Studies looking at countries which have *left* a currency union find that trade integration with the remaining members falls by about one-half from the level associated with monetary union in the year or so immediately following exit (Glick and Rose 2002). Accordingly, if Scotland were

---

[6]Thießen's study shows that in moving from a low to medium per capita income level there is a positive association between fiscal decentralization and growth, while the move from a medium to high level of per capita income level produces a negative association.

[7]The discussion here draws on de Mello (2000).

[8]The data were originally collected by the World Values Survey for the period 1980–81 to 1990–91.

[9]It is negatively related to both confidence in government and associational activity and positively related to civic cooperation.

[10]Evidence for this, though not directly based on Scottish data, is found in MacDonald (1999, 2000), Buiter (2000), Layard et al. (2000), Glick and Rose (2002) and Artis and Ehrmann (2000).

to leave the UK monetary union, it might experience a large and rapid fall in its trade with the rest of the UK, its largest trade partner.[11]

Weighing against the benefits, in a monetary union a region gives up two instruments of macroeconomic management: the exchange rate and monetary policy. This may not matter from a macroeconomic point of view (maintaining full employment and a stable price level) given one of two conditions: either macroeconomic shocks are symmetric with the rest of the currency area, or, if asymmetric, labour is mobile between regions.[12]

It is not entirely clear in the context of the UK that labour mobility is always going to be the best shock absorber. Although labour mobility is high within the UK, people may not have the necessary skills to migrate and it may take a considerable time for them to retrain. What is more, Scotland's well-known demographic imbalance suggests it is worth discouraging movement out of Scotland as a way of adjusting to adverse macroeconomic shocks (see Chapter 7). Moreover, the average correlation coefficient between business cycles in the UK regions is approximately 0.7 (de Grauwe and Vanhaverbeke 1993; Forni and Riechlin 2001; Barrios et al. 2003; Clark and van Wincoop 2001). This high regional business cycle correlation suggests that the role of macroeconomic stabilization should largely be left to CG. This pools risks: if Scotland suffers an adverse shock relative to the rest of the UK, its payments to the centre fall while its receipts from the centre increase.

In sum, Scotland breaking its link with the UK monetary union would have an adverse effect on its trade and investment, while there is no evidence of substantial asymmetric shocks which might weigh in favour of a separate currency and monetary policy.

CHARACTERISTICS OF EFFECTIVE DEVOLVED FINANCING

In this part of the chapter we consider the key objectives of an effective devolved fiscal system, its principal characteristics and the experience in other countries of fiscal federalism. An optimal system of financing will seek to balance equity and efficiency (achieve appropriate horizontal and vertical balance) without undermining macroeconomic stabilization. For Scotland this would mean trading off some equity in favour of greater allocative efficiency, with knock-on benefits for growth.

The principal characteristics of an optimal system are

(a) expenditures and own-source revenues well-matched through the assignment, devolution and sharing of an agreed range of taxes;

(b) appropriate intergovernmental transfer mechanisms to ensure equity considerations are not sacrificed excessively;

---

[11] In 2000, 51.3% of Scottish exports were to the rest of the UK, the remainder being to the rest of the world.

[12] The relevance of interregional labour mobility to the optimum currency area question was first discussed by Mundell (1961). Kenen (1969) argued that the more industrially diversified a country, the less asymmetric would be shocks. McKinnon (1963) argued that a high degree of openness, such as with Scotland's trade with the rest of the UK, suggested a fixed exchange rate because changes in nominal exchange rates could not affect the real exchange rate due to an absence of money illusion.

(c) provision for an agreed regional borrowing capacity, with appropriate fiscal discipline.

Taking the first of these characteristics, the essence of the argument is that there should be a link between the benefits of public goods and services and their price in the form of the tax raised to finance them. Any successful fiscal federalist solution should have taxation at the margin as an important component. This simply means that for any given fiscal settlement for Scotland, the ability to increase expenditure in one particular area has to be paid for either by a reduction in spending in another category or an increase in taxes in Scotland. It is useful here to set out some nomenclature relating to taxation (see also Ter-Minassian 1997).

An *assigned tax* is one whose proceeds are either shared between the different levels of government on the basis of derivation (i.e. tax revenue is attributed to the particular geographical area where it was generated) or equalization (i.e. on the basis of needs or resources).[13] A *devolved tax* is one for which the sub-central level of government possesses the power to vary the base and/or rate at which that tax is levied. As we saw earlier, the key idea underlying a tax system in which revenue is either assigned or devolved to the SCG level is that it communicates to households and business units the cost of consuming different levels of local public goods and services. Theoretically, this should result in a more efficient allocation of these goods.

Needs equalization 'involves the attribution of tax revenue (and explicitly public expenditure) to particular geographical areas or units of government on the basis of criteria other than derivation' (Heald 1990).

The *tax assignment problem* refers to the determination of the vertical structure of taxes within a fiscal federation. There is vertical imbalance when revenues raised by SCG are considerably less than expenditure—requiring some form of subsidy from central government, as with the block grant received by Scotland from Westminster.

The key point in designing a vertical tax structure is to attempt to match revenue raising by the region to its expenditure levels. However, some areas have higher taxable capacity—and so can provide more services for lesser tax levels—and as we noted above the mobility of people or capital between regions also presents difficulties for designing the vertical tax structure. Moreover, the mobility of economic agents increases the more local the level of government. A good example of this would be the number of households who use the services, such as art galleries and music, provided by Glasgow city council but choose to live outside the city boundary to avoid the (property) taxes levied to pay for these services.

This problem with differential regional taxes, combined with labour mobility, on the face of it suggests that the Scottish Parliament should avoid the differential taxation of labour—that is, personal income tax should not be devolved. However, strictly speaking the Parliament should avoid taxes which are not linked to any benefits on mobile households or firms, while taxing them for the benefits they do

---

[13]Heald (1990) notes that assigned revenues can contribute a sense of 'creating entitlement' to the revenues which he regards as 'very important aspect to the fiscal psychology of the relationship between devolved parliaments and the UK Treasury'.

receive from public services. Communicating to taxpayers the cost of consuming local public goods could result in an efficient allocation of these goods. So some devolution of income tax may well be appropriate, as is indeed the case at the moment in Scotland.

The same principle applies to capital taxes: levy taxes on capital to the extent that the government provides local inputs to business which increase the productivity of capital. However, capital is so mobile that the broad thrust of the literature on fiscal federalism is that in practice the ability to alter corporation tax should usually be left with the centre.

Taxing natural resources is not usually seen as a suitable means for raising revenue for local government since these resources are usually unevenly distributed across regions. It has also been argued that the extraction of profits (or 'economic rent') from natural resources should be the prerogative of the nation state and for the benefit of the whole nation (Norregaard 1997). Perhaps the most convincing argument against having a devolved natural resource tax in the Scottish case is the potential volatility of revenue from its key natural resource, namely North Sea oil.

Customs and excise taxes and local purchase taxes are usually not regarded as suitable for devolution, because it is undesirable to have rates differing dramatically between regions. This can lead to an inefficiently excessive amount of travelling over the border to avoid the tax or duty.

On the other hand, other minor taxes such as betting tax, stamp duty, vehicle licence, business licence taxes, TV taxes and various types of user fees for local services could all potentially be devolved to the Scottish Parliament (as they are in some other countries). Property taxes are also well-suited for devolution and they have already been devolved in the UK: in the case of non-domestic rates to the Scottish Parliament and in the case of council tax to the lowest tier of SCG, local government across the UK.

On the face of it, the unsuitability of the major taxes for devolution would seem to limit the possibility of addressing the vertical fiscal imbalance which currently exists in the UK. However, there is no reason why the key taxes discussed in this section should not be *assigned* to the SCG and this could represent the major revenue source for the Scottish Parliament.

The second characteristic of an optimal fiscal federalist system is the use of transfers from CG to SCG. Intergovernmental grants can have three roles in a federated tax system (see, for example, Oates 1996, 1999): fiscal equalization across regions, improving the functioning of the overall tax system, and internalizing spillovers to other regions. Theory suggests that to limit spillovers from one region to another, *conditional* grants should be used to finance a proportion of the SCG expenditures.[14] Such conditional grants are currently not part of the fiscal set-up in the UK, but would be necessary if components of expenditure with important spillover effects were to be devolved.

The objective of fiscal equalization ('horizontal equity') is usually thought to be best achieved through the use of *unconditional* grants. These transfers are usually

---

[14]That is, where the marginal social cost is equal to the marginal social benefit (Boadway and Hobson 1993).

Table 5.1. Sub-central government revenues (percentages).

	Tax revenues	Non-tax revenues	Grants
Belgium	79	3	19
Denmark	51	8	40
France	47	19	34
Italy	34	14	53
Netherlands	10	14	76
Spain	37	9	54
Sweden	75	6	20
UK	14	13	73

Source: OECD (2002, Table 3.3). Latest year. Percentages may not add to 100 due to rounding.

based on the 'fiscal need' and the 'fiscal capacity' of each region, so that regions with a high fiscal need–capacity ratio will receive a large transfer from the centre. Scotland may have a higher fiscal need due to its poorer health record and the greater geographical dispersion of its population compared with the rest of the UK. Unconditional grants increase regional income without affecting local spending priorities (which should depend on local preferences).

THE EXPERIENCE IN OTHER COUNTRIES

About 60% of public expenditure in Scotland already has been devolved to the Scottish Executive. The devolution of expenditures on health, education, housing and community amenities, social security and welfare, and general public services to SCGs is common in many EU countries—though not all together in any single country (OECD 2002, Table 3.6; see also Watts 1996). But in the division of taxing powers between SCG and CG, the UK differs from other countries.

Table 5.1 shows the composition of SCG revenues in eight EU countries. Most striking is the heavy reliance (almost three-quarters of total revenues) that the UK has on grants to SCGs as their main revenue source. SCG own-taxes in the UK amount to only 14% of SCG revenues (these figures are UK-wide). Apart from the Netherlands, the vertical imbalance is greatest in the UK.

Table 5.2 classifies SCG taxes by tax base. It shows that at the SCG level the UK is alone among the eight EU countries in heavy reliance on grants from CG together with an almost total dependency on property taxes as the single source of tax revenue. Table 5.3 gives a somewhat more detailed picture of SCG taxes in the same eight countries and Germany. Table 5.4 shows the structure of state revenues in three non-European federal countries.

One striking feature of Table 5.4 is the importance of grants from the centre to the sub-central tier of government even in well-developed federal systems—it ranges from 22 to 59%. The figure of 22% is in fact the lower bound internationally and indicates that in any new fiscal settlement for Scotland there will always be a block grant component.

The tying of SCG expenditures and own-revenues more closely together in many countries goes some way to imposing a hard budget constraint on SCG. This is

Table 5.2. Classification of sub-central government taxes by tax base, percentages (1999).

	Income and profits tax	Taxes on payroll and work force	Taxes on property	Expenditure taxes	Other taxes
Belgium	55		6	39	
Denmark	93		7		
France		4	52	11	34
Italy	8		22	26	45
Netherlands			63	38	
Spain	26		36	35	3
Sweden	100				
UK			99.7		0.3

Source: OECD (2002, Table 3.4). Percentages may not add to 100 due to rounding.

helpful in promoting rational resource allocation by SCG because it eliminates the moral hazard caused by the exclusive use of CG grants.

One way in which regions can supplement their revenue is by borrowing. There are four models of discipline for SCG debt: market discipline, 'collegiate' or administrative discipline, rules-based discipline, and targets set by CG. A few high-income countries do allow SCG borrowing, disciplined mainly by the capital markets. These include Canada, Finland, Portugal and Sweden. Four conditions are necessary for effective market discipline. Markets must not be required to treat governments as privileged borrowers; there should be an adequate information flow to lenders on SCG financial and economic conditions; bailouts should be excluded, to prevent moral hazard; and borrowers should have in place institutional arrangements which promote an adequate response to deteriorating credit ratings.

Given the high level of development of UK financial markets, one might think that such a system could work well. But there are dangers. Even in such a highly developed market economy as Canada, market discipline has not been tight, when judged by the rapid increase in provincial indebtedness and deterioration in provincial credit ratings. Only with a lag of more than a decade have the most indebted provinces acted meaningfully to contain growth in their indebtedness. Rules-based systems, where the rules are specified in law, are in place in the USA, Spain and Japan. Thus, for example, borrowing at some levels of SCG is limited to the estimated level of debt service capacity or another indicator of creditworthiness. A rules-based system has the advantages of transparency and even-handedness. The main disadvantage is that SCG may attempt to circumvent the rules, for example, by moving some spending off balance sheet or reclassifying current spending as capital spending.

In a collegiate system, the centre and region agree reasonable borrowing limits. There is an obvious political dimension in the bargaining process. The Australian system of administrative controls has thus been supplemented with efforts to introduce market-type discipline.

Direct control of SCG borrowing by CG is the system in effect in the UK for local government, whereby CG annually approves borrowing limits for local authorities, and restrictions may be placed on the loan characteristics, including term and type of

Table 5.3. Sub-central government taxes: eight EU countries.

Belgium	Regions have almost complete autonomy over 40% of their revenues (regional taxes) and rate autonomy, but not tax base autonomy, over the other 60%.	Federal country
Denmark	Income tax covers about 90% of SCG tax revenues. Each SCG has tax rate autonomy, but tax base set by central government. Municipalities' tax rates range from 13 to 22%. Upper and lower limits are constrained by CG	Unitary state with substantial subsidiarity to 275 municipalities and 14 county councils.
France	SCG does not control tax base. Communes, departments and regions vote independently on tax rates. Limits on rates are set by CG.	Regions have some legislative powers
Germany	Länder control 63% of tax revenue and 31% of expenditure taxes. Property tax a minor component of total SGC revenue.	Federal country
Italy	From 1992 tax responsibility transferred to SCG. From 2001 grants replaced with VAT sharing: SCG can vary the tax rate within limits set by CG.	Regional authorities have some powers comparable with federal countries
Netherlands	SCGs choose which taxes to levy within relevant Acts, and can vary tax rates.	Decentralized unitary state: 12 provinces and 548 municipalities
Spain	Tax sharing with central government, and SCGs can set their own income tax rates but not tax bases.	Regional authorities have some powers comparable with federal countries
Sweden	SCG tax revenue is from a single tax base: personal income. Freedom to set tax rates but not bases.	Unitary state, but guaranteed local rights to levy taxes and set tax rates
UK	Council tax on imputed capital value paid by all households, direct to local government; non-domestic rate set by Scottish and UK parliaments. Scottish Parliament can also alter the basic income tax rate within specified margins but not tax base. Size of block grants take into account level of local taxes raised.	Unitary state of four nations: 32 local authorities in Scotland

Source: extracted from OECD (2002).

loan. The main possible disadvantage is inflexibility, especially given the informational advantages on local needs that SCG may possess. An SCG allowed to borrow might add to the public-sector borrowing requirement and, in turn, interfere with CG macroeconomic policy. Internal stability pacts between levels of government

Table 5.4. Structure of state tax revenues (as a percentage of total tax income) and grants as a percentage of state income in three federal countries.

	Income tax	Property tax	Expenditure taxes	Other taxes	Grants as a percentage of state government income
Australia	0	30	41	29	59
Canada	43	4	40	13	22
USA	37	4	56	3	29

Source: Norregaard (1997, Table 3), based on the IMF *Government Finance Statistics Yearbook.*

are required to prevent this. The management of fiscal policy in federal systems is more complicated than in unitary systems.

In sum, the main message is that the vertical fiscal imbalance that we observe in the UK is at odds with the experience elsewhere. In particular, other countries place much greater reliance on addressing vertical fiscal imbalances using expenditure and income taxes, rather than relying almost exclusively on property taxes. Practically all countries (the main exception is the United States) have extensive equalization systems. And SCG typically have borrowing powers.

THE SCOTTISH PERSPECTIVE

In this section we turn to a more detailed discussion of the implications of fiscal federalism for Scotland and the rest of the UK. We start by giving a brief overview of the current picture with respect to taxation and spending in Scotland. We then go on to present a sketch of what a fiscal federalist system might look like for Scotland, based on the arguments made in previous sections. We discuss the choices for Scotland around the revenue raising issues, the design of a grant system, and the borrowing options. First, though, we set the scene in terms of the current Scottish position.

The Current Scottish Position

Under the Scotland Act (1998) various expenditure functions have already been devolved to Scotland, mainly in the areas of education, health, agriculture, economic development and transport, environment, law and home affairs and social work and housing. Reserved areas retained by Westminster include defence, employment, financial and economic matters, social security and international relations. This division appears to be rational in that expenditures on the reserved items yield UK-wide benefits and might also enjoy economies of scale. Moreover, the benefits generated by the devolved expenditures are probably more localized, and, as we argued in the first section, local polities are likely to be better placed to identify potential benefits than is distant central government.

Under the UK's current fiscal arrangements, in the period 2001–02, the gap between government expenditure (£39.4 billion) and revenue (£31.4 billion) in Scotland implies a non-oil budget deficit for Scotland in 2001–02 resulting in net borrowing of £8 billion, or a deficit of 10.3% of Scottish GDP. However, if all of the revenue from North Sea oil were to be apportioned to Scotland the gap between revenues and expenditure falls to £2.8 billion (or 2.9% of GDP) (see Scottish Executive 2003). Below, we return to some issues relating to oil revenues.

The current formula for spending allocation in Scotland is based on the Barnett formula (Edmonds 2001; McGregor and Swales 2003). This formula only relates to the expenditure items currently devolved to the Scottish Parliament, which means that approximately 40% of identifiable public expenditure in Scotland falls outside the remit of Barnett. The formula is a way of sharing *changes* (not the level) in public spending plans between the participating countries of the Union. Scotland receives a population-based share of the total changes in planned spending on analogous programmes in England or England and Wales. Since the formula is based on population shares, it does not necessarily reflect spending needs.

The Barnett formula does not seem to be a good platform on which to base a future fiscal federalist structure for Scotland as it focuses almost exclusively on the equalization function at the expense of allocative efficiency. Nor does it reflect the changing needs assessment, other than by arbitrarily managing downwards the initial spending share for Scotland. What are the alternatives?

Alternatives to the Barnett Formula

What does the forgoing theoretical analysis and comparative evidence suggest would be a sensible degree of fiscal federalism in Scotland? Some advocate fiscal autonomy. But this extreme approach has two drawbacks. First, the most efficient way to implement the kind of sophisticated social security systems which exist in most countries today is at the national or central level rather than at the subnational level. Secondly, macroeconomic stabilization should, for reasons noted earlier, be conducted mainly at the centre. In essence what the fiscal autonomy approach amounts to is devolving all three economic functions of government—allocative, equity and stabilization—to the Scottish Parliament. We refer to this model as the 'straw man' autonomy position since it does not currently exist in any unitary or federal country.

In this 'straw man' model all taxes—income, expenditure, corporation, North Sea oil, etc.—would be devolved to Scotland and the Executive would become responsible for all of Scotland's public spending needs, including a payment to Westminster for reserved services (see Heald (2003) for a further discussion of this).

The objective of equity has been abandoned in this case. Indeed, given the earlier findings on Scotland's net government funding deficit, there can be little doubt that the implementation of these policies would lead to a significant reduction in spending in areas which had previously been regarded as important for meeting Scotland's needs. This shortfall could be met by an unconditional lump sum grant (which is what the theory deems appropriate). However, the proponents of the fiscal autonomy view in fact eschew the use of such grants. Doubtless they would argue that in the longer run the potential success of the policy in stimulating growth would permit expenditure commensurate with needs. However, it is unclear how long that process would take. The failure of the fiscal autonomy model to address the equity issue properly is one important reason why we do not in practice observe it in any nation state.

A second important issue concerning the fiscal federalist position relates to the macroeconomic stabilization role of fiscal policy. At present, this is a Westminster function and in most discussions of fiscal federalism the stabilization role is classed with defence and foreign affairs as items which should be controlled from the centre.[15] However, the close correlation between the regional business cycles within the UK noted earlier is a compelling argument against devolving the stabilization role to the Scottish Executive. Given that many of the shocks within the UK are closely correlated, as noted earlier it does not seem efficient or cost effective to have a separate macroeconomic stabilization function for Scotland.

A third important issue relates to the suitability of devolving the key sources of revenue, such as North Sea oil, VAT, corporation tax and income tax. Consider, first, North Sea oil. Although there is certainly some independent academic support for the view that the vast bulk of North Sea oil lies within 'Scottish waters' it is not clear that this would be a particularly reliable source of revenue for the Scottish Parliament. Revenues from natural resources are not considered to be a good tax base at the regional level. For North Sea oil this conclusion is reinforced because of the variability of the price of oil and the fact that it is priced in US dollars: a depreciation in the value of the dollar, relative to sterling, decreases oil revenues and this effect can be quite dramatic. Therefore, we discount using oil revenues as a component of the tax base for the Executive.

VAT is also probably not well-suited to devolution. For one thing the tendency within Europe is towards the harmonization of VAT and this would preclude much, if any, variation within a national state. And from a practical perspective, because it is a multi-stage tax, the devolution of VAT would be an administrative nightmare. The devolution of both corporation tax and income tax would in principle be feasible (although there are considerable difficulties in unravelling the former), but the fiscal federalist literature indicates that care should be taken since they are taxes on potentially highly mobile firms and households.

An argument can be made for devolving corporation tax powers as well, along the lines of the current UK approach to corporate taxes within the EU. Clearly, though, for a small open economy and given the mobility of capital, increases could lead to a rapid movement of capital (presumably in the form of headquarters locations) from Scotland to the rest of the world. Some commentators have argued that there may be an important asymmetry here, in the sense that cuts in corporation tax could lead to an inflow of capital which in global terms would be minimal, but in Scottish terms could be highly significant. This policy would seem to have been pursued successfully in Ireland, and the new EU members, Estonia, Hungary, Latvia and Poland, all have corporation tax rates of less than 20% but it would not necessarily be suitable for Scotland (Alexander 2003; Krugman 1993).[16] And since other regions

---

[15]A classic example of mismanaged sub-central government spending and borrowing interfering with central government macroeconomic policy is that of Argentina during the period of its currency board, 1991–2001 (Cuevas 2003).

[16]New EU members: see 'Dancing an Irish jig', *The Economist*, 15 April 2004.

in the UK do not have the ability to change corporation tax, tax cuts in Scotland could produce a beggar-thy-neighbour outcome.

So there is a degree of complexity and uncertainty, particularly with respect to the issues of equity and stabilization, in the extreme case of fiscal autonomy. It goes too far in trying to address the efficiency function of fiscal policy at the expense of the equity and stabilization aspects. This is presumably why we do not observe the fiscal autonomy model operating currently in any nation state.

A Proposal for Scotland

Recognizing the above problems, what might a realistic fiscal federalist system look like for Scotland? Guided by the fiscal federalist experience of other countries, we propose an approach that avoids both the risks and volatility of autonomy and the poor incentive effects of the current status quo. In other words we seek a balance between allocative efficiency and equity. It should deliver a better balance between the horizontal and vertical aspects of fiscal policy and trade off some equity in favour of stimulating greater allocative efficiency.

This will be achieved by a system that

- extends the assignment of an agreed range of taxes and the devolution of a further range of taxes;
- preserves a significant equalization grant to ensure equity considerations are not sacrificed unduly, in line with good practice across the globe;
- provides for an agreed regional borrowing capacity.

We argued earlier that there is only limited scope for the *devolution* of the main sources of tax revenue. However, even assigning more tax revenues, without devolution of either tax rates or bases, would in itself represent a substantial step in hardening the budget constraint faced by the Scottish Executive and Parliament. We argued that North Sea oil is not a good tax revenue base for Scotland and therefore we do not believe it should be devolved or assigned. Although we also argued that VAT in Scotland should not be devolved, there is nothing to prevent the revenues raised from VAT being assigned to the Scottish Executive. The same is true of customs and excise duties. Income tax seems equally suited to assignment and also has the potential to be devolved. Indeed, there is already the possibility to alter income tax by 3% either way from the UK rate. So far this power has not been used. Some commentators have argued that the amount is essentially insignificant because it represents a very small proportion of total expenditure and taxes. We would argue on the basis of the experience in other countries, particularly Belgium and Denmark, that a wider discretionary band of ±7% would be more appropriate or perhaps even no limit at all. In principle, corporation tax is similar to income tax and would therefore seem a natural candidate for assignment.

In sum, our approach emphasizes assignment of revenues rather than full devolution of tax-raising powers. However, we propose the devolution for income tax (for all rates but not bases) and a package of minor taxes. Table 5.5 summarizes the assignment and devolution aspects of the various taxes.

Table 5.5. A summary of the assignment and devolution of taxes.

Type of tax	Assigned	Devolved	Reasons against assigning or devolving
Income	Yes	Possibly	Feasible, but potential problems due to mobility of tax source.
Corporation	Yes	Partial	Feasible, but difficulties in unravelling tax source. Serious potential problems over mobility of source.
VAT	Yes	No	Goes against EU harmonization. Practical administrative complexities.
Customs and excise	Yes	No	Can result in travel inefficiency problems (border shopping)
Other duties	Yes	Yes	In particular where these relate to user fees for local services
North Sea oil	No	No	Highly volatile and regionally unevenly distributed

As discussed earlier, it is likely that any fiscal settlement based on tax assignment/devolution would produce a fiscal deficit (an excess of expenditure over revenue) for Scotland. In order to deal with this horizontal imbalance, we would recommend an unconditional lump sum block grant determined on the basis of an assessment of Scotland's needs at the time of the move to a fiscal federalist system. However, experience in other countries suggests that this is not a straightforward exercise and it is likely to be an especially tricky issue in the UK context since it would be the first time such a decentralization of fiscal policy had taken place. One way of addressing this issue would be to have a lump sum block grant at the time of the changeover to the new system such that total revenues were equal to the current Barnett position. Over time this could be phased to the new level derived from an assessment of needs. We also believe that, at least in the short run, there should be some mechanism in place to protect the lump sum grant if Scotland did indeed succeed in raising economic growth and the overall tax take. Westminster needs to realize that in the longer term the UK budget could benefit from tax devolution to Scotland so that there should be an incentive for the Scottish polity to create greater tax efficiency in Scotland.

In our particular variant of the fiscal federal model, we propose that overall macroeconomic stabilization would remain with the central UK government. Could there be an additional discretionary role for the Scottish government to stabilize the economy, as the correlation between regional business cycles in the UK is not perfect? Paul Krugman, in Chapter 2, suggests that this would not be a useful way of using fiscal federalism in Scotland, essentially because it does not seem to have worked in other countries such as the US. However, in the US most states are constitutionally required to balance their budgets each year, which may explain why regional counter-cyclical policies have been unsuccessful. Although we recognize that the management of a limited counter-cyclical policy represents a serious challenge for a small open economy operating within a monetary union, we do think the flexibility to engage in such a policy could be useful, especially in the presence of asymmetric shocks which are known to be temporary. Clearly, such a policy would not be well-suited to dealing with permanent shocks.

Allowing a role for some stabilization, and given the move in the fiscal federalism case away from equity to efficiency, might also mean the Scottish Executive would wish to generate alternative sources of revenue. One possible source would be borrowing. One of the anomalies of the current devolution settlement is the fact that local authorities have a greater degree of fiscal autonomy than the Scottish Executive in respect of their facility to borrow in times when they face temporary falls in revenue.

While we are convinced that tax devolution or assignment would work in the direction of improving efficiency, how quickly the benefits from addressing the vertical imbalance in the current arrangements would appear would rather depend on how the politicians in Edinburgh responded to their new budget constraint. In practice, politicians might not understand or might strongly discount the effect of their spending decisions on the level of taxes. If politicians take years, perhaps decades, to recognize the new budget constraint, some equity would have been sacrificed without much, if any, increase in efficiency.

CONCLUSIONS

In this chapter we have considered the economic case for a form of fiscal federalism in Scotland. Our specific proposal involves the assignment and devolution of certain tax revenues to Scotland. We mean by this that in future a considerable proportion of taxes levied on Scottish tax bases should be returned to the Scottish Executive. There should be a better balance between Scottish Executive expenditure and assigned or devolved tax revenues. The Scottish budget, however, would continue to be supplemented by transfers from the Westminster budget in line with most informational practice.

In embarking on a fiscal federalist system, a needs assessment exercise might well have to be conducted in order to assess the size of the block grant to be provided by the centre. We also believe that any legislation creating tax assignment for Scotland should allow scope for further modification of the Scottish fiscal system—along the lines of the Spanish system, where regional finances are reviewed every five years.

Our suggestion falls short of fiscal autonomy for Scotland, either in the sense of independence with no shared obligations or in the sense of Scotland only making a sovereign contribution for access to shared services without any equalization mechanisms. We draw on the theory of fiscal federalism to argue for a smaller vertical imbalance between taxes retained in Scotland and public spending in Scotland. A closer matching of spending with taxes would better signal to beneficiaries the true costs of public spending in terms of taxes raised. It would create better incentives for politicians to provide public goods and services in quantities and at qualities that voters are actually willing to pay for. We reject proposals for fiscal autonomy because, in sharply reducing vertical imbalance in the Scottish budget, it would worsen horizontal balance between Scotland and the other UK regions. Scotland is insulated through the block grant. This risk-sharing mechanism would be lost with fiscal autonomy. So would risk-sharing in the face of macroeconomic shocks over the course of the business cycle.

Finally, any fiscal federalist proposal will clearly only work if the relevant institutional framework is in place, and what is especially important is that the Scottish polity respond positively to a new form of (hard) budget constraint, designed to ensure time-consistent behaviour. Clearly, it is impossible to predict *ex ante* how the local polity will react to a changed fiscal environment. However, we do not regard this uncertainty as a sufficient argument against addressing the important vertical fiscal imbalance that currently exists within the UK.

REFERENCES

Alexander, W. 2003. *Chasing the Tartan Tiger: lessons from a Celtic cousin?* The Smith Institute.

Artis, M. J. and M. Ehrmann. 2000. The exchange rate: a shock absorber or source of shocks? A study of four open economies. CEPR Discussion Paper 2550.

Barrios, S., M. Brulhart, R. J. R. Elliott and M. Sensier. 2003. A tale of two cycles: cofluctuations between UK regions and the Euro zone. *Manchester School* 71:265–292.

Bahl, R. W. and J. F. Linn. 1992. *Urban public financing in developing countries.* Oxford University Press.

Bell, D. N. F. and A. C. Christie. 2002. A new fiscal settlement for Scotland. *Scottish Affairs* 41(Autumn):121–140.

Boadway, R. and P. A. Hobson. 1993. Intergovernmental transfers in Canada. Tax Paper 96. Toronto: Canadian Tax Foundation.

Buchanan, J. M. and G. Brennan. 1980. *The power to tax.* Cambridge University Press.

Buiter, W. 2000. Optimal currency areas: why does the exchange rate regime matter? *Scottish Journal of Political Economy* 47(3):213–250.

Clark, T. E. and E. van Wincoop. 2001. Borders and business cycles. *Journal of International Economics* 55:59–85.

Cuevas, A. 2003. Reforming intergovernmental fiscal relations in Argentina. IMF Working Paper 2003.

Darby, J., A. Muscatelli and G. Roy. 2002. Fiscal federalism and fiscal autonomy: lessons for the UK from other industrialised countries. *Scottish Affairs* 41:26–54.

Davoodi, H. and H. Zou. 1998. Fiscal decentralisation and economic growth a cross-country study. *Journal of Urban Economics* 43:244–257.

De Grauwe, P. and W. Vanhaverbeke. 1993. Is Europe an optimum currency area? Evidence from regional data. In *Policy issues in the operation of currency areas* (ed. P. Masson and M. Taylor). Cambridge University Press.

De Mello, L. 2000. Can fiscal decentralisation strengthen social capital. IMF Working Paper 00/129.

Edmonds, T. 2001. The Barnett formula. House of Commons Economic Policy and Statistics Section, Research Paper 01/18.

Ehdaie, J. 1994. Fiscal decentralisation and the size of government: an extension with evidence from cross-country data. World Bank Policy Research Working Paper 1387.

Forni, M. and L. Reichlin. 2001. Federal policies and local economies: Europe and the US. *European Economic Review* 45:109–134.

Glick, R. and A. K. Rose. 2002. Does a currency union affect trade? The time-series evidence. *European Economic Review* 46:1125–1151.

Grossman, P. J. 1989. Fiscal decentralisation and government size: an extension. *Public Choice* 62:63–69.

Heald, D. 1990. Financing a Scottish Parliament: options for debate. Discussion Paper.

———. 2003. Funding the Northern Ireland Assembly: assessing the options. Northern Ireland Economic Council, Research Monograph 10.

Hines, J. R. and R. H. Thaler. 1995. The fly paper effect. *Journal of Economic Perspectives* 9:217–226.

Kenen, P. 1969. The theory of optimum currency areas: an eclectic view. In *Monetary problems in the international economy* (ed. R. Mundell and A. Swoboda). Chicago University Press.

Krugman, P. 1993. Lessons of Massachusetts for EMU. In *The transition to economic and monetary union in Europe* (ed. F. Giavazzi and F. Torres), pp. 241–261. Cambridge University Press.

Layard, R., W. Buiter, P. Kenen, A. Turner, W. Hutton and C. Huhne. 2000. The case for the Euro. Britain in Europe Campaign, London.

MacDonald, R. 1999. Exchange rate behaviour: are fundamentals important? *Economic Journal* 109:F673–F691.

———. 2001. The role of the exchange rate in economic growth: a Euro area perspective. In *How to promote economic growth in the Euro area* (ed. J. Smets and M. Dombrecht). Edward Elgar.

McGregor, P. G. and K. Swales. 2004. The economics of devolution/decentralisation in the UK: some questions and answers. Department of Economics, University of Strathclyde.

McKinnon, R. I. 1963. Optimum currency areas. *American Economic Review* 53:717–725.

McLean, I. and A. McMillan. 2002. The fiscal crisis of the United Kingdom. Nuffield College Working Papers in Politics, W10.

Mankiw, N. G., D. Romer and D. N. Weil. 1992. A contribution to the empirics of economic growth. *Quarterly Journal of Economics* 107:407–437.

Mundell, R. 1961. A theory of optimum currency areas. *American Economic Review* 51:657–665.

Norregaard, J. 1997. Tax assignment. In *Fiscal federalism in theory and practice* (ed. T. Ter-Minassian). International Monetary Fund.

Oates, W. E. 1985. Searching for Leviathan: an empirical study. *American Economic Review* 75:748–757.

———. 1994. Federalism and government finance. In *Modern public finance* (ed. J. Quigley and E. Smolensky). Harvard University Press.

———. 1996. Taxation in a federal system: the tax assignment problem. *Public Economic Review* 1:35–60

———. 1999. An essay on fiscal federalism. *Journal of Economic Literature* 37:1120–1149.

———. 2004. Toward a second generation theory of fiscal federalism. Unpublished paper.

OECD. 2002. *Fiscal decentralization in EU applicant states and selected EU member states.* Paris: Centre for Tax Policy and Administration.

Scottish Executive. 2003. Government revenue and expenditure in Scotland, 2000–2001.

Stine, W. F. 1994. Is local government revenue response to federal aid symmetrical? *National Tax Journal* 47:799–816.

Tanzi, V. 2001. Pitfalls on the road to fiscal decentralization. Carnegie Endowment for International Peace, Working Paper 19.

Ter-Minassian, T. (ed.). 1997. *Fiscal federalism in theory and in practice.* International Monetary Fund.

Thießen, U. 2003. Fiscal decentralisation and economic growth in high-income OECD countries. *Fiscal Studies* 24:237–274.

Tiebout, C. 1956. A pure theory of local expenditures. *Journal of Political Economy* 64:416–424.

Watts, R. L. 1996. *Comparing federal systems in the 1990s*. Institute for Intergovernmental Relations, Queen's University, Ontario.

Xie, D., H. Zou and H. Davoodi. 1999. Fiscal decentralisation and economic growth in the United States. *Journal of Urban Economics* 45:228–239.

Zhang, T. and H. Zou. 1998. Fiscal decentralisation, public spending, and economic growth in China. *Journal of Public Economics* 67:221–240.

PART 2
Opportunity

Skill Policies for Scotland

By James J. Heckman and Dimitriy V. Masterov[1]

INTRODUCTION

The Scottish economist Adam Smith attributed the wealth of a nation to the specialization and division of its labour force. In the first book of his magnum opus, he wrote:

> The difference of natural talents in different men is, in reality, much less than we are aware of; and the very different genius which appears to distinguish men of different professions, when grown up to maturity, is not upon many occasions so much the cause, as the effect of the division of labour. The difference between the most dissimilar characters, between a philosopher and a common street porter, for example, seems to arise not so much from nature, as from habit, custom, and education. When they came into the world, and for the first six or eight years of their existence, they were, perhaps, very much alike, and neither their parents nor playfellows could perceive any remarkable difference. About that age, or soon after, they come to be employed in very different occupations. The difference of talents comes then to be taken notice of, and widens by degrees, till at last the vanity of the philosopher is willing to acknowledge scarce any resemblance. But without the disposition to truck, barter, and exchange, every man must have procured to himself every necessary and conveniency of life which he wanted. All must have had the same duties to perform, and the same work to do, and there could have been no such difference of employment as could alone give occasion to any great difference of talents.

In this passage, Smith perceptively notes three basic economic forces that characterize modern economies. Individuals, who differ in talents and skills, benefit from pursuing their comparative advantage by specializing in what they do best, and through trade and cooperation. Initial differences in abilities become amplified through education and on-the-job learning; such investments make persons more productive in the tasks they pursue. Education and learning are a major source of both economic productivity and human differences.

---

[1] We thank Giacomo De Giorgi for providing very helpful research assistance with the British and Scottish data and for helpful comments. We thank Wendy Alexander, David Bell, Richard Blundell, Pedro Carneiro, Diane Coyle, Fernando Galindo-Rueda, Alissa Goodman, Lynne Pettler Heckman, Costas Meghir, John McLaren, Robert Pollak and Anna Vignoles for helpful comments and discussion.

Open markets encourage trade among diverse individuals and encourage investment in what we now call human capital. Specialization and division of labour associated with lifetime skill formation are major sources of economic growth and economic advantage. The modern economy is based on skills. A skilled workforce is a productive one, able to adapt to change and to innovate. Inequality in skills is a major determinant of inequality in earnings. Scotland needs a more skilled workforce if it is to grow and prosper. This chapter is about policies to foster skills in the Scottish workforce.

One way to foster skill is to promote immigration of skilled labour to Scotland. A more open and flexible labour market will encourage such immigration. Some advocate policies to discourage emigration. It might be argued that educating Scottish youngsters to work in London is a bad business. That ignores altruism on the part of Scottish parents or the benefits that accrue to UK and world society. Given the proper incentives, Scots will stay in Scotland. We focus most of our attention in this essay on policies to foster the skills of those born in or resident in Scotland.

Smith's observations about markets and skills apply to Scotland today. He properly emphasized the importance of acquiring skills in the workplace. Yet we have learned much more about the life cycle of skill formation than Smith knew at the time he wrote the above passage. We now know that, contrary to Smith's opinion, by age eight people are not all that similar. Basic human differences emerge much earlier and cannot all be attributed to workplace experience or even to education. A child's time spent with its family in its early years is crucial for its development. Economists and psychologists have investigated the full life cycle of learning and have come to a deeper understanding of the dynamics of the skill formation process. This new evidence changes the way we think about policies to foster skills.

The central message of an entire literature, and a main theme of this chapter, is that skills policy is not the same as educational policy. Schooling is only a part of the skill formation process. What schools can achieve largely depends on the quality of the students they work with. This in turn depends on the quality of family life. An effective skill formation policy must account for the role of the family in producing skills and motivation. Dysfunctional families produce impaired children. A successful skill formation policy encompasses family policy. The current emphasis in popular discussions of skill formation policy focuses too much attention on aspects of schooling such as per pupil expenditure in schools, tuition rates and the like, and too little on the role of the family and the role of the firm. Much learning takes place on the job after schooling is completed.[2] A comprehensive skill formation policy accounts for families, schools and firms, and their interactions.

The abilities and motivations of children emerge early and affect performance in schools and the work place. Bright, motivated children do better in school, are more likely to obtain higher education degrees and participate in workplace-based training. As Adam Smith noticed, initial differences among people are accentuated by educational and training choices. The downside of the dynamics of skill

---

[2]Heckman et al. (1998a) estimate that over 40% of post-family learning takes place after formal schooling ends.

and ability formation is that those who start with early deficits, accumulate further deficits. Remedial action at later ages is costly and becomes prohibitively costly if it is attempted too late.

The motto of the new economics of skill formation is that skill begets skill; motivation begets motivation. Skill formation is a dynamic, synergistic process and these synergies must be tapped if a successful policy is to be crafted.

The main lessons for Scotland from the modern literature are as follows.

- Skill formation is a life cycle process. It begins in the womb and continues in the workplace. Educational policy is only one aspect of a successful skill formation policy, and not necessarily the most important one.

- Families are major producers of skill. Dysfunctional families produce children with lower levels of ability and motivation than functioning, healthy families. A successful skills policy encompasses policies to promote successful families and to supplement failing ones. The growing proportion of out-of-wedlock births and single-parent families in Scotland and the UK bodes ill for the future development of the Scottish workforce because such families are known to produce impaired children who perform poorly in school, the workplace and society at large.

- Early advantages produce later advantages. Early disadvantages produce severe later disadvantages that are hard to remedy.

- Skills are multidimensional in nature. Both cognitive and non-cognitive skills are important in the workplace and in performance in schools. An emphasis on IQ or on success measured by achievement tests is misguided but conventional in policy discussions about skill formation around the world. Successful policy recognizes the multiplicity of skills and works with it.

- The heterogeneities in skills and abilities that open up at an early age produce heterogeneity in the economic returns to schooling. Rates of return to university education vary greatly among persons. The return to the marginal student is nowhere near as high as the return to the average student, although many scholars in the United Kingdom often fail to make this distinction and estimate average rates of return when discussing educational policy. They use methods which do not allow them to distinguish the marginal return from the average return. More sophisticated analyses show declining returns for marginal students. Simply put, university is not for everyone.

- Skills differ in their malleability over the life cycle. Contrary to the quote from Smith, IQ is more or less set by age eight and it varies greatly among persons. Non-cognitive skills are malleable until later ages. This has important implications for the design of policy.

- At current levels of spending, changes in conventional educational policies that receive most of the attention in the economics of education, such as reductions in pupil–teacher ratios or increases in traditional schooling quality, are unlikely to have dramatic effects on economic or social performance. When evaluated, they do not survive a cost–benefit test.

- Policies subsidizing university tuition and other schooling expenses need to be rethought. Abilities formed at early ages play a much more decisive role in accounting for disparities in college enrolment than tuition or the income facing children and their families at the age children contemplate going to college.
- There is a well-established empirical regularity found in most societies that children from families with higher incomes are more likely to go to school and achieve higher education. This empirical regularity is usually interpreted to mean that credit constraints affect school choice and that tuition policy is the appropriate solution. However, the weight of the empirical evidence from many countries suggests another interpretation with vastly different policy implications. Families with higher incomes provide better early environments for their children. Interventions in the early years are far more likely to be effective in promoting college attendance than tuition supplements or scholarships paid at a later age. Children lacking ability and motivation do not make good college students.
- The problem of credit constraints—bright children denied university education because of low family income—is greatly overstated in popular discussions of educational policy in England, Scotland and the US and exerts disproportionate influence on policy discussions everywhere. Fewer than 8% of students are constrained in this sense in the US or the UK. Targeted subsidies for these constrained students are economically justified, but raising tuition for the others may also be a prudent policy. This kind of policy will raise support for education by channelling educational funds toward students who benefit most from them and by screening out unproductive, low-quality students for whom schooling is a poor investment.
- Post-school, on-the-job training (OJT) is a productive activity with a high economic rate of return. The return is higher for the most able and so this form of investment is disequalizing. It perpetuates, and even exacerbates, initial disadvantages.
- During periods of transition to new technologies or open markets, certain skills become obsolete. Workers adapted to one technology and way of doing business may be ill-suited to new modes of production and trade. Retraining younger and more able workers to higher levels of skill can be a sound investment.
- Public job training programmes targeted towards older displaced workers and the less able have a sorry track record. Remedial training for such people is simply not effective, so there are better uses for those funds. Wage subsidies and policies that promote flexibility in the labour market are far more likely to promote employment than job training. Such subsidies should be cohort-specific to avoid creating a new generation of unskilled workers dependent on government for their livelihood.
- Tax reforms are not likely to increase human capital accumulation dramatically, although they can promote capital formation and raise wages.

This chapter elaborates and documents these points. The next section presents some basic facts about the Scottish labour market and trends in Scottish education. Our analysis will place the situation in context with that of other developed nations. The following section reviews the evidence that supports the claims made in this section. Then we discuss interventions that have proved to be effective in the past. We draw on two papers by Heckman (2000a) and Carneiro and Heckman (2003) that present more detailed support for these arguments. We also draw on the academic literature on the UK. The final section concludes with policy recommendations for Scotland.

COMPARING ENGLAND, SCOTLAND AND THE US

In order to design effective policies, it is necessary to have a clear understanding of the problems they are intended to address. This requires getting straight the facts about Scotland. This task is not a simple one for all of the aspects of the Scottish economy because many studies neglect Scotland and do not distinguish uniquely Scottish problems. When we can use Scottish data, we will. Otherwise, we will draw on evidence from the UK as a whole. With a few notable exceptions, the empirical patterns are very closely linked, which leads us to believe that our analysis is at least qualitatively correct and our policy recommendations are appropriate. Our comparative advantage lies in being able to offer a fresh perspective, bringing our expertise on US data to bear on Scottish issues.

We consider several dimensions of the Scottish economy as a background for a discussion of skill formation policy: wage premiums for skilled labour, wage inequality, unemployment and worklessness, illegitimacy, crime, educational attainment and participation, and skills of the labour force. Like many countries and regions in the world, Scotland has experienced a shift in demand toward more skilled labour. This has produced a premium for those who have skills as well as wage inequality between those who have skills and those who do not. Scots have responded to the rising economic return to schooling by increasing their participation in higher education. The Scottish participation rate in higher education is increasing while among recent cohorts it is stagnating in the US and the UK.

At the same time, there are major sources of concern for Scotland. Worklessness is increasing; levels of literacy and numeracy are low and are not increasing in the younger cohorts. There is clear evidence of social pathology in the sense of more out-of-wedlock births, high crime rates and the like. Given the evidence that out-of-wedlock children acquire poorer lifetime skills than others, an emerging Scottish underclass should be a major source of concern addressed in any comprehensive skill formation policy.

There is also a growing group of middle-age workers caught up in the dynamics of production transformation. Trained to work in obsolescent technologies, their skills are maladapted to the new economy, especially at current wage levels. The case for public job retraining is weak, especially for middle-age and low-ability workers. More creative thinking is required to devise policies to ease their transition, promote their employability and at the same time equip their children with the skills needed to work in the new economy.

123

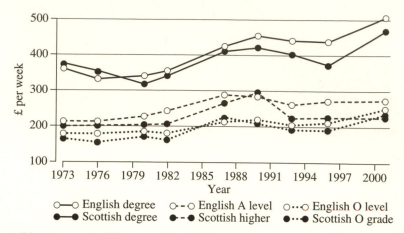

Figure 6.1. Average weekly gross wages. Males and females from the General Household Survey. Wages are shown in two-year averages and in 1995 pounds. The O levels category contains City and Guilds crafts; BTEC/SCOTVEC first or general diploma; O level; GCSE grades A–C or equivalent. A levels category contains GMVQ advanced; A level or equivalent; RSA advanced diploma or certificate; BTEC/SCOTVEC national certificate (CSYS); SCE higher or equivalent; AS or equivalent and trade apprenticeship certification. Degree category contains higher degree; NVQ level 5; first degree.

Wage Inequality and Education

Educational attainment and basic literacy have become increasingly important because of the rising premium for skilled labour found in many countries. Since the late 1970s, the economic return to education (the economic benefit of attending school) has risen.[3] Growth in overall wage inequality for both men and women is substantial.

A rise of the wage skill premium occurred in Scotland and England. Figure 6.1 shows that the growth of average weekly gross wages of English and Scottish workers increases with their educational level.[4] The skill wage premium for those with a degree or higher is rising with respect to A levels/Highers. This is a combination of both a rise in wages for the highly educated and a flat A level profile in the last 15 years. The same is true with respect to O levels/O grades. The widening wage differentials we observe in Figure 6.1 are also apparent in the real hourly wage trends for the 10th, 50th and 90th percentiles[5] of the UK and US wage distributions analysed by Gosling and Lemieux (2001). They find that in both countries, women

---

[3] See the time-series on US returns to education in Card and DiNardo (2002).

[4] Scottish and English school qualifications differ. Until 1986 the Scottish equivalent of O levels were O grades, and afterwards Standard Grades. Until 1999 Scottish students completed Highers and then CSYS in the following year as their certificates for post-school education, equivalent to the two-year A level in England. Since 1999 they have been replaced gradually by the Higher Still programme of Highers and Advanced Highers.

[5] Percentiles measure relative positions in the distribution of hourly wages. The 90th percentile line represents the average wages for those whose wages are equal to or greater than 90% of the people in the sample, the 10th percentile is the bottom 10%, and the 50th percentile is the median line.

have higher rates of wage growth relative to men, and wage growth is larger in the UK than the US.[6] The 10th (bottom) decile in the UK has apparently not lost ground in real terms and has actually experienced substantial wage growth, especially for women. The UK's 50th percentile has improved significantly as well. Although the difference between the highest paid and the lowest paid worker has grown both in the UK and the US, in the US the least skilled have lost ground in real terms while they have not in the UK.[7] It is clear, however, that growth in inequality took place mostly during the 1980s, and inequality remained mostly stable in the 1990s. Growth in inequality has been similar in England and Scotland, although there has been some slight divergence in the last decade (see Bell 2004).

The primary force generating the skill premium is skill-biased technical change. As documented in Machin and Van Reenen (1997), the shift in the demand for skilled workers has occurred in many sectors of the economy and is found in all countries where it has been studied. As noted by Nelson and Phelps (1966) and Schultz (1975), those with more education and skill are better able to cope with, and benefit from, changes and opportunities that open up with increased trade and new technology. A more-skilled workforce can create new technologies and opportunities. However, as noted by Adam Smith in *The Wealth of Nations*, not everyone should be equally skilled or trained in the same fashion. Comparative advantage operates among people as well as among nations. Scotland needs a full portfolio of skills, but it should increase its weight on skilled workers.

Employment and Worklessness

Historically, England has had slightly higher employment and slightly lower unemployment rates than Scotland for all age groups, though the trends have converged in recent years. Labour force withdrawal rates are very similar.

In the UK, worklessness is becoming increasingly common, while the opposite is true for the US, especially for single mothers. Dickens and Ellwood (2003) summarize the effect of policies under the Blair government and compare them to the policies in the US during the same period. They argue that the British reforms focused on increasing employment of individuals who faced few benefits from entering the labour market.[8] However, simultaneous reforms offset these employment incentives by improving out-of-work benefits.[9] The net effect seems to have boosted

---

[6]It is important to note that women still earn less than men.

[7]The analysis of Blundell et al. (2003) cautions us that selective dropouts from the low end of the wage distribution bias upward these figures. Their adjusted estimates make the US and UK experiences appear more similar, as real wages at the bottom of the UK distribution may be declining.

[8]The Working Families Tax Credit (WFTC) raised in-work benefits for those with children, and the Childcare Tax Credit provided increased childcare support for working low-income families. Moreover, the lowest income tax rate was reduced from 20 to 10%. National Insurance reforms lowered fees for those with low wages and a National Minimum Wage of £3.60 per hour was introduced for workers older than 22. Non-financial incentives included improvements in childcare provision.

[9]Benefit rates for out-of-work families with children were raised. Child Benefit rates, which are non-means tested and paid to every household with children, were increased. Income Support rates for low-income families with children raised, while those for families without children were not.

employment (see Gregg and Harkness 2003). The Clinton strategy in the US was quite different. Out-of-work benefits were cut and time limits were introduced. EITC payments to low-wage workers increased. After these reforms, benefits for workers were substantially higher than for those out of work.

Dickens and Ellwood (2001) show that in England, the rise in worklessness took place over a period with stable unemployment and employment rates that have remained unchanged between 1979 and 1999.[10] However, the overall statistics obscure some important facts about worklessness. Nickell (2004) notes that unemployment among men with no qualifications has risen from 7% in 1979 to 12% in 1999, though unskilled women experienced no such change. Moreover, inactivity among working-age men has risen from 4.7 to 15.9%, while inactivity among working-age women has fallen from 34.6% to 26.9%. An increase in the labour force participation of married women with employed partners has disguised a decrease in participation of single women with children. For men the rise in inactivity has been among married men whose partners cease to work and among single men. Households where both partners are working and households where neither partner is working have become more common.[11] This is true for Scotland as well. Bell and Jack (2002) report that from 1992 to 2001, the fraction of workless households in all working-age households rose from 17 to 22%. The fraction of households where all adults are employed rose from 54 to 57%, while the fraction where only some adults work fell from 30 to 21%.

Worklessness has increased markedly for the youngest cohorts. Murray (2001) studied the change in employment among males aged 18–24 between 1989 and 1999. He showed that worklessness rose from 20.5 to 31.2%, and that attrition from the labour force was highest for those between the ages of 20 and 24. Faggio and Nickell (2003) showed that for men inactivity was concentrated among low-skill individuals. Gregg and Wadsworth (2003) attributed the recent drop in unemployment among the low-skilled to a transition to worklessness rather than improved employment. Figure 6.2 shows that Scotland and England share this trend. Increased participation in higher education is not the reason behind this disturbing trend. It is linked to declining real wages and higher social benefits.

To put these numbers in perspective, Dickens and Ellwood (2001) estimate that in the US in 1999, less than 5% of two-parent families with children were workless. Such families without children are only marginally more likely to be without work. For single parents with children, worklessness has fallen from a peak of 44% in 1982 to about 27% in 1999 (see Dickens and Ellwood 2001). The corresponding number for single parents without children is slightly above 20%. As noted by Nickell (2004)

---

[10]Since 1998, there has been a slight decline in worklessness and a simultaneous increase in the employment rate for all of the groups in the UK as measured in the Labour Force Survey (see Shaw 2004). The decrease in worklessness has been especially large for lone parents with children. However, the rates reported in Shaw (2004) are slightly lower in 1998 than the ones in Dickens and Ellwood (2003), who use the Family Expenditure Survey (FES), which leads us to believe some of the difference in the rates may be due to differences in the sample selection criteria.

[11]Between 1979 and 1999, the percentage of households where both partners are employed in all two-adult households has increased from 55 to 64%. The corresponding change in households where neither partner is working was from 4 to 8%.

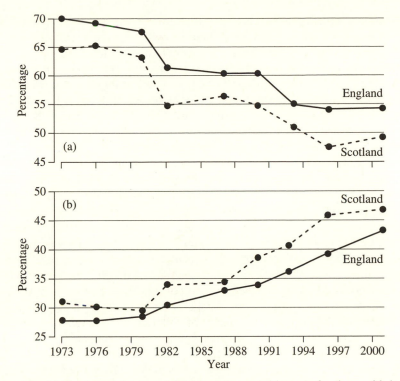

Figure 6.2. (a) Employment rate and (b) labour force attrition rate for those with low or no qualifications. *Source:* data for men and women aged 16–64 from the General Household Survey.

this cross-country difference is explained in part by generous welfare benefits in the UK. However, Dickens and Ellwood (2001) argue that the movement of people into work has not done much to decrease relative poverty. Individuals who enter the labour market increase their income, but they usually do not earn high wages. This is because worklessness is closely linked with education and skill, and it is concentrated among the less skilled and educated persons.

Illegitimacy and Poverty

Murray (2001) shows that the illegitimacy rate, defined as the percentage of children born to unmarried mothers, increased from 5% to nearly 40% in England between 1950 and 2000.[12] Almost all of that increase has occurred in the last 20 years. Haskey (2001) shows that both the number of one-parent families and the number of children living in such families rose between 1984 and 2000, though both trends appear to have slowed in recent years. In 1986, one-parent families represented 14%

---

[12] High illegitimacy rates are not only confined to poor neighbourhoods. However, there does seem to be strong link between social class (as measured by occupation) and out-of-wedlock births. See Murray (1994).

of all families with dependent children. In 1991 the figure was 20%. By 2000, one-parent families comprised 25% of all families with dependent children and 23% of all dependent children were from one-parent families. Moreover, the percentage of all families with dependent children headed by lone mothers has increased at a rapid rate since 1971 (see Haskey 2001). It is now just under 1 in 4, while in the 1970s it was 1 in 12. Kiernan (2001) reports that although lower than the US in 1975 and 1985, the rate of out-of-wedlock births per 100 births in the UK exceeded the US rate by 1999. In Scotland, non-married households with dependent children comprise 40% of all households with dependent children.[13]

These changes in family structure have occurred on a short time-scale, and they have far-reaching consequences for the offspring of such families. For instance, in 2001 in Scotland, only 48% of lone parent households with dependent children were employed with about half working only part-time, while 90% of couples with children have at least one partner employed.[14] Employment is closely linked with poverty. Bell and Jack (2002) report that only 5% of the households where everyone worked were poor[15], and only 10% of households where at least one person worked were poor. However, 38% of households where no adults worked were in poverty. The corresponding numbers for the percentage of children in poverty were 11%, 22% and 67%. At the same time, the percentage of children living in absolute poverty in Scotland has fallen and the percentage of children living in relative poverty has remained stable or fallen slightly.[16] This suggests that generous government benefits have offset some of the negative effect.

McLanahan and Sandefur (1994) observe that children from single-parent households are more likely to be poor, and have health and psychological problems. They are also more likely to engage in crime, report worse labour market outcomes and have unstable marriages. DeLeire and Kalil (2002) find that American teenagers from unmarried families are less likely to graduate high school or attend college. They are also more likely to smoke and drink at a young age. McLanahan and Sandefur (1994) confirm that various outcomes for stepchildren are similar to those of children from single-parent families. Ginther and Pollak (2003) show that even joint biological children from blended families (families containing stepchildren and their half-siblings who are the biological children of both parents) have inferior outcomes relative to children reared in traditional nuclear families. Stepchildren are also at a greater risk for abuse by step-parents and cohabiting partners (see Daly and Wilson 1998). The problem of broken homes and out-of-wedlock births has serious implications for the skills and performance of the next generation.

---

[13]We define non-married households as cohabiting couples, lone parents and other households. A dependent child is a person in a household aged 0–15 (whether or not in a family) or a person aged 16–18 who is a full-time student and in a family with parent(s).

[14]Data are from the SCROL database of the 2001 Census, available at http://www.scrol.gov.uk/scrol/common/home.jsp. A dependent child is a person in a household aged 0–15 (whether or not in a family) or a person aged 16–18 who is a full-time student in a family with parent(s). Part-time is defined as working 30 hours or less a week. Full-time is defined as working 31 or more hours a week.

[15]That is, with income less than 60% of median household income after housing costs.

[16]Relative poverty uses a benchmark that changes from year to year, i.e. the proportion of mean or median income from all sources in the relevant year.

Many analysts dismiss this research because correlation, even with extensive statistical controls, does not establish causation. One stylized fact from this literature is that controlling for factors such as long-term family income, parental education and cognitive ability greatly diminishes the effect of family structure on child outcomes (see, for example, Ginther and Pollak 2004). This suggests that at least some of the disadvantages of non-traditional child-rearing can be offset by improving home environments. However, it is not clear which policies should be chosen since the current literature does not determine the causal mechanisms producing these relationships. For instance, divorce and family resources may be jointly determined and outcomes may simply reflect common unobserved factors.

There is, however, an emerging literature that uses parental death as a natural experiment. The death of a parent has a smaller negative effect on children than divorce.[17] For instance, Cherlin et al. (1995) use NCDS data to compare the behavioural outcomes of British adults who experienced divorce or parental death as children with adults reared in intact families. One advantage of their study is that they control for various pre-divorce characteristics of the family and the child, such as pre-existing emotional problems, cognitive achievement and socioeconomic status. They find that by age 23, both men and women with divorced parents are more likely to leave home because of friction and to have their first child born outside of marriage. Moreover, while experiencing the death of a parent seems to exert a similar effect, it is usually much smaller. This is a consistent finding, and suggests that some portion of the benefits from marriage is not purely a matter of increased resources. A carefully tailored policy needs to bolster family structure as well as compensate for the lack thereof with educational interventions like enriched pre-schools, which we discuss in this chapter.

Crime in England, Scotland and the US

In recent years, serious crime rates are higher in England[18] than in the United States. This pattern is evident in both surveys of crime victims as well as the reported police statistics. Langan and Farrington (1998) analyse data from the 1995 victim surveys. They show that robbery, assault, burglary and motor vehicle theft are all higher and generally rising in England. The major exception to this pattern is the murder rate, which is nearly six times higher in the US despite the large drop in the late 1990s. Langan and Farrington (1998) also show that an offender's risk of being caught, convicted and sentenced to incarceration has risen in the US for all types of crime[19], but has fallen in England for all but murder. Moreover, for all offences, courts in the US hand down longer sentences and confinement is generally also longer (although both the length of sentences and time served are rising in England for violent crimes).

---

[17] For comparisons of parental death and divorce, see Lang and Zagorsky (2001), Corak (2001) and Biblarz and Gottainer (2000).

[18] Crime data include Wales unless otherwise specified.

[19] The measured types of crime are murder, rape, robbery, assault, burglary and motor vehicle theft.

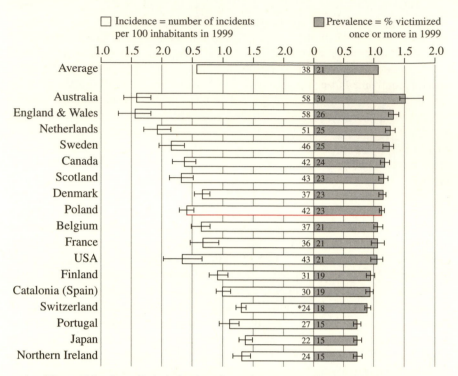

Figure 6.3. Overall victimization. Countries are sorted by prevalence rates. Incidence rates for Switzerland are estimated. *Source:* Van Kesteren et al. (2001).

Figure 6.3 examines the incidence and prevalence of overall victimization in 1999.[20] Prevalence rates are defined as the percentage of those aged 16 or more who experienced a specific crime once or more in a given year. Incidence rates express the number of crimes experienced by each 100 people in the sample. In terms of both prevalence and incidence, England has significantly higher rates than Scotland and the US, which are not essentially different. When incidence is high relative to prevalence, we can surmise that crime is concentrated in the sense that a few people experience the bulk of it, and are prone to repeated victimization. The gap is very wide in England and Wales and the US. By this measure, Scotland's crime seems to be somewhat more evenly distributed.

Another alarming statistic is the estimated number of children who have parents with a serious drug problem. A recent report[21] by the Advisory Council on the Misuse of Drugs (2003) infers that there are between 40 800 and 58 700 children in Scotland who have a parent who is a problem drug user. This represents about 4–6% of the one million children under 16. However, fewer children, only about 1–2%, live with a problem drug user.

---

[20]This is based on Van Kesteren et al. (2001). This report uses data from the International Crime Victims Survey. It avoids the problem of differential reporting and definitions involved in using police data by using a common survey instrument across countries.

[21]'Hidden harm: responding to the needs of children of problem drug users.'

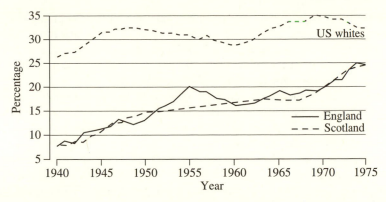

Figure 6.4. Percentage of residents with at least a college degree by country and year of birth (five-year moving averages). Data from Quarterly Labour Force Survey (QLFS) 2002 and Current Population Survey (CPS) 2000. US sample contains only whites. UK data are separated by place of residence. In the UK, the college category contains those who have at least degree level qualifications. For the US, those with four-year college, professional and terminal degrees are included.

Crime is also related to educational attainment, skill levels and the returns to market activities. Machin and Meghir (2000) find that falling wages of unskilled workers led to increases in crime in England and Wales between 1975 and 1996. They also find the level of criminal activity and the returns to crime are similarly closely linked, while increased deterrence is negatively linked with crime, suggesting several approaches to stemming crime.

Educational Attainment

How have Scottish youth responded to the new demand for skills? Here we look at educational responses because they are easily studied. Evidence for other sources of skill, such as on-the-job learning, is less easily obtained. Figure 6.4 compares higher educational attainment of Scottish, English and US cohorts born after 1940. The percentage of each cohort with at least a college degree has increased in both Scotland and England over time, especially for those born after the late 1960s.[22] Both the levels and their rates of growth are fairly similar in England and Scotland, with

---

[22]Much of the jump in college attainment for those born after 1960 can be attributed to the reconstitution of the polytechnics as university institutions in 1992. This shift in supply essentially doubled the number of universities in the UK (see Lowe 2002). Huisman et al. (2003) attribute the expansion in polytechnics and college sector between 1989 and 1994 to formula funding, which uses a core plus margin model. This formula means that institutions receive between 5 and 10% of their funding (the margin) as a function of how many additional students they were able to recruit at a lower price. This led them to expand vacancies until the marginal cost of each student equaled the average. A similar university expansion was enabled by raising tuition fees to approximately 30% of instructional costs, and giving these fees to the university for all the additional students they attracted. Overall, enrolments in higher education were growing by more than 10% per year in the early 1990s. By 1994, this expansion was halted, though since 1998 a number of initiatives have been taken to widen and deepen participation. At the same time, however, higher education in the 1990s has become less affordable as grants were replaced by loans, and a system of student fees was introduced. However, Callender and Kemp (2000) argue that the UCAS data show no reduction in enrolment of students from lower classes.

the fraction of college graduates approaching one-quarter for recent cohorts. In the US, the percentage of residents with at least a degree is higher, and the acceleration in enrolment begins earlier, though it is less steep than comparable rates for Scotland and England. There appears to be a decline in attainment for those born after 1969. This pattern has not emerged in England or Scotland.

Historically, the fraction of the population with low or no qualifications has declined. However, this proportion has been virtually constant for some years. The fraction of dropouts has grown in the US, relative to older cohorts, though it is still considerably lower than in the UK.

One area of concern is the stagnation in participation (as opposed to completion) in post-compulsory education. In the US, college enrolment has stagnated for recent cohorts, even as completion is rising. Completion rates cannot increase indefinitely, though there is still a lot of room for it to grow since the US college dropout rate is approximately 40%. In England, both staying-on rates after 16 and college participation are stagnating for the youngest cohorts (see Blanden and Machin 2003). These trends are troubling. It is important to also note that the UK has a much lower higher education dropout rate of 18% (Smith and Naylor 2001). This suggests that stagnation in participation is much more likely to begin exerting a downward pull on completion in the UK since the two rates are much closer together. However, until recently, the age participation index for Scotland does not seem to be stagnating, as it is in England.

Literacy and Numeracy

The news on basic workforce skills is not so encouraging. Scotland, the UK and the US have a thick lower tail of barely literate and numerate persons, who are a drag on productivity and adaptability and who are a source of social problems. We use data from the International Adult Literacy Survey (IALS)[23] to examine literacy and numeracy of adults of working age (16–65 years). Three dimensions of literacy are used. Prose literacy is defined as the knowledge and skills required to understand and use information from texts such as newspaper articles and fictional passages. Document literacy is defined as the ability to locate and use information from timetables, graphs, charts and forms. Quantitative literacy is defined as applying arithmetic operations, either alone or sequentially, to numbers embedded in printed materials, such as calculating savings from an advertisement or the interest earned on an investment. These data allow us to compare the distributions in US, Scotland, England, Germany and Sweden. The IALS grouped the scale scores into five empirically determined levels, with level 1 representing the lowest ability level and level 5 representing the highest. In Figures 6.5–6.7, we plot the proportion of each gender group falling within a particular level of literacy by country and the 95% confidence intervals for these estimates. Because a small proportion of people tested at the highest skill categories, we collapse levels 4 and 5 together. Relative to the US and England, Scotland has a lower proportion of people with the highest levels

---

[23]More information on the IALS is available in documents located at http://www.nald.ca/nls/ials/introduc.htm and IALS (2002).

of literacy and especially numeracy, though the difference is usually not precisely determined. Germany and Sweden perform better than the English-speaking countries. McIntosh (2003) examines these data. Those with good to excellent literacy skills enjoy a sizeable wage premium over those who do not, even accounting for their schooling attainment. Moreover, he finds that the younger cohorts do not have better skills than older ones. Younger cohorts are no better or even worse on literacy and numeracy, respectively.

In light of the encouraging performance of Scottish students on the 2000 Programme for International Student Assessment (PISA) survey of 15-year-olds (see Education and Young People Research Unit (2002)), it is surprising to see the literacy of the youngest Scots may not be improving. Figure 6.8 shows the means and the 95% confidence intervals for the overall reading score from the Progress In Reading Literacy Survey (PIRLS)[24] for 4th graders from several OECD countries in 2001. Scotland's students perform significantly worse than students in England and Sweden, though Scotland's performance is not significantly different from that of US or of Germany.

Scottish youth are going to colleges at higher rates than their parents and participation is increasing rather than stagnating as it is in England and the US. At the same time, there is a serious problem with the bottom half of the skill distribution as measured by their numeracy and literacy. The growth in worklessness and crime—linked to declining wages of the unskilled—bodes ill for the Scottish economy. Social polarization as measured by income inequality across skill groups is increasing. One way to address these problems is to invest in the skills of the young and possibly also to upgrade the skills of the adult workforce. We now turn to evidence on the effectiveness of various interventions.

LESSONS ON SKILL FORMATION FROM AROUND THE WORLD

A major lesson from recent research for effective policy analysis is that the skills acquired in one stage of the life cycle affect both the endowments and the technology of learning at the next stage. Human capital is produced over the life cycle by families, schools and firms, although most discussions of skill formation focus on schools as the major producer of abilities and skills.

A major determinant of successful schools is successful families. Schools work with what parents bring them. They operate more effectively if parents reinforce them by encouraging and motivating children. Job training programmes, whether public or private, work with what families and schools supply them and cannot remedy 20 years of neglect. Scottish skill formation policy should be based on this basic principle.

Figure 6.9a summarizes the major findings of an entire literature. It plots the economic rate of return to human capital at different stages of the life cycle for a person of a given ability. The horizontal axis represents age, which is a surrogate for the agent's position in the human life cycle. The vertical axis represents the rate

---

[24]The PIRLS database is accessible at http://lighthouse.air.org/timss/.

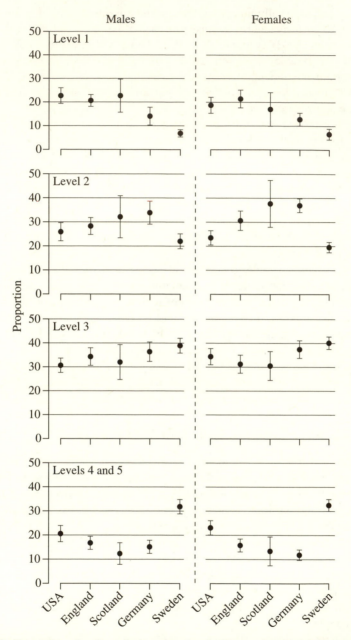

Figure 6.5. Proportion of each gender in a given level of International Adult Literacy Survey (IALS) Prose Literacy Scale. The scale scores were grouped into five levels of increasing difficulty. Sample restricted to adults between 16 and 65 at the time of the survey (1996 for the UK, 1994 for the US and Germany and 1994–95 for Sweden). Standard errors are calculated as described in IALS (2002). Scale: 95% confidence interval.

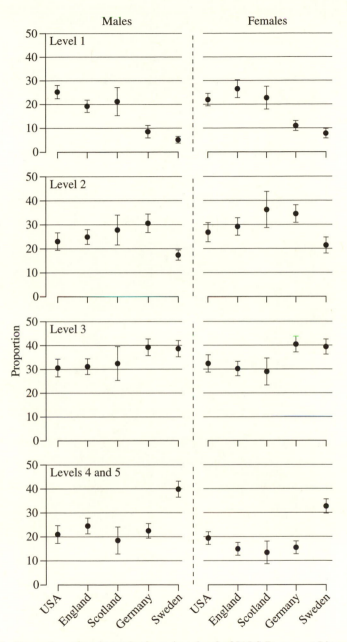

Figure 6.6. Proportion of each gender in a given level of IALS Document Literacy Scale. The scale scores were grouped into five levels of increasing difficulty. Sample restricted to adults between 16 and 65 at the time of the survey (1996 for the UK, 1994 for the US and Germany and 1994–95 for Sweden). Standard errors are calculated as described in IALS (2002). Scale: 95% confidence interval.

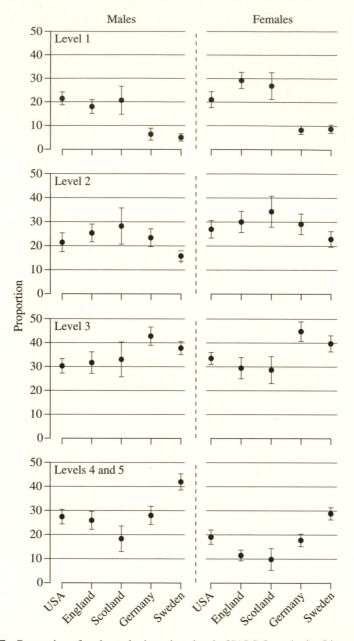

Figure 6.7. Proportion of each gender in a given level of IALS Quantitative Literacy Scale. The scale scores were grouped into five levels of increasing difficulty. Sample restricted to adults between 16 and 65 at the time of the survey (1996 for the UK, 1994 for the US and Germany and 1994–95 for Sweden). Standard errors are calculated as described in IALS (2002). Scale: 95% confidence interval.

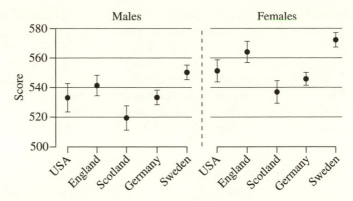

Figure 6.8. Overall reading by gender and country. *Source:* data are from the Progress In Reading Literacy Survey (PIRLS) for 4th graders conducted in 2001.

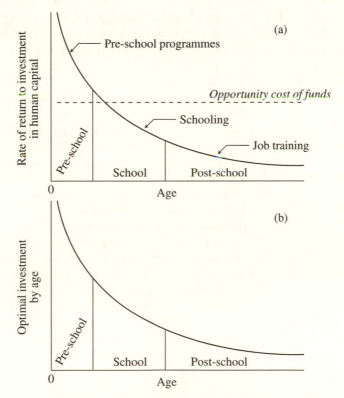

Figure 6.9. (a) Rates of return to human capital investment initially setting investment to be equal across all ages. (b) Optimal investment levels.

of return to investment assuming the same investment is made at each age. Holding everything else constant, the rate of return to a pound of investment made while a person is young is higher than the rate of return to the same pound made at a later

137

age. Returns are higher for more able people (i.e. the schedule shifts outward for the more able). Early investments are harvested over a longer horizon than those made later in the life cycle. In addition, because early investments raise the productivity (lower the costs) of later investments, human capital is synergistic. Learning begets learning; skills (both cognitive and non-cognitive) acquired early on facilitate later learning. For an externally specified cost of funds (represented by the horizontal line with intercept in Figure 6.9a), an optimal investment strategy is to invest less in the old and more in the young. Figure 6.9b presents the optimal investment quantity counterpart of Figure 6.9a.

Figure 6.9a is also an empirical description of the economic returns to investment at current levels of spending in most economies around the world. The return to investment in the young is quite high; the return to investments in the old and less able is quite low. A socially optimal investment strategy would equate returns across all investment levels. A central conclusion of a vast body of research summarized and extended in Heckman (2000a) and Carneiro and Heckman (2003) is that at current investment levels in most countries, efficiency in public spending would be enhanced if human capital investment were directed more toward the young and away from older, less-skilled and illiterate persons for whom human capital is a poor investment.

The recent literature in the economics of human development challenges a convention that equates skill with intelligence. It demonstrates the importance of both cognitive and non-cognitive skills in determining success both in the labour market and in schooling. Both types of skill are affected by families and schools, but they differ in their malleability over the life cycle, with non-cognitive skills being more malleable than cognitive skills at later ages. Differences in levels of cognitive and non-cognitive skills by family income and family background emerge very early and persist. Schooling widens these early differences, as Adam Smith noted.

Current educational policy discussions focus on tested academic achievement as the major output of schools. Proposed systems for evaluating school performance are premised on this idea. While cognitive ability is an important factor in determining schooling and labour market outcomes, non-cognitive abilities, although harder to measure, also play an important role. Early childhood interventions primarily improve non-cognitive skills, with substantial effects on schooling and labour market outcomes, but only weakly affect cognitive ability. Mentoring programmes in the early teenage years can also affect these skills. Current evaluations of skill formation policy focus too much on cognitive ability and too little on non-cognitive ability.

Sources of Skill Differences

There is a strong relationship between family income and college attendance. Parents with higher incomes are more likely to send their children to college. Blanden and Machin (2003) show that there are substantial differences in UK college participation rates across family income classes that have, if anything, increased in recent years. Vignoles and Galindo-Rueda (2003) present supporting evidence. This pattern is found in many other countries (see the essays in Blossfeld and Shavit (1993)). In the late 1970s or early 1980s, college participation rates started to increase in the UK, Scotland and the US in response to increasing returns to schooling. The increase was greatest for youth from the top family income groups. Such differential educational responses by income class promise to perpetuate or widen income inequality across generations and among social groups.

There are two interpretations of this evidence that are not necessarily mutually exclusive. The common interpretation of the evidence, and the one that guides much policy discussion around the world and in the UK and Scotland (Vignoles and Galindo-Rueda 2003; Blanden and Machin 2003), is the obvious one. Credit constraints mean poor families cannot afford to send their children to college. A second interpretation emphasizes long-run factors associated with higher family income. It notes that families with high income in a child's adolescent years are more likely to have high income throughout the child's life at home. Better family resources in a child's formative years are associated with higher quality of education and better environments that foster cognitive and non-cognitive skills. Both interpretations of the evidence are consistent with a form of borrowing constraint. The first, more common, interpretation is clearly consistent with this point of view. But the second interpretation is consistent with another type of borrowing constraint: the inability of a child to buy the parental environment and genes that form the cognitive and non-cognitive abilities required for success in school and the labour market.

A vast quantitative literature surveyed and extended in Heckman (2000a) and Carneiro and Heckman (2003) suggests that the second interpretation is by far the more important one. Controlling for ability formed by the early teenage years, parental income plays only a minor role in explaining college attendance and graduation. The evidence from the US and the UK suggests that at most 8% of youth are subject to short-term borrowing constraints that affect their post-secondary schooling despite the enormous attention lavished on this problem. Most of the family income gap in enrolment in higher education is due to long-term factors that determine the abilities needed to benefit from participation in college. Adjusting for long-term family factors (measured by ability or parental background) mostly eliminates ethnic or racial gaps in schooling in American data.

The first-order explanation for gaps in enrolment in college by family income is long-run family factors that are crystallized in ability. Short-run income constraints play a role in creating these gaps, albeit a quantitatively minor one. While there is scope for intervention to alleviate these short-term borrowing constraints, one should not expect to reduce the enrolment gaps substantially by eliminating such constraints, or fiddling with tuition rates, although discussions in Scotland focus on these policies.

Family Income and Enrolment in College

Children whose parents have higher incomes have access to better-quality primary and secondary schools. Children's tastes for education and their expectations about their life chances are shaped by those of their parents. Educated parents are better able to develop scholastic aptitude in their children by assisting and directing their

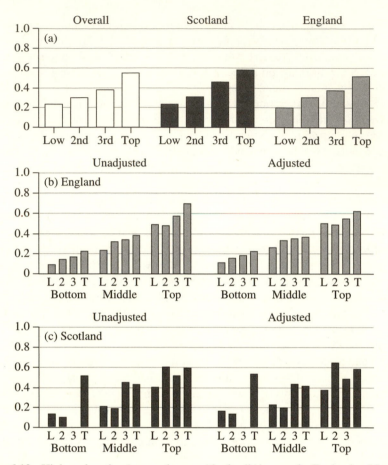

Figure 6.10. Higher education (men and women) by family income for England and Scotland (British Cohort Study). Note that higher education includes both vocational and academic degree. Adjusted by paternal education.

studies. By age 8, intelligence as measured by IQ tests seems to be fairly well set (see the evidence summarized in Heckman (1995)). Non-cognitive skills appear to be more malleable until the late adolescent years (see Carneiro and Heckman 2003). The influences of family factors present from birth through adolescence accumulate to produce ability and college readiness so the scope for tuition policy to promote college attendance is restricted by the stock of adolescent ability. A large literature supports the importance of early investment.

Adjusting Family Income Gaps Using Ability or Other Long-Term Family Factors

Figure 6.10a, based on the analysis of Carneiro and Heckman (2002, 2003), shows that a pattern found in many countries is present in England and Scotland as well. Children from higher-income families are more likely to participate in higher education. In Scotland, the top quartile (i.e. the top 25% of the family income distribution) has an average enrolment rate of almost 60% against an enrolment rate of 25% for the bottom quartile. The differences in England are less dramatic but still substantial.

The left (unadjusted) panel of Figure 6.10b shows how the English differentials are changed when we condition on terciles (33% points) of ability as measured in a student's adolescent years. Top corresponds to children who are at the top third of the cognitive ability distribution and so on. Within each ability group, we classify participation rates in higher education (HE) by family income. The chart shows that ability is a major determinant of college participation. Within ability groups, children from the top income groups are more likely to go to college. Adjusting for an additional long-run factor (father's education) reduces, but does not fully eliminate, the family income effect (see the right-hand panel of Figure 6.10b).

Unfortunately, this calculation for Scotland is less reliable because the sample is small and the standard errors of the estimates are large (see Figure 6.10c). The big spikes shown there arise from a small number of observations. Results from the larger English sample shown in Figure 6.10b show a more consistent pattern, whose broad characteristics are by no means absent in the Scottish data. Ability appears to be the major determinant of participation in higher education in all countries. Dearden et al. (2004) replicate the Carneiro and Heckman (2003) US analysis for England. They find that after controlling for ability, family background and other characteristics, individuals in the top income quartile are 7–8% more likely to stay on in post-compulsory schooling after age 16. They also find that there is little evidence of any credit constraints for higher education.

Policies that improve the financing of the education of identified constrained subgroups will increase their human capital and may well be justified on objective cost–benefit criteria. The potential economic loss from delay in entering college can be substantial. Given standard economic values for attending college, and assuming schooling is delayed one year, the costs of the delay are 9% of the lifetime value of schooling in the US data (see Carneiro and Heckman 2003). For identified constrained subgroups, the benefits to reducing delay and promoting earlier college completion, higher college quality and graduation are likely to be substantial.

In designing policies to harvest these benefits, it is important to target the interventions. Broad-based policies generate deadweight, although they promote a sense of equality and fairness. Dynarski (2001) and Cameron and Heckman (1999) estimate that 93% of President Clinton's Hope Scholarship funds, which were directed toward high-achieving children who largely came from middle-class families, were given to children who would have attended school even without the programme. Such policies dissipate scarce funds and forego revenue that is better invested in productive educational ventures. We discuss tuition policy below. While targeting those identified as constrained is good policy, it is important not to lose sight of the main factors accounting for the gaps in Figure 6.10a: family background factors crystallized in ability.

Early Test Score Differentials

Important differences in ability across family types appear at early ages and persist. These are found in the UK (Vignoles and Galindo-Rueda 2003; Feinstein 2003) and in the US (Carneiro et al. 2003b), and similar patterns are found for other tests and in many other datasets. Feinstein (2003) finds that there is a 13 percentile difference in an index of cognitive development at 22 months between British children from high and low socioeconomic status ('SES') families. By 118 months, this difference widens to 28 percentile points.[25] This means that there was considerable pre-school educational inequality in the UK in the 1970s. This kind of inequality is present in the US as well. Ability gaps open up early and persist. This is true for many measures of verbal and mathematical ability. Having access to more and higher-quality resources that contribute to improving cognitive ability early in life affects skill acquisition later in life (see Heckman 1995).

Controlling for the long-term family factors, including mother's education, mother's ability and family structure, substantially reduces the gaps in rank scores across income groups. Measured long-term family factors play a powerful role, but they do not fully eliminate the gaps.

The emergence of early test score differentials is not limited to cognitive measures. At early ages, differences in US children's behaviours and attitudes across income groups are also evident, as Figure 6.11a illustrates.[26] The figure presents average percentile ranks in the anti-social behaviour score by family income quartile. Motivation, trustworthiness and other behavioural skills are important traits for success in life. The evidence summarized in Carneiro and Heckman (2003) shows that non-cognitive skills matter greatly in labour markets and for success in school. Hence, understanding the gaps in these behavioural skills across different income groups (and how to eliminate them) is also important for understanding the determinants of economic success. Figure 6.11b presents percentile ranks of the scores for behavioural measures adjusted for mother's education and cognitive ability as well as family structure. Adjusting for early family background factors substantially reduces gaps in non-cognitive skills across income groups. Comparing adjusted cognitive and non-cognitive test scores reveals the importance of long-term factors in reducing the gaps in behavioural scores across these groups. Although non-cognitive ability gaps across income quartiles cannot be eliminated at later ages, controlling for mother's ability, educational attainment of the parents, family structure and location significantly reduces the gaps in ranks in non-cognitive abilities across these groups at both early and later ages. Vignoles and Galindo-Rueda (2003) present similar evidence for the UK.

Good families promote cognitive, social, and behavioural skills. Bad families do not. Children from broken homes or single-parent families suffer both cognitive and

---

[25] Using data from the British Cohort Study, Feinstein (2003) finds that the percentile rank on the cognitive development index at 22 months predicts educational attainment at age 26, though scores at 46 months yield better predictions. High SES children with low scores are much more likely to improve their scores than low SES children with poor scores.

[26] Mothers were asked 28 age-specific questions about frequency, range and type of specific behaviour problems that children age four and over may have exhibited in the previous three months. Factor analysis was used to determine six clusters of questions, one of which is anti-social behaviour. The responses for each cluster were then dichotomized and summed. Anti-social behaviour consists of measures of cheating and telling lies, bullying and cruelty to others, not feeling sorry for misbehaving, breaking things deliberately (if age <12), disobedience at school (if age >5), and trouble getting along with teachers (if age >5).

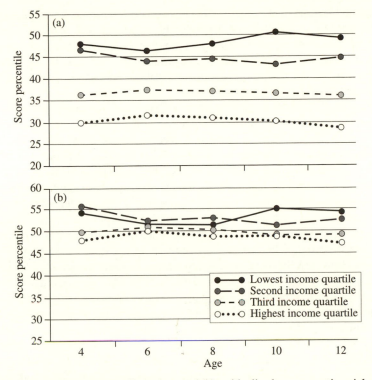

Figure 6.11. (a) Average percentile rank on and (b) residualized average anti-social score by income quartile. *Source:* Carneiro and Heckman (2003), data from the National Longitudinal Survey of Youth (NLSY79). (a) The income measure we use is average family income between the ages of 6 and 10. Income quartiles are then computed from this measure of income. (b) Residualized on maternal education, maternal AFQT and broken home at each age (we use AFQT corrected for the effect of schooling).

non-cognitive deficits. The relevant policy issue is to determine what interventions in bad families are successful.

The Evidence on the Importance of Non-cognitive Skills

Much of the neglect of non-cognitive skills in analyses of earnings, schooling and other life outcomes is due to the lack of any reliable method for measuring them. Many different personality and motivational traits are lumped into the category of non-cognitive skills. Psychologists have developed batteries of tests to measure these skills (see, for example, Sternberg 1985). Companies use these tests to screen workers, but they are not yet used to ascertain college readiness or to evaluate the effectiveness of schools or reforms of schools. The literature on cognitive tests ascertains that one dominant factor ('g') summarizes cognitive tests and their effects on outcomes. No single factor has emerged as dominant in the literature on non-cognitive skills and it is unlikely that one will ever be found, given the diversity of traits subsumed in the category.

Studies by Bowles and Gintis (1976), Edwards (1976) and Klein et al. (1991) demonstrate that job stability and dependability are traits most valued by employers as ascertained by supervisor ratings and questions of employers, although they present no direct evidence on wages and educational attainment. Perseverance, dependability and consistency are the most important predictors of grades in school (Bowles and Gintis 1976).

Heckman and Rubinstein (2001) present the cleanest evidence on this point using evidence from the General Education Degree (GED) testing programme in the United States. The GED programme is a second-chance programme that administers a battery of cognitive tests to self-selected high school dropouts to determine whether or not their level of academic attainment is equivalent to that of high school graduates. If they pass the test, GED recipients are eligible to apply to college. The GED recipients are as smart as ordinary high school graduates who do not go on to college and also smarter than other high school dropouts. They earn more than other high school dropouts, have higher hourly wages, and finish more years of high school before they drop out. When measured cognitive ability is controlled for, however, GED recipients earn the same or less, have lower hourly wages, and obtain lower levels of schooling than other high school dropouts. Some unmeasured factors therefore account for their relatively poor performance compared with other dropouts. Heckman and Rubinstein (2001) identify these factors as non-cognitive skills noting that a subsequent analysis should parcel out which specific non-cognitive skills are the most important. The fact that someone has received the GED sends a mixed signal. They are smarter (have higher cognitive skills) than other high school dropouts and yet at the same time have lower levels of non-cognitive skills. Both types of skill are valued in the market and both affect schooling choices. These findings challenge the conventional signaling literature, which assumes there is a single skill that determines socioeconomic success. They also demonstrate the folly of a psychometrically oriented educational evaluation policy that assumes that cognitive skills are all that matter for success in life.

While IQ is fairly well set by age 8, motivation and self-discipline are more malleable at later ages (Heckman 2000a). Given the evidence on the quantitative importance of non-cognitive traits, social policy in Scotland should be more active in attempting to alter them, especially in children from disadvantaged environments who receive poor discipline and little encouragement at home. This more active social-policy approach would include mentoring programmes and stricter enforcement of discipline in the schools. We present evidence on the value of such interventions later in this chapter. Such interventions would benefit the child and society but at the same time might conflict with widely held values of sanctity of the family for those families that do not value self-discipline and motivation and resent the imposition of what are perceived as middle-class values on their children.

Summary

Long-term environmental factors crystallized in cognitive and non-cognitive abilities play a major role in accounting for gaps in schooling attainment across socioeconomic groups. Short-term borrowing constraints and tuition factors that receive

prominent attention in current policy discussions do not. Short-term credit constraints do, however, affect a small group of persons, and targeted-subsidy policies
appear to be cost effective for those persons. One cannot expect tuition-reduction
policies to eliminate the substantial gaps in schooling attainment according to socioeconomic background. Gaps in levels of cognitive and non-cognitive skills open up
early and are linked to family environments at early ages, not parental income in
the adolescent years. Non-cognitive skills substantially determine socioeconomic
success later in life.

ANALYSES OF SPECIFIC POLICIES

This part of the chapter applies these lessons to the analysis of specific policies,
drawing on studies from the US and the UK. We do not discuss subsidies justified by
human capital externalities. Although such externalities have played a prominent role
in the recent revival of growth theory by leading economic theorists, an accumulating
body of evidence (see, for example, Acemoglu and Angrist 2001; Heckman et al.
1996; Heckman and Klenow 1998) suggests that these theoretical possibilities are
empirically irrelevant.

The Returns to Schooling

Few topics in empirical economics have received more attention than the economic
return to schooling. By now there is a firmly established consensus that the mean
return to a year of schooling, as of the 1990s, exceeds 10% and may be as high as 17–
20% (Carneiro et al. 2001b). An extra year of college can raise earnings by as much
as 17%. This return is higher for more-able people (Taber 2001) and for children
from better backgrounds (Altonji and Dunn 1996). Those from better backgrounds
and with higher ability are also more likely to attend college and earn a higher
rate of return from it. The synergy or complementarity suggested in Figure 6.9a is
confirmed in estimates of ability and background on earnings. Both cognitive and
non-cognitive skills raise earnings through promoting schooling and through their
direct effects on earnings. (See the evidence in Taber (2001), Heckman et al. (2001)
and Carneiro et al. (2001a, 2003a).) Table 6.1 presents a summary of the mean
rate of return to schooling for different ability groups. The annual return to college
is substantially higher for persons with greater ability. Those at the top 95% of the
ability distribution have rates of return almost twice those at the bottom 5%. Students
at the margin of attending college or not attending have substantially lower returns
at each ability level than those who attend college (compare row 4 with row 2.)

The research of Carneiro et al. (2001a, 2003a) and Cunha et al. (2004) shows
that returns to schooling are lower for people who are less likely to attend college.
Carneiro et al. (2003a) compare the marginal returns for people at various levels
of the probability of attending college. Marginal students earn less than average
students. The message of this finding and of Table 6.1 is that college is not for
everyone, because, in general, ability greatly affects rates of return. Meghir and
Palme (2003) find that in Sweden the returns to compulsory schooling are highest

Table 6.1. Return to one year of college for individuals at different percentiles of the math test score distribution.

	5%	25%	50%	75%	95%
Average return in the population	0.1121 (0.0400)	0.1374 (0.0328)	0.1606 (0.0357)	0.1831 (0.0458)	0.2101 (0.0622)
Return for those who attend college	0.1640 (0.0503)	0.1893 (0.0582)	0.2125 (0.0676)	0.2350 (0.0801)	0.2621 (0.0962)
Return for those who do not attend college	0.0702 (0.0536)	0.0954 (0.0385)	0.1187 (0.0298)	0.1411 (0.0305)	0.1682 (0.0425)
Return for those at the margin	0.1203 (0.0364)	0.1456 (0.0300)	0.1689 (0.0345)	0.1913 (0.0453)	0.2184 (0.0631)

Source: Carneiro and Heckman (2003), data for white males from high school and beyond.

for those with above-median ability. In fact, most of the overall increase in earnings for their sample was driven by the high-ability subgroup from poor backgrounds. This body of evidence suggests that early ability differences affect returns on later investments.

Raising Schooling Quality

The most commonly suggested reforms for schools are reductions in class size, summer school programmes and increases in teacher salaries and per-student expenditures. Krueger (1999, 2003) suggests that these interventions are likely to be cost effective, although the benefit–cost ratios he presents are very low. Some of the evidence on the success of such initiatives is based on experimental evidence, such as that from the Tennessee Student–Teacher Achievement Ratio (STAR) programme, which has been widely publicized. Evidence from this programme has been mixed; kindergarten students in smaller classes initially have higher test scores than those in larger classes, but in later grades, treatment and control group students' test scores move much closer together, although there is still a small positive effect of the programme (see Hanushek 2000; for an opposing view, see Krueger (1999)). There is no evidence that reductions in class size of the sort reported in the Tennessee STAR experiment will substantially affect earnings or reduce the substantial skill gaps across socioeconomic groups. Even if the test score gains from reductions in class size can be shown to last, test scores are only weakly linked to earnings later in life (Cawley et al. 1999; Heckman and Vytlacil 2001).

Studies linking measures of schooling quality directly to lifetime earnings and occupational achievement have recently appeared. There is a growing consensus based on these studies that within current ranges of funding in most developed economies, changes in measured inputs such as class size and spending per pupil have only weak effects on the future earnings of students (see Heckman et al. 1996; Hanushek 1998, 2002).

Even if one takes the most favourable estimates from the literature and combines them with the best-case scenario for the costs of raising schooling quality, decreasing the pupil–teacher ratio by five pupils per teacher does not turn out to be a wise investment. Such a reduction in the ratio, keeping the number of students enrolled the same, would require the addition of new teachers, and the addition of new classroom and school facilities. Accounting only for the costs of adding new teachers, Carneiro and Heckman (2003) estimate that a decrease of five pupils per teacher would cost about $790 per student.[27] They estimate that even on a relatively optimistic assumption of a 4% increase in future earnings resulting from a decrease in the pupil–teacher ratio by five pupils per teacher, there is a negative present value of between $2600 and $5500 per 1990 high school graduate at standard discount rates (5–7%). Dearden et al. (2002) report what an entire literature finds: in developed countries, returns to improvements in schooling quality are minuscule or non-existent, and rarely survive a cost–benefit test (see also Dustmann et al. 2003). Bell and Sarajev (2004) report that, despite spending nearly 25% more per capita on education in Scotland relative to England, this difference is not apparent in higher wages for full-time Scottish employees, conditional on individual and labour market factors. Pouring more funds into schools to lower class sizes by one or two pupils or to raise spending per pupil by a few hundred pounds will not solve the problems of the Scottish primary and secondary school system, nor will it substantially stimulate the college going of the poor.

The literature in economics does not say that school quality does not matter.[28] Hanushek (1971, 1997), Murnane (1975) and Hanushek and Luque (2000, 2003) all show that individual teachers matter in the sense of raising the test scores of students. Conventional measures of teacher quality do not, however, predict who are the good teachers. Giving principals more discretion in rewarding and punishing teachers would be a more effective way to use local knowledge than increasing measures of dubious predictive value. Bureaucratization of public schools hinders use of this knowledge. Although the effects of schooling quality vary across environments and additional funding for some schools may be justified in certain cases, marginal improvements in school quality are unlikely to be effective in raising lifetime earnings and more fundamental changes are required if one hopes to see a significant improvement in our educational system.

Choice and Competition in Schooling

Currently in Scotland, there is very little choice in schools and the incentives for excellent performance by teachers and pupils are muted. School choice has been advocated as a reform to improve the quality of educational services. Proponents of school choice argue that competition among schools to attract students will force schools to decrease costs and increase the quality of services provided. Additionally, by having parents actively choose the schools attended by their children, school choice systems would likely increase the degree of parental involvement in children's

---

[27] In 1990 dollars, equivalent to about £630 in 2004.

[28] Machin and McNally (2003) find large gains in reading and English for 11-year-old students who were exposed to the Literacy Hour programme between 1996 and 1998. At this age the effect is about 2–2.5 percentage points for reading and about 3% more children achieving level 4 or above in English. There are also some weak improvements in GSCE performance at age 16. Unlike most interventions in school quality, the Literacy Hour focused on curricular content and class management and not on lowering the pupil–teacher ratio.

schooling. Opponents of school choice argue that increased competition among schools will lead to increased stratification and inequality among students as well as a dilution of basic schooling standards; and that poor parents lack the information and the ability to make informed decisions for their children. Hence, school choice systems would be most beneficial to those, the richer families, already able to exercise choice in the current system.

Voucher experiments provide data for empirical studies concerning school choice. Experiments that give tuition vouchers to public-school students so that they may attend private schools have been conducted in several US cities, including Milwaukee, Cleveland, Minneapolis and New York (prominent studies include Witte (2000), Peterson and Hassel (1998) and Rouse (1997)). Researchers do not agree on whether vouchers have any impact on students' educational achievement. Recent research (see Peterson and Hassel 1998) shows important differences in parental satisfaction. Relative to parents not allowed to exercise choice, parents under school choice systems are more likely than other parents to report satisfaction with their children's school. But these voucher experiments are often limited in their scale, and it is difficult to generalize any findings from them to the national level. Any national voucher programme will most likely have large general-equilibrium effects that cannot be estimated from small-scale experiments (see Urquiola and Hsieh 2002).

Other researchers have studied the effect of introducing competition among public schools into the monopolistic setting of the US public school system. Evidence from these studies indicates that increased school competition and student and parental choice improves the quality of schools, as measured by test scores and by parental and student satisfaction with learning. Contrary to the view that competition siphons resources away from the public sector to its detriment, Hoxby's (2000) research suggests that when public schools are subject to greater competition both from parochial and other private schools, the performance of all schools increases. Higher levels of achievement are produced at lower cost. Making schools more competitive in salaries and rewarding excellent performance by students as well as teachers will promote productivity.

The conventional argument of educational planners against choice in schools is that parents and students are not able to make wise choices. The available evidence points to better outcomes from increased school competition but it is far from definitive. Policies that promote such competition are much more likely to raise schooling performance than policies that increase schooling quality and do not change the organization of schools (see also Chapter 8). Exact quantitative trade-offs, however, are not available (see Hanushek 2000, 2002).

Early Childhood Investments

The evidence summarized earlier shows that both cognitive and non-cognitive abilities affect schooling and economic success and that socioeconomic differences in cognitive and non-cognitive skills appear early and, if anything, widen over the life cycle of the child. Parental inputs are important correlates of these skills. Yet the policy interventions supported by this evidence are far from obvious, because the exact causal mechanisms through which good families produce good children are not yet well understood. Perhaps for this reason, most societies have been reluctant to intervene in family life, especially in the early years.

There is a profound asymmetry in popular views about family life and schooling. On the one hand, there is a widespread belief that offering choice of school is not beneficial implying that parents cannot make wise choices about their children's schooling. But if that is true, then how can parents be trusted to make correct decisions in the pre-school years, which recent research has demonstrated to be so important for lifetime success? The logical extension of the paternalistic argument that denies the wisdom of parental sovereignty in choosing schools would suggest that the state should play a far more active role in the pre-school life of the child. That is a position that few would accept, however.

Paternalistic interventions in the early life of children in dysfunctional families may be appropriate, though. If one is to violate the principle of family sovereignty anywhere in the life cycle, the case for doing so is strongest at the pre-school stage (and only for some groups), not at later stages of formal schooling, for which the argument paternalistic is most often made. Dysfunctional families and environments are major sources of social problems and, as established earlier in this chapter, the proportion of children growing up in dysfunctional families in Scotland and the UK is increasing.

Although there are several early interventions in the UK, such as Sure Start and Effective Provision of Pre-School Education (EPPE), we do not know of any extensive evaluations of their long-term effects. However, if US evidence is any indication of their potential, they should prove to be fairly successful. Recent small-scale studies of early childhood investments in children from dysfunctional families and disadvantaged environments have shown remarkable success and indicate that interventions in the early years can effectively promote learning. They demonstrate that interventions that good families routinely provide can remedy the failings of bad families. Early childhood interventions of high quality raise achievement and non-cognitive skills, but they do not raise IQ. Disadvantaged subnormal IQ children (average 80) in Ypsilanti, Michigan, were randomly assigned to the Perry Preschool Program, and intensive treatment was administered to them at ages 3–4. The treatment consisted of a daily 2.5 hour classroom session on weekday mornings and a weekly 90 minute home visit by the teacher on weekday afternoons to involve the mother in the educational process. The length of each pre-school year was 30 weeks, beginning in mid October and ending in May. The average child–teacher ratio for the duration of the programme was 5.7. Treatment was then discontinued, and the children were followed over their life cycle.

Evidence on the treatment group, now about 35 years old, indicates that those enrolled in the programme have higher earnings and lower levels of criminal behaviour in their late 20s than did comparable children randomized out of the programme. Reported benefit–cost ratios for the programme are substantial. Measured through age 27, the programme returns $5.70 for every dollar spent. When returns are projected for the remainder of the lives of programme participants, the return on the dollar rises to $8.70 (see Table 6.2). A substantial fraction (65%) of

Table 6.2. Perry Preschool: net present values of costs and benefits through age 27.

1. Cost of pre-school for child, ages 3–4	12 148
2. Decrease in cost to government of K-12 special education courses for child, ages 5–18	6 365
3. Decrease in direct criminal justice system costs of child's criminal activity, ages 15–28[a]	7 378
4. Decrease in direct criminal justice system costs of child's projected criminal activity, ages 29–44[a]	2 817
5. Income from child's increased employment, ages 19–27	8 380
6. Projected income from child's increased employment, ages 28–65	7 565
7. Decrease in tangible losses to crime victims, ages 15–44	10 690
Total benefits:	43 195
Total benefits excluding projections[b]	32 813
Benefits minus costs	31 047
Benefits minus costs excluding projections[b]	20 665

Notes: all values are net present values in 1996 dollars at age 0 calculated using a 4% discount rate. [a]Direct criminal justice system costs are the administrative costs of incarceration. [b]Benefits from projected decreased criminal activity (4) and projected income from increased employment (6) are excluded. *Sources:* Karoly et al. (1998) and Barnett (1993).

the return to the programme has been attributed to reductions in crime (Schweinhart et al. 1993).

Recent estimates of the rate of return to the Perry Preschool Program are 13% (W. S. Barnett, personal communication, 2002). This number looks low relative to the 15–20% return for schooling reported by Carneiro and Heckman (2003). However, it should be compared with the return for low-ability students, because the Perry programme only recruited low-ability children. Recall that Table 6.1 shows that the return to one year of college for the average individual in the 5th percentile of the ability distribution is 11% and the return to college for the average individual in the 5th percentile of the ability distribution not attending college is only 7%. (Most of the population at this percentile of the ability distribution is not attending college, so the latter is the relevant number for the comparison.) For individuals at the 25th percentile of the ability distribution, higher than the percentile rank for the Perry participants, this return rises to 9.5%. (The returns to maternal inputs at early ages are very high for normal children; 13% is a lower bound on the return for normal children.) The return to the Perry programme is very high.

Evidence on the more universal Head Start programme is less clear, but the programme is quite heterogeneous and is much less well-funded than the Perry Preschool Program. Currie and Thomas (1995) find short-term gains in test scores for all children participating in Head Start; most of those gains decayed quickly, however, for African-American children after they left the programme. Currie and Thomas conclude that either differences in local-programme administration or in quality of schooling subsequent to the Head Start programme are at the root of the differences between the outcomes for black and white children. Ramey et al. (1988) note that the schools attended by the Perry Preschool children were of substantially higher quality than those attended by the typical Head Start child. In addition, the Perry programme also taught parenting skills and arguably put better long-term environments in place for the children. The failure in subsequent years to support the initial positive stimulus of Head Start may account for the decline in the impact of Head Start over time, and may account for its apparent ineffectiveness compared with the Perry Preschool Program. In a more recent paper, Garces et al. (2002) find substantial long-term effects of Head Start on high school graduation, college attendance, earnings and crime. The largest effects are for individuals whose mothers have less than a high school education. Among whites in this group, attending Head Start leads to a 28% increase in the probability of high school graduation, a 27% increase in the probability of college attendance and a 100% increase in earnings measured in the early 20s. For blacks, the likelihood of being booked or charged with crime is 12% lower for those who attended Head Start than for those who did not.[29]

As noted earlier, an emphasis on cognitive test scores is misplaced. It appears that early childhood programmes are most effective in changing non-cognitive skills, although they also raise achievement test scores (as opposed to IQ). Enriched interventions very early on in life can raise IQ (see Cunha et al. 2005). We also note that eventual decay of initial gains in test scores, like those found in regard to the Head Start programme, were found for programmes like Perry Preschool as well, but the long-term evaluations of these programmes are quite favourable in terms of participants' success in school and society at large. The fade-out effects in test scores found for the Head Start programme do not imply that participation in the programme has no long-term beneficial effects. Head Start may improve the lifetime prospects of its participants, despite yielding only short-term gains in test scores, which may not measure many relevant dimensions of social and emotional skills.

The Perry intervention affected both children and parents. Parents in the programme improved their education and labour force activity and reduced their participation in welfare. Successful enrichment programmes like Perry Preschool foster long-term improvements in the home environment that carry over to the child long after the programme has terminated. Head Start offers a much lower quality staff who are also paid accordingly, part-time classes for children and limited parental involvement. The programme terminates without any substantial intervention into or improvement in the home environments of the disadvantaged children. Given the potential for success of such programmes (as exhibited by the Perry Preschool experiment), more studies of the long-term impacts of various types of small-scale and broad-based early intervention programmes are warranted. Calculations by Donohue and Siegelman (1998) indicate that if enriched early intervention programmes were targeted toward high-risk, disadvantaged minority male youth in the US, the expected savings in incarceration costs alone would more than repay the substantial costs of these enriched programmes.

An important lesson to draw from the Perry Preschool Program, and indeed from the entire literature on successful early interventions, is that the social skills and

---

[29]There is also new evidence that suggests that Head Start may not have any effect. Imai (2004) uses a difference-in-differences approach rather than the family fixed effects method. He finds no effect whatsoever on cognitive outcomes or problem behaviour.

motivation of the child are more easily altered than IQ. There also tends to be a substantial improvement in the children's social attachment. These skills affect performance in school and in the workplace. Academics have a bias toward believing that cognitive skills are of fundamental importance to success in life. Because of this, the relatively low malleability of IQs after early ages has led many to proclaim a variety of interventions to be ineffective. Yet the evidence from the Perry Preschool Program and the evidence summarized in Carneiro and Heckman (2003) reveals that early intervention programmes are highly effective in reducing criminal activity, promoting social skills, and integrating disadvantaged children into mainstream society. The greatest benefits of these programmes are their effects on socialization and not those on IQ. These programmes may be very effective as antidotes to adverse family environments. Enriching the educational and nurturing content of the recently expanded early child care system will pay off in producing a more skilled and emotionally competent workforce.

Interventions in the Adolescent Years

How effective are interventions in the adolescent years? Is it possible to remedy the consequences of neglect in the early years? Just as early intervention programmes have a high pay-off primarily because of the social skills and motivation they impart to the child and the improved home environment they produce, so do interventions that operate during the adolescent years, and for the same reasons. Programmes aimed at intervening in the lives of children in their teenage years attempt to redress the damage of bad childhoods. Although these programmes do not raise participants' IQ, there is some evidence that they can affect their social skills (non-cognitive abilities), because the prefrontal cortex, which controls emotion and behaviour, is malleable until the late teenage years (Shonkoff and Phillips 2000).

Carneiro and Heckman (2003) summarizes evidence on the effects of adolescent interventions on education, earnings and crime rates. The available schooling literature demonstrates that providing disadvantaged students with financial incentives to stay in school and participate in learning activities can increase schooling and improve employment outcomes. It should be noted that although programmes providing such incentives have been proved to influence employment and earnings positively, and often to reduce crime, they do not perform miracles. The impacts are modest, but positive.

The evidence on programmes aimed at increasing the skills and earnings of disadvantaged youth suggests that sustained interventions targeted at adolescents still enrolled in school can positively affect learning and subsequent employment and earnings. Interventions for dropouts are much less successful. It is important to remember that the interventions conducted by such programmes only partly alleviate and do not reverse early damage caused by poor family environments.

Tuition Policy

Tuition policy is hotly debated in Scotland and elsewhere. The recent prohibition on student contributions in Scotland and the introduction of optional variable fees in England exemplify the sensitivity of this issue. Although in both countries these decisions were accompanied by additional measures intended to aid students from disadvantaged backgrounds, most of the past beneficiaries of such programmes have been students from relatively wealthy backgrounds.[30] The middle class has a strong political interest in getting the rest of society to pay the college bills for its children (Peltzman 1973), and yet free, or heavily subsidized, tuition is viewed as an egalitarian policy.

Recent analyses challenge this widely held premise. The studies of Cameron and Heckman (2001) and Keane and Wolpin (2001) show that variation in tuition fees plays only a minor role in accounting for schooling attendance gaps by family income status. Far more important are the abilities determined at early ages. College attendance is promoted by shaping these abilities.

One might therefore argue that charging tuition and raising standards may be a better policy than subsidizing tuition for everyone. The increased tuition can help meet the costs of college (and other educational expenditures) and ration places to those with a greater demand for schooling. Merit-based scholarships targeted to bright but poor children (e.g. the bottom income quartile of the top ability group in the right half of Figure 6.10b) can make sure that deserving students go to school. Our evidence that the returns to college are lower for marginal and low-ability students shows that college is not for everyone. The absence of any clear evidence of substantial human capital externalities at current levels of funding suggests that there is considerable scope for raising fees and charging people for the benefits they will achieve, benefits which largely accrue to themselves. Under the guise of equality of opportunity, current public policy in Scotland subsidizes those from more advantaged environments rather than going to the root of family problems that cause disadvantages in skills and motivation that appear early and persist throughout life unless treated early.

Private and Public Job Training

Because of a lack of data, the returns to private-sector training are less well studied than the returns to public-sector training. Studies by Lynch (1992, 1993), Lillard and Tan (1986), Bishop (1994) and Bartel (1992) find sizeable effects of private-sector training on earnings in the US (see also United States Department of Labor 1995). Most of these studies do not attempt to control for the bias that arises because more-able and more-motivated persons are more likely to undertake training, so estimated rates of return overstate the true returns to training by combining them with the return to ability. Upper-bound estimates of the return to training for marginal entrants range from 16 to 26% and are comparable with those obtained from education (see Mincer 1993). Somewhat smaller returns are found in data for the UK. These studies typically do control for ability and this accounts for the lower estimated returns than those found in the American studies. Blundell et al. (1999) estimate that employer-provided training (EPT) that leads to a qualification results in 7.8% return for the

---

[30]Moreover, the additional funds available in England may impair Scotland's ability to attract and retain staff, professors and students.

male worker. EPT that does not involve formal qualification leads to a return of 8.3%. Non-employer-provided training has zero effect. Male workers who experience five or more training courses during the time of the study earn 12.5% more.[31] There is also some evidence that EPT with qualifications is not firm-specific, so that workers who change employers will still gain from the experience. EPT provides sizeable gains, especially considering that 13% of the Scottish working-age population participated in training in 2000.[32]

An important feature of private-sector training is that the more-skilled and more-able participants in such training do more investing in human capital even after they attain high skill levels. Different types of training and learning have strong complementarities with respect to one another. Blundell et al. (1999) find that those with more education (including previous training) and higher cognitive ability are much more likely to participate in training. The same patterns are found in the US (see Carneiro and Heckman 2003). Low-skilled and low-ability persons typically do not participate in private-sector training. The lack of interest of private firms in training disadvantaged workers indicates the difficulty of the task and the likely low return to this activity.

The best available evidence indicates that public training programmes are an inefficient transfer mechanism and an inefficient investment policy for low-skilled adult workers. In evaluating any public project, it is necessary to account for the welfare costs of raising public funds as well as the direct costs of providing the services. It is also necessary to estimate accurately the time series of the returns to any investment in human capital and to discount it appropriately to compare with project costs. Heckman and Smith (1998) take experimental estimates from the evaluation of a major US job training programme, the Job Training Partnership Act (JTPA), and make alternative assumptions about benefit duration, costs, welfare costs, interest rates for discounting and the welfare cost of public funds. Accounting for these factors vitally affects the estimates of the economic return to training. Especially important is the assumption about benefit duration. The JTPA evaluation followed participants for only 30 months. When the benefits of the training provided are assumed to persist for seven years, the estimated effects are larger in absolute value.[33] But conventional evidence on the effectiveness of public-sector training reports treatment effects without accounting for costs, and so these evaluations overstate net benefits.

Heckman et al. (1999) present a comprehensive survey of the economic return to public-sector training. Martin and Grubb (2001) provide a useful summary of some general lessons from the empirical literature on job training. Public job training includes classroom education, make work, subsidized employment and job search.

---

[31] The corresponding effects for females are 10%, 14%, 0% and 7.8%.

[32] Calculated from the Scottish Household Survey 2000. Working age includes those between 16 and 65 living in private residences.

[33] Seven years has been selected as the measure here because Couch (1992) shows that one intensive wage subsidy programme has annual benefits of that duration. On the other hand, Ashenfelter (1978) estimated a 13% annual depreciation rate of the first round impact on earnings, which suggests that an assumption of no depreciation is grossly at odds with the evidence.

The rate of return to classroom training is sizeable (see Heckman et al. 2000a). The rates of return for other components of training, however, are generally lower, although subsidized work appears to have a large pay-off. Even when an activity such as job search assistance is profitable, the scale of and gains from the activity are low. Based on the empirical record, one cannot expect substantial benefits from job training (see the evidence Heckman et al. (1999)).

There is also considerable evidence of heterogeneity in response to treatment in job training (Heckman et al. 1997). Treatment is found to be most effective for those at the high end of the wage distribution. It has no effect for those at the bottom. So there are substantial gains to be realized from targeting treatment. The information required to do so effectively, however, is generally not available (see Heckman et al. 2002). The returns to job training for older workers and displaced workers are very low.

Scotland has seemingly been more successful at job training than England. However, the results mirror the outcomes in the US. McVicar and Podivinsky (2003) use age eligibility requirements to estimate the effect of the New Deal for Young People (NDYP) in Scotland. They find that NDYP increased outflows from long-term unemployment, but almost half of this outflow was not into employment, but into education and training. This achievement is hardly a success. Blundell et al. (2003) argues that the effect of NDYP for the UK as a whole is small: about 17 000 more employed per year; but the cost is small as well.

A comparison of the job training programmes discussed in this section suggests a few important lessons. First, you get what you pay for. The recently terminated American JTPA programme cost very little but produced very few results. An exception to the rule is the return to classroom training, which is substantial (Heckman and Lochner 2000). Second, the effects of treatment vary substantially among subgroups (Heckman et al. 1999). Third, job training programmes also have effects on behaviour beyond schooling and work that should be considered in evaluating their full effects. Reductions in crime may be an important impact of programmes targeted at male youth. The evidence summarized in Heckman et al. (1999) indicates that the rate of return to most US and European training programmes is close to zero, although the benefits to certain groups may be substantial, and some may pass cost–benefit tests. We cannot look to public job training to remedy or alleviate substantially skill deficits that arise at early ages. They have also proved to be ineffective in equipping middle-age workers for the modern economy.

Tax and Subsidy Policy

Progressive income taxes of the sort in place in the United Kingdom retard skill formation. In addition, generous social welfare payments of the sort recently implemented in the UK discourage work and hence investment in workplace-based skills. UK tax rules tend to encourage investments made on-the-job over investments in formal schooling, especially schooling that requires substantial out-of-pocket or tuition costs. Tax rules in the United Kingdom tend to promote human capital formation over physical capital formation but tax reductions which encouraged capital accumulation would raise the wages of all workers. Although many of these effects of the current tax system on human capital investment may be unintended, they may nevertheless be substantial and may favour certain workers as well as certain types of investment over others. But based on studies for the US, we find that tax reforms are unlikely to have substantial effects on skill formation.

The costs of investment in human capital are foregone earnings net of taxes plus any additional tuition or out-of-pocket expenses. Higher proportional taxes reduce the costs of spending an hour in school by the amount they reduce the return of working an hour in the market. In a regime with flat (proportional) taxes in which the only human capital investment cost is foregone income, changes in the level of the flat wage tax will have no effect on human capital accumulation, because increases in the tax rate reduce the return by the same proportion as they reduce the cost. On the other hand, if tuition expenses are not tax deductible, as they are not in the UK, a higher tax rate discourages investment in human capital, because it lowers the returns to investment more than the costs, discouraging human capital investment. The progressiveness in the current UK tax schedule discourages human capital investment still further. The gain in earnings resulting from human capital investment causes some individuals to move up into a higher tax bracket. For such individuals, the returns from investment are taxed at a higher rate, but the cost is expensed at a lower rate.

Taxes on physical capital are another important component of the tax system that can affect human capital investment decisions. The level of human capital investment declines when the after-tax interest rate increases, because the discounted returns to investment are then lower. Reducing the tax on interest income can have a beneficial effect both on capital accumulation and on real wages. Heckman et al. (1998b, 2000b) and Heckman (2001), estimate that for the US economy, a revenue-neutral move to a flat tax on consumption in the steady state would raise the wages of both skilled and unskilled workers and raise aggregate output by 5% while raising the wages of college graduates and high school graduates equally (7%). Such a move would barely affect overall inequality in earnings while promoting the accumulation of greater levels of both human capital and physical capital.[34] The major effect of such a reform, however, would be on physical capital and its feedback effects on wages through the increased productivity of labour. It would have only a small effect on human capital accumulation. Tilting the bias in the tax system toward capital and away from human capital would improve the earnings of both capital and labour in the long run.

Reductions in tax on interest income are often either ignored or misrepresented. Populists see such a move as favouring capital and hence rich people. They ignore the crucial point that higher levels of capital stock raise the wages of all workers in a roughly uniform way.

---

[34] In order to account for the constancy of capital's share over time in the US economy, they use a Cobb–Douglas (in capital) model, and hence assume no capital–skill complementarity. Although some others claim to find such complementarity, they are hard-pressed to explain the near constancy of the capital share over time. This absence of capital–skill complementarity is the reason for the absence of any substantial effects on earnings inequality from a revenue-neutral move to a consumption tax.

The Problem of Skill Transition

Skill-biased technical change operates to make workers trained under old regimes obsolete at prevailing wages in new regimes. This phenomenon operates with a vengeance in transition economies in Eastern Europe and Latin America that have opened up markets and now trade at world prices. These factors are also operating in Scotland.

Younger workers trained under old technologies can, and have, adapted to new technologies through retraining and education. For older workers, with more limited horizons of working life and lower levels of skill and ability, such re-education is rarely economically efficient. In the long run, the economy adjusts to a new, higher level of skill requirements, but the long run can last 30 years or longer and the disadvantaged workers created by technical change pose serious social and economic problems. Based on the best available evidence, the most economically justified strategy for improving the incomes of low-ability, low-skill adults is to invest more in the highly skilled, tax them, and then redistribute the tax revenues to the poor. Some would argue that the Blair government has done just this in creating incentives not to work by raising transfer benefits.

However, many people view the work ethic as a basic value and would argue that cultivating a large class of transfer recipients breeds a culture of poverty and helplessness. If value is placed on work as an act of individual dignity, because of general benefits to families, and especially the early environments of young children and because of benefits to communities and society as a whole, then society may be prepared to subsidize inefficient jobs. Increased subsidies to employment induce people to switch out of criminal activities (Lochner 1999). Subsidies induce labour supply and output that partly offsets the cost of the subsidy, and so they are a cheaper alternative than welfare (Phelps 1997). The problem with giving such subsidies to adults is that they may discourage skill formation among the young if the subsidies are extended to them (see Heckman et al. 2003). To alleviate these adverse incentive effects, wage subsidies should be given on a cohort-specific basis.

Current thinking does not recognize the need to distinguish policies for different cohorts. Subsidizing work through the Earned Income Tax Credit (US) or Working Families Tax Credit (UK) can reduce the incentives to acquire skills and so perpetuate poverty across generations. Raising earnings today makes it more expensive to forego current earnings to improve one's future skills. This effect is strengthened by progression in the British tax system. Even though a policy that subsidizes work only for the old is inequitable across generations, it is socially efficient because it encourages the young to acquire the skills needed in the modern workplace. The policy prescription based on a firm empirical literature is to invest in the young and subsidize the work of the old, and the less able, and not invest in them. A little intergenerational inequity in the short run can promote efficiency in the long run.

SUMMARY

This chapter presents a framework for thinking about human capital policy in Scotland. It stresses the need to recognize the nature of the human capital accumulation process and the multiplicity of actors and institutions that determine human capital investments. Good policy recognizes heterogeneity in skills and human ability in designing policies to foster skill. It stresses the need to conduct cost–benefit analyses to rank proposed policies rigorously.

Because human capital is an investment good, it is important to account for the life-cycle dynamics of learning and skill acquisition in devising effective policies. Schooling is only one phase of a lifetime skill accumulation process. Families, firms and schools all create human capital.

Learning begets learning. The empirical evidence summarized in this chapter demonstrates the importance of the early years in creating the abilities and motivations that affect learning and foster productivity. Recent research has also demonstrated the importance of both cognitive and non-cognitive skills in the workplace and in the skill acquisition process. Non-cognitive skills are a form of human capital. Some of the most effective interventions operate on non-cognitive skills and motivations. Evidence from dysfunctional families reveals the value of healthy ones. We have demonstrated the first-order importance of abilities and motivation in producing skills. Cognitive and non-cognitive deficits emerge early, before schooling, and, if uncorrected, create low-skilled adults. A greater emphasis needs to be placed on family policy. Studies of a limited set of small-scale, high-quality interventions reveal that early cognitive and non-cognitive deficits can be partly remedied. This raises a new set of questions about whether or not society should respect the sanctity of the family in regard to certain dysfunctional groups.

The evidence shows that schools and teachers matter, but that it is difficult to use conventional measures of teacher quality to assess who is a good teacher. Principals and parents know this. Schemes to improve productivity in schools should allow agents to use their local knowledge to create the right incentives. Movement toward choice, competition and local incentives will likely foster productivity in the classroom. The evidence also shows that education policies based on objective quality measures (class size, teacher salaries, and the like) that receive most of the attention in public policy debates are unlikely to produce dramatic gains in Scottish educational achievement. At current levels of educational support, marginal changes in conventional quality measures yield only modest benefits and often fail a cost–benefit test.

Much of the evidence that is alleged to support the existence of widespread credit market problems in the financing of college education is found upon examination to be weak. At the same time, there appears to be a small group of secondary school graduates (about 8%) who are credit constrained and for whom a targeted transfer policy may be effective.

Scotland should seriously consider devising a more selective tuition policy by charging those who benefit most and providing relief for the small minority of bright but poor children. This is one way to raise revenue and promote equality in the society at large. Persons who benefit from education should pay for it. This will raise money for further skill investment and will help ration scarce resources. Scholarships to a small group of bright but poor children are justified on cost–benefit grounds.

Targeting the persons who can benefit from interventions will improve the efficiency of the interventions. The trick is in identifying the groups for whom the interventions are likely to be effective. In many human capital programmes this has proved to be an elusive goal.

The recent literature stresses the need to carefully assess the full life-cycle stream of the costs and benefits of human capital interventions. Tax policy is unlikely to be a strong lever to pull to foster human capital development but tax policy that fosters physical capital accumulation can have a substantial beneficial effect on wages.

We have stressed carefully the need to develop cohort-specific strategies. Middle-age workers whose skills have become obsolete make poor investments. The young and the more able make good investments. A better policy for the older displaced workers is to subsidize their employment and to make markets flexible. Younger workers should be trained with skills to enhance their productivity. Subsidizing the young directly will discourage skill formation and perpetuate poverty across the generations.

We have not discussed immigration policy in this chapter. Flexible labour markets and incentives for excellence will attract top flight persons trained elsewhere to come to Scotland. They will also encourage Scots to stay, and promote a culture of excellence in the nation.

REFERENCES

Acemoglu, D. and J. Angrist. 2001. How large are the social returns to education? Evidence from compulsory schooling laws. In *NBER macroeconomics annual 2000* (ed. B. Bernanke and K. Rogoff), pp. 9–59. Cambridge, MA: MIT Press.

Altonji, J. and T. Dunn. 1996. The effects of family characteristics on the return to education. *Review of Economics and Statistics* 78:692–704.

Ashenfelter, O. 1978. Estimating the effect of training programs on earnings. *Review of Economics and Statistics* 6:47–57.

Barnett, W. S. 1993. Benefit–cost analysis of preschool education: findings from a 25-year follow-up. *American Journal of Orthopsychiatry* 63:500–508.

Bartel, A. 1992. Productivity gains from the implementation of employee training programs. NBER Working Paper 3893.

Bell, D. 2004. The Scottish labour market: supply or demand failure? *Scottish Economic Policy Review*. Unpublished Mimeo, Department of Economics, University of Stirling.

Bell, D. and G. Jack. 2002. Worklessness and polarisation in Scottish households. Scottish Economic Policy Network Discussion Paper, University of Stirling.

Bell, D. and V. Sarajev. 2004. Is Scottish education really better? Scottish Economic Policy Network Discussion Paper, University of Stirling.

Biblarz, T. and G. Gottainer. 2000. Family structure and children's success: a comparison of widowed and divorced single-mother families. *Journal of Marriage and the Family* 62:533–548.

Bishop, J. 1994. Formal training and its impact on productivity, wages and innovation. In *Training and the private sector: international comparisons* (ed. L. Lynch). University of Chicago Press.

Blanden, J. and S. Machin. 2003. Educational inequality and the expansion of UK higher education. CEP Working Paper.

Blossfeld, H. P. and Y. Shavit. 1993. *Persistent inequality: changing educational attainment in thirteen countries*. Boulder, CO: Westview Press.

Blundell, R., L. Dearden and C. Meghir. 1999. Work-related training and earnings. UCL Working Paper.

Blundell, R., H. Reed and T. Stoker. 2003. Interpreting aggregate wage growth: the role of labor market participation. *American Economic Review* 93: 1114–1131.

Bovenberg, A. L. and B. Jacobs. 2001. Redistribution and education subsidies are Siamese twins. CEPR Discussion Paper 3099.

Bowles, S. and H. Gintis. 1976. *Schooling in capitalist America*. New York: Basic Books.

Browning, E. 1987. On the marginal welfare cost of taxation. *American Economic Review* 77:11–23.

Callender, C. and M. Kemp. 2000. Changing student finances: income, expenditure and the take-up of student loans among full- and part-time higher education students in 1998/9. DfEE Report RR213.

Cameron, S. and J. Heckman. 1993. The nonequivalence of high school equivalents. *Journal of Labor Economics* 11:1–47.

——. 1999. Can tuition policy combat rising wage inequality? In *Financing college tuition: government policies and educational priorities* (ed. M. Kosters). Washington, DC: American Enterprise Institute Press.

——. 2001. The dynamics of educational attainment for black, Hispanic, and white males. *Journal of Political Economy* 109:455–499.

Card, D. and J. DiNardo. 2002. Skill biased technological change and rising wage inequality: some problems and puzzles. NBER Working Paper 8769.

Card, D. and A. Krueger. 1992. Does school quality matter? Returns to education and the characteristics of public schools in the United States. *Journal of Political Economy* 100:1–40.

Carneiro, P., K. Hansen and J. Heckman. 2001. Removing the veil of ignorance in assessing the distributional impacts of social policies. *Swedish Economic Policy Review* 8:273–301.

——. 2003. Estimating distributions of treatment effects with an application to the returns to schooling. *International Economic Review* 44:361–422.

Carneiro, P. and J. Heckman. 2002. The evidence on credit constraints in post-secondary schooling. *Economic Journal* 112:705–734.

——. 2003. Human capital policy. In *Inequality in America: what role for human capital policy?* (ed. J. Heckman and A. Krueger). Cambridge, MA: MIT Press.

Carneiro, P., J. Heckman and D. Masterov. 2003. Labor market discrimination and racial differences in premarket factors. NBER Working Paper 10068.

Carneiro, P., J. Heckman and E. Vytlacil. 2001. Estimating the rate of return to education when it varies among individuals. University of Chicago Working Paper.

Cawley, J., J. Heckman and E. Vytlacil. 1999. On policies to reward the value added by educators. *Review of Economics and Statistics* 81:720–727.

Cherlin, A., K. Kiernan and P. Chase-Lansdale. 1995. Parental divorce in childhood and demographic outcomes in young adulthood. *Demography* 32:299–318.

Coleman, J. 1966. *Equality of educational opportunity*. Washington, DC: US Department of Health, Education, and Welfare, Office of Education.

Corak, M. 2001. Death and divorce: the long-term consequences of parental loss on adolescents. *Journal of Labor Economics* 19:682–715.

Couch, K. 1992. New evidence on the long-term effects of employment training programs. *Journal of Labor Economics* 10:380–388.

Cunha, F., J. J. Heckman and S. Navarro. 2004. Counterfactual analysis of inequality and social mobility. University of Chicago Working Paper.

Cunha, F., J. J. Heckman, L. Lochner and D. V. Masterov. 2005. Interpreting the evidence on life cycle skill formation. In *The handbook of education economics* (ed. F. Welch and E. Hanushek). New York: North-Holland.

Currie, J. and D. Thomas. 1995. Does Head Start make a difference? *American Economic Review* 85:341–364.

Daly, M. and M. Wilson. 1998. *The truth about Cinderella: a Darwinian view of parental love*. London: Weidenfeld & Nicolson.

Dearden, L., J. Ferri and C. Meghir. 2002. The effect of school quality on educational attainment and wages. *Review of Economics and Statistics* 84:1–20.

Dearden, L., L. Granahan and B. Sianesi. 2004. Credit constraints and returns to the marginal learner. IFS Working Paper.

DeLeire, T. and A. Kalil. 2002. Good things come in threes: single-parent multigenerational family structure and adolescent adjustment. *Demography* 39:393–413.

Department of Work and Pensions. 2004. Households below average income (HBAI) analysis 2002/3: figures for Scotland using the range of low income thresholds 1994/95–2002/03.

Dickens, R. and D. Ellwood. 2001. Whither poverty in Great Britain and the United States? The determinants of changing poverty and whether work will work. NBER Working Paper 8253.

——. 2003. Child poverty in Britain. In *The labour market under new Labour: the state of working Britain* (ed. R. Dickens, P. Gregg and J. Wadsworth), pp. 291–305. New York: Palgrave Macmillan.

Donohue, J. and P. Siegelman. 1998. Allocating resources among prisons and social programs in the battle against crime. *Journal of Legal Studies* 27:1–43.

Dustmann, C., N. Rajah and A. van Soest. 2003. Class size, education, and wages. *Economic Journal* 113(485):F99–120.

Dynarski, S. 2001. Does aid matter? Measuring the effects of student aid on college attendance and completion. Harvard University Working Paper.

Education and Young People Research Unit. 2002. Programme for international student assessment: Scottish Report. (Available at http://www.scotland.gov.uk/library3/education/pisa.pdf.)

Edwards, R. 1976. Individual traits and organizational incentives: what makes a good worker? *Journal of Human Resources* 11:51–68.

Faggio, G. and S. Nickell. 2003. The rise in inactivity among adult men. In *The labour market under new Labour: the state of working Britain* (ed. R. Dickens, P. Gregg and J. Wadsworth), pp. 40–52. New York: Palgrave Macmillan.

Feinstein, L. 2003. Inequality in the early cognitive development of British children in the 1970 cohort. *Economica* 70:73–97.

Garces, E., T. Duncan and J. Currie. 2002. Longer-term effects of Head Start. *American Economic Review* 92:999–1012.

Ginther, D. and R. Pollak. 2003. Family structure and children's educational outcomes: blended families, stylized facts, and descriptive regressions. NBER Working Paper 9628.

Gosling, A. and T. Lemieux. 2001. Labour market reforms and changes in wage inequality in the United Kingdom and the United States. NBER Working Paper 8413.

Gregg, P. and S. Harkness. 2003. Welfare reform and the employment of lone parents. In *The labour market under new Labour: the state of working Britain* (ed. R. Dickens, P. Gregg and J. Wadsworth), pp. 98–115. New York: Palgrave Macmillan.

Gregg, P. and J. Wadsworth. 2003. Workless households and the recovery. In *The labour market under new Labour: the state of working Britain* (ed. R. Dickens, P. Gregg and J. Wadsworth), pp. 32–39. New York: Palgrave Macmillan.

Hanushek, E. 1971. Teacher characteristics and gains in student achievement: estimation using micro-data. *American Economic Review* 61:280–288.

———. 1997. Budgets, priorities, and investment in human capital. In *Financing college tuition: government policies and social priorities* (ed. M. Kosters). Washington, DC: AEI Press.

———. 1998. The evidence on class size. In *Earning and learning: how schools matter* (ed. S. E. Mayer and P. Peterson), pp. 131–168. Washington, DC: Brookings Institution.

———. 2000. Further evidence of the effects of Catholic secondary schooling: comment. *Brookings-Wharton Papers on Urban Affairs*, pp. 194–197.

———. 2002. Evaluating the impact of school decentralization on educational quality: comments. *Economia: Journal of the Latin American and Caribbean Economic Association* 2:303–305.

Hanushek, E. and J. Luque. 2000. Smaller classes, lower salaries? The effects of class size on teacher labor markets? In *Using what we know: a review of the research on implementing class-size reduction initiatives for state and local policymakers* (ed. S. Laine and J. Ward), pp. 35–51. Oak Brook, IL: North Central Regional Educational Laboratory.

———. 2003. Efficiency and equity in schools around the world. *Economics of Education Review* 22:481–502.

Haskey, J. 2001. One-parent families—and the dependent children living in them—in Great Britain. *Population Trends* 109:46–57.

Heckman, J. 1995. Lessons from the bell curve. *Journal of Political Economy* 103:1091–1120.

———. 1999. Education and job training: doing it right. *Public Interest* 135:86–107.

———. 2000a. Policies to foster human capital. *Research in Economics* 54(1):3–56.

———. 2000b. Accounting for heterogeneity, diversity and general equilibrium in evaluating social programmes. *Economic Journal* 111:F654–F699.

———. 2001. Micro data, heterogeneity, and the evaluation of public policy: Nobel Lecture. *Journal of Political Economy* 109:673–748.

Heckman, J. and P. Klenow. 1998. Human capital policy. In *Policies to promote capital formation* (ed. M. Boskin). Stanford, CA: Hoover Institution.

Heckman, J. and L. Lochner. 2000. Rethinking myths about education and training: understanding the sources of skill formation in a modern economy. In *Securing the future: investing in children from birth to college* (ed. S. Danziger and J. Waldfogel). New York: Russell Sage Foundation.

Heckman, J. and Y. Rubinstein. 2001. The importance of noncognitive skills: lessons from the GED testing program. *American Economic Review* 91:145–149.

Heckman, J. and J. Smith. 1998. Evaluating the welfare state. In *Econometrics and economic theory in the 20th century: the Ragnar Frisch Centennial Symposium* (ed. S. Strøm). Cambridge University Press.

Heckman, J. and E. Vytlacil. 2001. Identifying the role of cognitive ability in explaining the level of and change in the return to schooling. *Review of Economics and Statistics* 83:1–12.

Heckman, J., A. Layne-Farrar and P. Todd. 1996. Human capital pricing equations with an application to estimating the effect of schooling quality on earnings. *Review of Economics and Statistics* 78:562–610.

Heckman, J., J. Smith and N. Clements. 1997. Making the most out of social experiments: the intrinsic uncertainty in evidence from randomized trials with an application to the national JTPA experiment. *Review of Economic Studies* 64:487–535.

Heckman, J., L. Lochner and C. Taber. 1998a. Explaining rising wage inequality: explorations with a dynamic general equilibrium model of earnings with heterogeneous agents. *Review of Economic Dynamics* 1:1–58.

———. 1998b. General equilibrium treatment effects: a study of tuition policy. *American Economic Review* 88:381–386.

Heckman, J., R. LaLonde and J. Smith. 1999. The economics and econometrics of active labor market programs. In *Handbook of labor economics* (ed. O. Ashenfelter and D. Card), vol. 3. Amsterdam: Elsevier.

Heckman, J., N. Hohmann, M. Khoo and J. Smith. 2000a. Substitution and dropout bias in social experiments: a study of an influential social experiment. *Quarterly Journal of Economics* 115:651–694.

Heckman, J., L. Lochner and C. Taber. 2000b. General equilibrium cost benefit analysis of education and tax policies. In *Trade, growth and development: essays in honor of T. N. Srinivasan* (ed. G. Ranis and L. K. Raut), Chapter 14, pp. 291–393. Amsterdam: Elsevier.

Heckman, J., J. Hsee and Y. Rubinstein. 2001. The GED is a 'mixed signal': the effect of cognitive and noncognitive skills on human capital and labor market outcomes. University of Chicago Working Paper.

Heckman, J., C. Heinrich and J. Smith. 2002. The performance of performance standards. *Journal of Human Resources* 37:778–811.

Heckman, J., L. Lochner and R. Cossa. 2003. Understanding the incentive effects of the EITC on skill formation. University of Chicago Working Paper.

Herrera, C., C. Sipe, W. McClanahan, A. Arbreton and S. Pepper. 2000. Mentoring school-age children: relationship development in community-based and school-based programs. Philadelphia, PA: Public/Private Ventures.

Hoxby, C. 2000. Does competition among public schools benefit students and taxpayers? *American Economic Review* 90:1209–1238.

Huisman, J., F. Kaiser and H. Vossensteyn. 2003. The relations between access, diversity and participation: searching for the weakest link? In *Access and Exclusion: International Perspectives on Higher Education Research* (ed. M. Tight), vol. 2, pp. 1–28.

IALS. 2002. *International Adult Literacy Survey Microdata User's Guide*. Statistics Canada.

Imai, K. 2004. Re-assessing the impacts of Head Start on children's outcomes. Cornell University Working Paper.

Karoly, L., P. Greenwood, S. Everingham, J. Hube, M. R. Kilburn, C. P. Rydell, M. Sanders and J. Chiesa. 1998. *Investing in our children: what we know and don't know about the cost and benefits of early childhood interventions*. Santa Monica, CA: Rand Corp. ED 419 621.

Keane, M. and K. Wolpin. 2001. The effect of parental transfers and borrowing constraints on educational attainment. *International Economic Review* 42:1051–1103.

Kiernan, K. 2001. Cohabitation and divorce across nations and generations. CASE Working Paper 65.

Klein, R., R. Spady and A. Weiss. 1991. Factors affecting the output and quit propensities of production workers. *Review of Economic Studies* 58:929–954.

Krueger, A. 1999. Experimental estimates of education production functions. *Quarterly Journal of Economics* 114:497–532.

——. 2003. Inequality, too much of a good thing. In *Inequality in America: what role for human capital policies* (ed. J. Heckman and A. Krueger). Cambridge, MA: MIT Press.

Lang, K. and J. Zagorsky. 2001. Does growing up with a parent absent really hurt? *Journal of Human Resources* 36:253–273.

Langan, P. and D. Farrington. 1998. *Crime and justice in the United States and England and Wales, 1981–96*. Washington, DC: Bureau of Justice Statistics.

Lillard, L. and H. Tan. 1986. *Private sector training: who gets it and what are its effects?* Santa Monica, CA: RAND, R-3331-DOL/RC.

Lochner, L. 1999. Education, work, and crime: theory and evidence. University of Rochester Working Paper.

Lowe, R. 2002. Higher education. In *A century of education* (ed. R. Aldrich). London: Routledge Falmer.

Lynch, L. 1992. Private-sector training and the earnings of young workers. *American Economic Review* 82:299–312.

———. 1993. *Training and the private sector: international comparison*. University of Chicago Press.

Machin, S. and S. McNally. 2003. The literacy hour. IZA Discussion Paper 1005.

Machin, S. and C. Meghir. 2000. Crime and economic incentives. IFS Working Paper 00/17.

Machin, S. and J. Van Reenen. 1997. Technology and changes in skill structure: evidence from seven OECD countries. IFS Working Paper 98/04.

McIntosh, S. 2003. Skills in the UK. In *The labour market under new Labour: the state of working Britain* (ed. R. Dickens, P. Gregg and J. Wadsworth), pp. 291–305. New York: Palgrave Macmillan.

McLanahan, S. and G. Sandefur. 1994. *Growing up with a single parent: what hurts, what helps*. Harvard University Press.

McVicar, D. and J. Podivinsky. 2003. Has the new deal in Scotland helped young people helped out of unemployment and into jobs. Scottish Economic Policy Network Research Paper.

Martin, J. and D. Grubb. 2001. What works and for whom: a review of OECD countries' experience with active labour market policies. *Swedish Economic Policy Review* 8:9–56.

Meghir, C. and M. Palme. 2003. Ability, parental background and educational policy: empirical evidence from a social experiment. IFS Working Paper 03/05.

Mincer, J. 1993. Investment in US education and training. Columbia University Discussion Paper 671.

Murnane, R. 1975. *The impact of school resources on the learning of inner city children*. Cambridge: Ballinger.

Murray, C. 1994. Underclass: the crisis deepens. IEA Health and Welfare Unit, Choice in Welfare Series 20.

———. 2001. The British underclass: ten years later. *Public Interest* 145:25–37.

Nelson, R. and E. Phelps. 1966. Investment in humans, technological diffusion, and economic growth. *American Economic Review* 56:69–75.

Nickell, S. 2004. Poverty and worklessness in Britain. *Economic Journal* 114:C1–C25.

Peltzman, S. 1973. The effect of government subsidies-in-kind on private expenditures: the case of higher education. *Journal of Political Economy* 81:1–27.

Peterson, P. and B. Hassel. 1998. *Learning from school choice*. Washington, DC: Brookings Institution Press.

Phelps, E. 1997. *Rewarding work: how to restore participation and to self-support free enterprise*. Harvard University Press.

Ramey, C., D. Bryant, F. Campbell, J. Sparling and B. Wasik. 1988. Early intervention for high-risk children: the carolina early intervention program. In *14 ounces of prevention: a casebook for practitioners* (ed. R. Price, E. Cowen, R. Lorion and M. Ramos-McKay), pp. 32–43. Washington, DC: American Psychological Association.

Rouse, C. 1997. Private school vouchers and student achievement: an evaluation of the Milwaukee Parental Choice Program. NBER Working Paper 5964.

Schultz, T. 1975. The value of the ability to deal with disequilibria. *Journal of Economic Literature* 13:827–846.

Schweinhart, L., H. Barnes and D. Weikart. 1993. *Significant benefits: the high/score Perry Preschool Study through age 27*. Ypsilanti, MI: High Scope Press.

Shaw, M. 2004. Work and worklessness among households. Office of National Statistics News Release. (Available at http://www.statistics.gov.uk/pdfdir/work0104.pdf.)

Shonkoff, J. and D. Phillips (eds). 2000. *From neurons to neighborhoods: the science of early childhood development*. Washington, DC: National Academy Press.

Smith, A. 1776. *An inquiry in the nature and causes of the wealth of nations*. London: Strahan and Cadell.

Smith, J. and R. Naylor. 2001. Dropping out of university: a statistical analysis of the probability of withdrawal for UK university students. *J. R. Statist. Soc.* A 164:389–405.

Sternberg, R. 1985. *Beyond IQ: a triarchic theory of human intelligence*. Cambridge University Press.

Taber, C. 2001. The rising college premium in the eighties: return to college or return to unobserved ability? *Review of Economic Studies* 68:665–691.

United States Department of Labor. 1995. *What's working (and what's not): a summary of research on the economic impacts of employment and training programs*. Washington, DC: US Department of Labor.

Urquiola, M. and C. Hsieh. 2002. When schools compete, how do they compete? An assessment of Chile's nationwide school voucher program. Cornell University Working Paper.

Van Kesteren, K., P. Mayhew and P. Nieuwbeerta. 2001. *Criminal victimisation in seventeen industrialised countries: key findings from the 2000 International Crime Victims Survey*. The Hague: WODC.

Vignoles, A. and F. Galindo-Rueda. 2003. Class ridden or meritocratic? An economic analysis of recent changes in Britain. CEP Working Paper.

Witte, J. 2000. *The market approach to education: an analysis of America's first voucher system*. Princeton University Press.

Starting Life in Scotland

By Heather E. Joshi and Robert E. Wright

Scotland, in line with the rest of Europe, is experiencing low rates of childbearing and its population is ageing. There is an increasing proportion of elderly people in the population, with more people who are growing old than growing up. The 'birth dearth' and 'population greying' are not unconnected: low fertility is the key influence on the age structure of a population as well as the rate of population growth.

The main focus of this chapter is on cradles rather than graves. We look at the conditions into which new Scots are being born. We look at the circumstances of individual families in the context of economic opportunities and public policies. These circumstances affect both the timing and probability of family formation, and also influence the life chances of those who are born. They therefore matter for their own sake as well as in terms of the demographic trends.

One of the main features of low fertility throughout Europe is that childbearing is being postponed to ages towards and above 30 and away from ages in the teens or the 20s, which was the norm in previous generations. In many countries this postponement is socially selective, for it is the more highly educated women with careers to combine with children who are delaying childbearing. The new evidence presented in this chapter shows how the polarization of family formation is particularly strong in Scotland—and that family polarization has several related dimensions. It appears that the reproduction of Scottish population is more characterized by the reproduction of disadvantage than the reproduction of excellence.

POPULATION AGEING IN SCOTLAND

Before turning to details of how many cradles are being filled (and by whom), it is important to take stock of the changing size and structure of the Scottish population as a whole and, in the next section, in the European context. In essence, population ageing is the redistribution of relative population shares away from the younger towards the older age groups. It is caused by interactions between the three main demographic variables: fertility, mortality and migration. Like most industrialized nations, the population of Scotland is expected to age rapidly over the next few decades. At the same time Scotland is the only country in the UK whose absolute numbers are expected to decline from the 5 062 011 people counted on Census Day, 29 April 2001 (General Register Office for Scotland (GROS) 2003; Shaw 2003).

If current demographic trends continue, one outcome of the ageing process will be a large increase in the number of individuals of pension age and a sizeable decrease in the number of people of working age. This will result in an increase

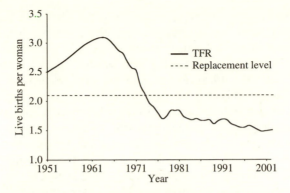

Figure 7.1. Total fertility rate, Scotland, 1951–2002.

in the demand for state-supplied health care, housing, pensions and other services consumed by the elderly (see Wright 2002a). At the same time, the population base that is expected to pay for this increase—essentially people of working age—will become progressively smaller, both in absolute numbers and as a share of the total population (see Wright 2002b). There is a growing consensus that the Scottish government will quickly find itself without the necessary resources to accommodate the changes in demand caused by population ageing. Nevertheless, it will be expected to increase expenditure in these areas. If it does not, or cannot, it will pay dearly at the ballot box, since a greying electorate will not vote for a government they see as ignoring their interests.

The main cause of Scotland's population ageing is low fertility. Figure 7.1 shows the total fertility rate for the period 1951–2002 in Scotland compared with the UK as a whole.[1] In 1951 in Scotland, it was 2.5 births per woman, well above the so-called replacement level, the number that is required in the long term to replace a generation, of 2.1 births per woman. In the 1950s, and into the early 1960s, fertility increased—the 'baby boom'—peaking at 3.1 births per woman in 1964. However, since 1965 the trend has been downwards. Currently, the total fertility rate is less than 1.5 births per woman, which is well below replacement and is less than half the rate at the peak of the baby boom. Over the past two decades, the total fertility rate in Scotland has been below that for the United Kingdom as a whole. It is the lowest of the four UK countries.

In what used to be the most prolific childbearing ages, the 20s, women's fertility has declined continuously since the mid 1960s. The trend is in the opposite direction for women in their 30s. In fact, among women aged 30–34, fertility has recently overtaken the rates for women under 30. Women over 30 now account for nearly half of all births. The proportion of teenage women giving birth has always been relatively low and it also fell during this period. Teenage mothers represented 8.5% of all births in Scotland in 2001, compared with 7.4% in the UK as a whole.

---

[1] This indicator summarizes childbearing in each year as the total number of children a woman currently this age would have between the ages of 15 and 49 experiencing this year's chances of having a birth at each age.

Falling mortality—delayed departure to the grave—has also played a role in population ageing. As in most industrialized countries, there has been a considerable increase in life expectancy in Scotland across all age groups during the past century. For example, in 1951, life expectancy at birth was 68.7 years for women and 64.4 years for men. By 2001, it had risen to 78.6 years for women and 73.1 years for men. However, despite this impressive progress, improved mortality has not been a main determinant of population ageing. The fact that older people are living longer reinforces the ageing of the population, but it is not a key cause because mortality has declined at all ages and therefore its effect on the age distribution has largely been largely neutral (see Wright (2004b) for a formal demonstration of this point).

Migration has also been a factor contributing to population ageing although, like mortality, its overall impact has been very small. Throughout most of the period 1951–2001 the number of emigrants from Scotland was larger than the number of immigrants, leading to population loss. However, currently the number of immigrants is roughly equal to the number of emigrants. Immigrants and emigrants both tend on average to come from the younger age groups. This means that for most of this period Scotland lost more young people than it gained, which clearly contributed to population ageing. However, the scale of net migration has not been particularly large when measured relative to the total size of the population: it never exceeded 1% of the total population (and rarely reached 0.5%).

There is a view that (on average) those people who emigrate are more skilled and more educated (and perhaps younger) than the people who immigrate. That is, even though the overall numbers balance out at present, Scotland is a net loser as emigration is eroding the skill and education base of the population. We are aware of no solid empirical evidence that supports this claim, although the Scottish population is somewhat better educated than the rest of the UK on average. There are unfortunately no data currently available for an adequate analysis, although there is a project currently underway—the Scottish Longitudinal Study—that is linking data from the 1991 and 2001 censuses to allow comparison of a larger sample of individuals who have moved between the constituent countries of the United Kingdom.

In sum, the current demographic situation in Scotland is a population with below-replacement level fertility, gradually decreasing mortality and zero net migration (see Anderson 2004). If there are no major changes in these factors, particularly fertility, the ageing of the population will accelerate quite dramatically in the coming decades. While it is not possible to foresee the future, it is possible to project what the age distribution of the population will look like given a precise set of assumptions. The population projections for Scotland produced by the Government Actuary's Department (GAD) are based on an extrapolation of the demographic situation prevailing in 2001 (see GAD 2002; GROS 2003; Wright 2004a). They assume in their principal projection that a below-replacement level total fertility rate of 1.6 live births (which is slightly higher than the current rate) will prevail indefinitely, that life expectancy at birth will increase to 82.6 years for women and to 77.6 years for men by 2041, and that the net migration will be a constant excess at emigration over immigration of 1000 people per annum (compared with the current level of about zero). The projection period covers four decades, beginning in 2001 and ending in 2041.

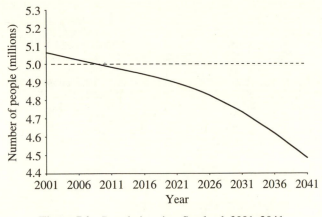

Figure 7.2. Population size, Scotland, 2001–2041.

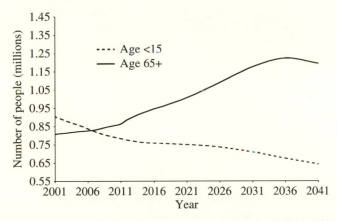

Figure 7.3. Population in different age groups, Scotland, 2001–2041.

On these assumptions, the Scottish population would continue to decline in absolute numbers. Figure 7.2 shows the projected size of the Scottish population in the period 2001–2041, to fall below five million in 2009 and continue to decline to below four million by 2041. There would also be a large increase in the number of people aged 65 and older and a large reduction in the number of people aged 15 and younger. As shown in Figure 7.3, the number of people aged 65 and older is projected to rise from about 800 000 in 2001 to about 1.2 million by 2041, while the number aged under 15 is projected to fall from about 900 000 to 650 000. In percentage terms, the share of the 65+ group is set to increase from 16 to 27% of the total population with the share of the under 15 group decreasing from 18 to 14%. Very soon, the population aged 65 and older is projected to outnumber those under 15. Recent revisions (GROS 2004), increasing projected net inward migration in the early years, delay the decline in population slightly but do not change the overall picture. Even on the altered assumptions, Scotland's population is projected to reach about 4.5 million in four decades.

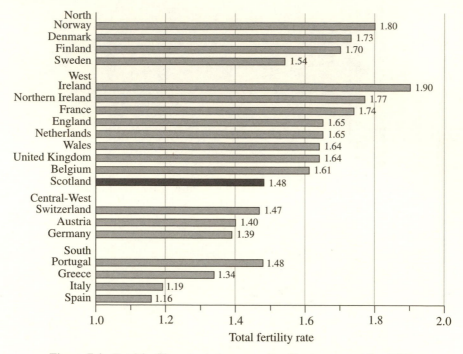

Figure 7.4. Total fertility rates in larger western European countries, 2002.

Scottish Fertility in a European Perspective

If we look at the situation across Europe, fertility has fallen everywhere in the last decades of the twentieth century but varies considerably between countries. Currently, only Albania and the Faroe Islands have total fertility rates above the replacement level of 2.1 births per woman. Figure 7.4 illustrates the broad regional pattern in the larger countries of Western Europe of fertility declining as one moves from North to South and from the Atlantic seaboard towards central Europe. Much of Scandinavia, France and Ireland are maintaining fertility rates nearer the replacement level (at least over 1.7), while fertility is very low in central and southern Europe. A 'Eurovision Contest' for low fertility would be won by Spain (1.16) with Italy (1.19) being a close runner-up. Bulgaria, Latvia and the Czech Republic, although not shown in the figure, also have total fertility rates below 1.2 births per woman.

Within the United Kingdom, Scotland currently has the lowest fertility rate. However, in this cross-national comparative perspective, its fertility rate is squarely in the middle of the European distribution, on a par with Portugal and Switzerland rather than Scotland's immediate neighbours across the Irish or North Sea. It is worth noting that in the relatively minor matter of the teenage fertility rate, Scotland resembles the rest of the UK where it in turn exceeds most of the rest of Europe.

QUANTITY OF BIRTHS OR QUALITY OF CHILDREN?

The long-term viability of population decline will depend on the productivity of upcoming generations being maintained, or preferably enhanced, by increasing investment in children's skills and abilities. This means somehow, publicly or privately or both, investing in the health and education of the new generation, so that they are better equipped not only to experience a good quality of life, but also to become more productive citizens able to contribute to supporting the growing burden of old age dependency.

The New Home Economics school of thought refers, somewhat awkwardly, to child 'quality' substituting for child 'quantity'. For all the infelicity of the expression, particularly the eugenic overtones, it is worth understanding that it is not only the number of births which matters. Children born into poverty have not only a poor experience of life during childhood, but a poorer chance of development, of enjoying opportunities for themselves and of becoming productive citizens (see Gregg et al. 1999; Bynner et al. 2000; Feinstein 2003; McCulloch and Joshi 2001, 2002; Pevalin 2003). We look next at the prospects for children being born in Scotland.

For details of the propensity to bear children by different groups within Scotland, we turn to data collected in wave 11 of the British Household Panel Survey (BHPS), which covers the period 2000–2001 (see Brice et al. 2001a,b). For women aged 45–49 who have reached the end of their childbearing span, the number of children reported is 1.6. This value corresponds closely to the fertility level assumed in the GAD's population projections discussed above, although there is some suggestion that, for this generation, the BHPS estimates understate the level of fertility[2]. Even though the BHPS may have missed out some mothers, it does suggest that more highly educated women start motherhood later, but by age 45 the differences according to educational level diminish. The women with higher education or 'any qualifications beyond basic school-leaving' each averaged 1.5 children, while those with 'no qualifications' averaged 1.8 children. It follows that the increase over time in the proportion of the female population with higher qualifications has contributed to the downward trend in fertility, although this may reflect the lengthening of the average childbearing period for such women rather than a reduction in the fertility of each complete cohort. The flight from early childbearing has particularly involved more educated women. We can also note from Graham and Boyle (2003) that fertility rates are lower in urban than rural areas, which they attribute to there being more students, more expensive housing and more female employment in urban areas. Whether a buoyant labour market for women need be a deterrent to childbearing is a question we consider later. The key question, of course, is how far will today's twenty-somethings catch up or even overtake their predecessors, and whether more women are going to remain childless in Scotland than elsewhere in the UK.

---

[2]The BHPS suggests that around one in three of women reaching the end of their childbearing span in Scotland are childless as opposed to the estimate of one in six based on the General Household Survey (a smaller sample, supplied by ONS) and for women this generation in England and Wales (ONS Birth Statistics Series FM1, Table 10.3).

CHILDREN OF THE NEW CENTURY: THE MILLENNIUM COHORT STUDY

Current births in Scotland

We now turn to new evidence on those Scots who have been born into the twenty-first century, the members of the Millennium Cohort Study[3] (Smith and Joshi 2002; Shepherd et al. 2003). These data were collected mostly during the year 2001 on children born between the end of November 2000 and January 2002 in Scotland, at the time the children were nine months old. They are part of a major UK-wide study to which some comparison will be made. The survey allows us to look at the costs and benefits of childbearing from the point of view of their parents and also at prospects for the children. Are they all starting out life in equally favourable circumstances, or is there a polarization in their early conditions? Are some less likely, right from the outset, to be able to fulfil their potential for a high quality of life and a significant contribution to the Scottish economy?

The survey suggests that smaller family size, along with a possibly greater prevalence of childlessness, are the reasons behind the lower fertility rate observed in Scotland. Teenage mothers may be notorious but they were not in fact very numerous, constituting only 8% of mothers by their age at the time of the survey child's birth. Half of the mothers were 30 years of age and older. Both proportions are slightly higher than in the UK as a whole: though Scotland has fewer births altogether, these births are more spread across the age range.

Polarization of Starting Childbearing by Age and 'Disadvantage'

Classifying the mothers by age when they had their first child (rather than at the time they had their child in the Millennium Cohort) identifies those who had started their families early, including those currently having second or later births at older ages. We have somewhat arbitrarily defined 'early-starters' as having a first (live-born) child under the age of 21. They constitute 24% of the Scottish sample. We have also arbitrarily drawn a line to divide the other mothers into middling and late-starters, setting 28 as the age threshold for a 'late starter'. Those who had their first births at age 28 or older constitute 43% of the Scottish sample. We use this grouping of families for two reasons. First, early childbearing has consequences for the family as a whole and not just for the first born. Secondly, this grouping is used to distinguish within the group of currently older mothers those who had deferred childbearing until or after their late 20s from those who started earlier and are currently adding to their families.

As with the current age of mothers, Scotland has slightly more early entrants to motherhood and slightly more 'deferrers' than the UK sample as a whole. Within Scotland, early-starters are most common in the 'disadvantaged' areas and the deferred families most common in the other areas. About half of the mothers outside the disadvantaged wards had started childbearing 'late' and only about one-sixth had

---

[3] Another feature of this survey is that children living in areas of high child poverty were oversampled to focus on the current government's objective of alleviating child poverty (Plewis 2004).

Table 7.1. Selected demographic characteristics of the Millennium Cohort Study mothers by age at first birth Scotland and the United Kingdom.

	Mother's age at first ever live birth				
	Scotland				
	Early ⩽20	Middle 21–27	Late 28+	All	All UK
Proportion of mothers starting in age group	24%	33%	43%	100%	
Average age of mother at interview (years, months)	23, 6	28, 8	33, 9	29, 7	29, 7
Proportion where cohort baby is first born	39%	37%	55%	45%	43%
Average number of children in household	2.0	1.9	1.6	1.8	1.9
Proportion of lone mothers	33%	13%	5%	14%	14%
Proportion of couples, legally married[a]	35%	69%	84%	70%	71%
Average age of fathers at interview (years, months)	28, 2	31, 10	35, 8	33, 0	33, 0
Current age difference between mothers and fathers (years, months)[a]	4, 5	3, 1	1, 7	3, 3	3, 3
Average current age of lone mothers (years, months)	22, 0	26, 8	33, 2	2, 0	25, 5
Proportion of lone mothers who never lived with cohort baby's father	67%	46%	56%	59%	56%
Proportion of lone mothers living with baby's grandparents	34%	21%	7%	26%	21%
Proportion with low qualifications (none + NVQ 1)	32%	15%	5%	15%	20%
Proportion with tertiary qualifications (NVQ 4 and 5)	6%	30%	59%	37%	34%
Maximum unweighted sample size[b]	592	751	925	2268	17 864

[a]Base is all natural mothers with resident or part-time resident partner. [b]Unweighted sample of natural mothers, with known age at first birth, before deletion of missing cases on other variables.

started early. However, in disadvantaged wards the proportion who had started early is just over a third and the proportion who started late is just under a third. Table 7.1 summarizes a number of other ways in which the demographics of early and late childbearing differ in Scotland. Those who had started earliest were more likely to have had more subsequent births, suggesting that earlier starts are associated with slightly larger families.

Lone Motherhood is More Prevalent among Early-Starters

At the time of the survey, 14% of all the mothers were living without a partner. This proportion is more than double that among early-starters (33%), but compares with only 5% among late-starters. Those living in couples were more likely to be legally married the older they started childbearing—the mothers who started young are almost twice as likely to be co-habiting with their partner, if they have one, than to be legally married to him. Those mothers currently living alone were, with an average age of 25, younger than the mothers who were living with partners. Of those mothers not living with a partner at the time of the survey, 59% had never lived with the cohort baby's father. This proportion rises to 67% among the mothers who had started childbearing youngest. Some of the mothers living without partners were living with the baby's grandparents (i.e. their own parents) and this is also more likely among the youngest group of mothers (34%) than among the older ones (7%). Thus early childbearing in Scotland, as elsewhere, is more likely mean starting without a partner and either remaining or becoming unpartnered.

Polarization between the Early and Late Mothers by Education, Health and Area

We can also see from Table 7.1 that the early-starters have fewer educational qual-ifications than late-starters: 32% of early-starters have low qualifications (none or the lowest NVQ level), compared with 5% of the women who had their first child at or over age 28. Nearly 60% of these late starters were qualified at the tertiary level, compared with only 6% of the early starters. Putting this the other way round, of the mothers who were highly qualified by the time of the interview, only 3% had started childbearing at or before age 21, and 71% had started at age 28 or over. The generally higher levels of educational attainment in Scotland are reflected in a lower proportion of mothers with low or zero levels of qualification (15% in Scotland versus 20% in the UK as a whole) as well as the higher proportion with tertiary level qualifications (37% versus 34%). The association of early childbearing with educa-tional disadvantage and unstable partnerships could be either cause or effect, or both, and the interpretation of this association is discussed below. For the moment, we should consider an early start to childbearing as a marker of a set of disadvantageous circumstances—whatever their making— from which many of newborn Scots are setting out.

Mothers were also asked whether their pregnancy with the current cohort child was a 'surprise'. A much higher proportion of early-starters (72%), even those who are no longer themselves teenagers, reported that it was a surprise, although as many as 24% of late-starters were also surprised about their pregnancy. When further asked if they felt 'unhappy or sad' about the prospect of having the baby, far fewer agreed— only 4% of late-starters were unhappy about the prospect of having the baby, but 20% among early-starters.

There are also large differences in the proportion of mothers in the different groups who ever tried to breastfeed. The survey suggests that 82% of late-starters attempted to breastfeed, while the figure for early-starters is only 42%. It is also worth noting that Scotland has distinctly lower rates of breastfeeding than the UK

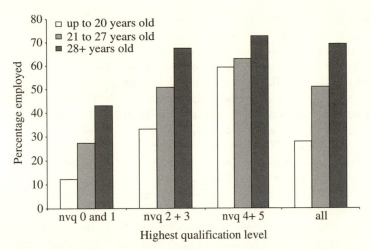

Figure 7.5. Percentage of mothers employed when Millennium Cohort Study child aged 9 months by education and age at motherhood, Scotland.

as a whole—66% versus 71%. Among early-starters, the rates are also lower in the rest of the UK.

The Polarization Carries Over into Housing and Environment

The same kind of contrast is apparent across various indicators of the environment by age at first motherhood. Nearly 40% of the sample of babies in Scotland was found to be living in disadvantaged areas at age nine months.[4] The proportion is much lower if their mothers had started childbearing late (27%) and much higher for mothers who had started childbearing young (58%). These contrasts are almost as strong for early- and late-starters who have since moved on to have further children. This suggests that the disadvantages surrounding early first motherhood are carried through into later stages of family building, and it makes sense to look at all early mothers regardless of their current age. For example, nearly half (49%) of early-starters were living in flats, compared with (19%) of late-starters; 51% of early-starters are housed in local authority dwellings compared with only 6% of late-starters. The problem of 'damp and condensation' was reported by 16% of early-starters and by 6% of late-starters.

Employment Status and Income Reflect the Same Polarized Pattern

The educational differences discussed above are also reflected in differences in occupational attainment. Among late-starters, 58% of those who had ever had a job had managerial or professional occupations compared with only 5% for early-starters. Of the latter group 72% had predominantly routine or semi-routine occupations in

---

[4]These were identified in the survey design as electoral wards with high rates of families claiming means-tested benefits, and the survey results confirmed that they were characterized not only by low incomes, but by generally less pleasant neighbourhood amenities.

175

their latest job compared with 14% for late-starters. It is worth remembering that they are all mothers with babies aged nine months old. How many of them were currently employed, combining motherhood with paid work? Only 16% overall were working full-time at the time of the survey and 2% were still on maternity leave. The probability of being in full-time work increases with the age at which the woman became a mother—only 6% for early-starters but 23% for late-starters. More of the Scottish mothers were combining motherhood with part-time work (38% overall) but again it was late-starters who were more likely to be doing so—46% compared with 23% for early-starters. The chances of employment are associated with education but differences in education do not account for all of the differences in employment rates by age of motherhood: as Figure 7.5 shows, there are sharp differences within education groups by age of motherhood. Most of the women in couples are living with another earner so the fact that they may not themselves be earning does not mean that the family has no income. However, 7% of the couples had nobody earning. Joblessness within families is highly correlated with poverty, and this rate was much higher (22%) for early-starters than late-starters (2%). Not only are the younger mothers less likely to have jobs themselves, but so are their partners. Among the mothers living without partners, 71% were not earning, and again the chances of this being the case were greatest for early-starters—79% compared with 50% for lone mothers who had their first child at or over 28.

Turning to sources of income provided by the state, 35% of the families were receiving at least one of the means-tested benefits listed in the note to Table 7.2. The proportion for early-starters was 72% and 13% for late-starters. A preliminary inspection of the family income data sets an arbitrary threshold for 'low' family income at £350 per week for couples, £235 for lone parents, and counts all other cases, including the 8% who did not report their income, as not having low income. On this basis, 40% of the families are classified as having 'low or very low' income, but again this hides a span from 75% to 20% between early- and late-starters.

How does the concentration of low income among the early-starters compare with the concentration of such low income in disadvantaged areas? This question is relevant to the issue of how policy should be designed to reach families in need. The answer is that there are roughly as many 'poor' in other areas as in 'disadvantaged' areas. Therefore, were anti-policy poverty to be targeted only on the families living in these places, almost half the 'poor' would be missed and almost half the target area population would be 'non-poor'. While areas are convenient for targeting many types of social policy, they miss some potential beneficiaries (see Joshi 2001).

Would targeting by age of first motherhood be any more efficient at reaching low-income families? This assumes it would be practicable to target all mothers who had ever had a birth below a given age, set here at 21, not just those who are still very young. In one sense, it would be more efficient, because such a high proportion, 75%, of the early mothers are 'poor'. On the other hand, early mothers, even when the threshold is set at 21, are a relatively small group. There are substantial numbers on low income (over half) who started childbearing after 21, or about 22% of the whole population. Early mothers are found in both types of area but there are not very many of them among the 'non-poor'. Of all low-income families, 44% were

Table 7.2. Earnings and finances of Millennium Cohort Study mothers by age at first birth Scotland and the United Kingdom.

| | Mother's age at first ever live birth | | | | |
| | Scotland | | | | |
	Early ≤20	Middle 21–27	Late 28+	All	All UK
Proportion in social class: management/professional[a]	5%	25%	58%	35%	34%
Proportion in social class: semi-routine/routine[a]	72%	38%	14%	35%	36%
Proportion employed, full-time	6%	14%	23%	16%	13%
Proportion employed, part-time	23%	37%	46%	38%	35%
Proportion of couples with two earners	29%	51%	68%	55%	51%
Proportion of couples, no earners	22%	5%	2%	7%	6%
Proportion of lone parents who are 'workless'	79%	65%	50%	71%	78%
Proportion of all in workless families	42%	14%	4%	16%	16%
Proportion who receive means-tested benefits (MTB)[b]	72%	37%	13%	35%	35%
Proportion in low/very low income band[c]	75%	42%	20%	40%	40%
Analysis by birth order: proportion in low/very low income band[c]					
Cohort baby first born	80%	47%	21%	40%	40%
Cohort baby not first	73%	40%	18%	41%	41%
Analysis by type of area: proportion in low/very low income band[c]					
Living in disadvantaged ward	82%	54%	30%	57%	57%
Living in other areas	67%	35%	16%	30%	30%
Proportion experiencing financial difficulties[d]	14%	9%	5%	9%	10%
Maximum unweighted sample size[e]	592	751	925	2268	17 864

[a]ONS-NSEC based on current or last occupation of those who ever had one. 74 unweighted cases are missing on occupation for the early mothers, 14 for the middle and 14 for the late mothers.

[b]MTB refers to those who receive one or more of the following: Jobseekers' Allowance, Income Support, Working Families Tax Credit or Disabled Persons Tax Credit.

[c]Low income is below £12 200 net income per annum for lone parents and £18 200 per annum for couples.

[d]Financial difficulties refers to those who are finding it difficult or very difficult to manage financially.

[e]Unweighted sample of natural mothers, with known age at first birth, before deletion of missing cases on other variables.

early-starters, 54% lived in disadvantaged areas and 28% satisfied both criteria. Were age to be used as a criterion for identifying families at risk of poverty, it would be necessary to investigate whether 21 was the best cut-off age. Age could also be used in conjunction with other criteria; perhaps to identify those at risk outside designated 'disadvantaged' areas, rather than to disqualify those within them. This question warrants further investigation but this very simple illustration may show the limitations of using single indicators to target populations on low income—unless of course income itself can be used as the criterion for eligibility.

Table 7.2 also reports a subjective measure of financial circumstances. When the mothers were asked how they were managing financially, only 5% of late-starters reported that they were finding it 'difficult' or 'very difficult' to manage, but the share of early-starters reporting difficulties was much higher at 14%.

High Malaise also among Early-Starters

Finally, we have reports from the mothers about other aspects of parenthood, for example, whether they have 'enough time to spend with their child'. Late-starters, particularly those who are employed, are more likely than early-starters to report that they do not have enough time to spend with their baby; 84% of early-starters reported that they have 'plenty of time' with their baby compared with only 62% for late-starters. However, this extra time with the baby does not seem to outweigh the relative difficulties faced by these different groups of mothers of young babies. In answer to a simple question designed to detect post-natal depression, mothers were asked if they 'felt low or sad' since the cohort baby's birth. This was more likely for early-starters—41% compared with 26% for late-starters.

Asked about their current state of mind on a set of questions selected from the malaise inventory, 32% of early-starters scored as having high 'malaise' (i.e. three or more out of nine symptoms) compared with 18% for late-starters. Mothers were also asked to rate themselves on a 'life satisfaction in general' scale that ranges from 1 (low) to 10 (high). Most scored between 8 and 10, indicating a generally high level of satisfaction. However, 16% scored themselves at 6 or less, 28% among early-starters and 10% among late-starters. This difference suggests that younger mothers seem to be having a more difficult time in their child's first year of life. This is not only a cost to them personally but is also potentially a cost to their baby.

INTERPRETING THE DIFFERENCES BETWEEN EARLY AND LATE FAMILY FORMATION

The evidence from the Millennium Cohort Study tells us a lot about the different sorts of families involved in the trend towards postponed childbearing. In Scotland, as in the rest of the UK, families where childbearing has been delayed are generally better off (Hobcraft and Kiernan 2001; Kiernan 1997). The residual minority having children exceptionally early are characterized by a number of disadvantages. Part of the answer to this is that women who postpone childbearing are generally combining motherhood with employment, and may indeed have timed their family-building to allow them to establish their careers first, as well as (relatively) secure partnerships with their children's fathers. The opposite is likely to be the case for early and teenage mothers. However, it would be unwise to assume that the disadvantages we observe are all consequences of early childbearing. It is also likely that those who had poor prospects, of either educational advancement or of good jobs, choose (or fail to avoid) to become mothers early, and would not be doing well in education or employment anyway.

Although no survey can provide direct evidence on what would have happened to the early mothers if their first child had come later, there is recent work on other British data which has been able to address this issue. For example, Ermisch and Pevalin (2003) and Hawkes (2003) (each looking at Great Britain-wide data) conclude that early disadvantage influences the likelihood of early childbearing more than giving birth early influences poor educational attainments. Ermisch and Pevalin also conclude that the poor labour market record of teenage mothers in the 1970 Birth Cohort Study is largely due to earlier disadvantages. While this implies that the adverse consequences of teenage motherhood are often overstated, Ermisch and Pevalin do find that original disadvantages are compounded as a result of early motherhood, particularly in respect of mental health and of later partnerships. These other studies suggest, though they cannot prove, that the disadvantages observed among those who started childbearing early are unlikely to be just the result of unwise decisions to forgo better life opportunities. It is more likely the case that in many cases the course taken by very young mothers was not unreasonable, given their bleak alternatives and disadvantaged family circumstances. Whatever the balance of cause, choice and consequence, there are likely to be cumulative mechanisms at work. Furthermore, whatever brought about early motherhood, it was not a choice made by the child. Likewise, later-born children stand a better chance of finding themselves with parents better equipped, emotionally and financially, to bring them up.

The polarization in timing of childbearing by the woman's level of educational attainment seen here is not internationally universal, though it is found in the rest of the UK and in southern European countries such as Spain and Italy. The differentials are much smaller in Sweden and France, for example (see Ekert-Jaffé et al. 2002; Gutierrez Domench 2003). The analysis in the first paper cited suggests that the greater dispersion in age of starting childbearing in Britain might be attributable to worse opportunities for prolonged education, training or employment for women in their late teens, along with fewer opportunities for less-skilled women to become part of a two-earner couple. For the more highly skilled, combining employment with motherhood is increasingly likely, when they are ready for it, particularly in countries which have long-established regimes of 'family friendly' policies in employment and childcare (such as Sweden and France). Where these facilities are not universal, women with less earning power are more likely to see participating in the labour market and home-making as alternative, and not complementary, activities. Those who do end up starting early may have less reason to wait than those who do not, although we have little evidence of early childbearing being a conscious strategy.

POLICIES TO MAKE CHILDBEARING AND EMPLOYMENT MORE COMPATIBLE

In the Scandinavian countries and France there is a more compressed age range for childbearing. These countries have better-developed sets of policies aimed at aiding the combining of employment and motherhood across the whole social spectrum. At the centre of these policies is some form of subsidized childcare. In Scandinavia there are policies that allow for significant leave from the labour market, for fathers as well as mothers, and the periods of paid leave are longer than those available in the UK. Policies to spread such facilities in Scotland might have the effect of reducing the delay by late-starters and even averting some childlessness among high earners. They are less likely to accelerate early motherhood by those not engaged in the labour market. Paradoxically, though, they could encourage delay by early-starters. There would still be a positive effect on total fertility if such policies reduced the number of women remaining childless or permitted late-starters to have more children, although stable or buoyant job prospects would also help. International evidence on aiming policies at demographic targets is not very encouraging, however (see Graham and Boyle 2003).

The main argument for these policies is not so much the demographic impact as the fact that they improve choice and the quality of life at all ages of motherhood. There is a range of policies which facilitate the compatibility of motherhood and employment, including employment practices, hours of work, parental leave, tax and social insurance provisions, poverty relief, childcare provisions, opening hours of commercial and public services, and the child-friendliness of public spaces (Dex and Joshi 1999). We focus here on just two of the areas on which the Millennium Cohort Study provides evidence: employment leave for fathers and the provision of affordable childcare.

Child-rearing is no longer just a mother's business. For that reason the survey interviewed fathers as well as mothers, when they were present and willing to answer. In the survey 86% of families consisted of two parents and in Scotland 88% of the fathers identified responded. Few of these fathers actually quit jobs on the arrival of a baby, but many took some form of leave. For example, 76% of fathers in Scotland took some 'time off work' at the time of the birth (compared with 79% for the UK). Only half of these reported taking paternity leave, and very few mentioned parental leave. Most in fact used annual or sick leave. We cannot tell whether this leave was paid or unpaid. In addition, we cannot tell if these fathers would have preferred to take more leave, particularly if it was paid. However, it would seem that the practice of fathers taking leave could be encouraged, especially for the partners of early mothers, as they report the lowest rates of leave-taking.

Table 7.3 summarizes some other indicators of fathers' involvement with the children in Scotland. These measures are roughly similar in Scotland and the UK as a whole, with one notable exception: 66% of Scottish fathers report changing the baby's nappy 'at least once a day' compared with a UK average of 57%.

Within Scotland, fathers' involvement with their babies is affected by their labour force status. For example, 60% of those employed full-time report they 'do not spend enough time with the baby', compared with only 6% of those out of employment. However, as with mothers, having plenty of time with the baby is not enough to compensate the effect of being out of work on general life satisfaction. Fathers who are not employed are most likely (39%) to report a low life satisfaction score compared with 11% of the fathers employed full-time. If fathers were able to increase their parenting activities without dropping out of employment, there could be benefits of combining employment with fatherhood as well as motherhood.

Table 7.3. Fathers' involvement with Millennium Cohort Study babies in Scotland and the United Kingdom. (FT, full-time; PT, part-time; NE, non-employed.)

| | Employment status of father | | | | |
| | Scotland: weighted data | | | | |
	FT	PT	NE	All	All UK
Proportion who look after baby on their own at least once a day	28%	53%	53%	31%	31%
Proportion who look after baby on their own less than once a week	38%	16%	21%	36%	41%
Proportion who change their baby's nappy at least once a day	65%	72%	74%	66%	57%
Proportion who change their baby's nappy less than once a week	13%	12%	18%	13%	20%
Proportion indicating that they spend plenty of time with baby	17%	63%	87%	25%	21%
Proportion indicating that they do not spend enough time with baby	60%	20%	6%	53%	57%
Proportion indicating low life satisfaction (6 or less out of a scale of 10)	11%	21%	39%	14%	15%
Maximum unweighted sample size[a]	1424	51	179	1654	12 882

[a]These totals relate to cases who had partner information, who answered number of hours worked each week.

However, childcare is still mainly the mothers' responsibility, although fathers play an important role in the portfolios of arrangements. Among mothers in employment when their child was nine months old, around one-quarter relied on the fathers as the main source of childcare, fewer if the mother's job was full-time. The largest category of main childcare arrangement was grandparents (36% in Scotland and 31% in the UK as a whole). Including other sources of informal help such as neighbours, friends and other relatives, and the mother remaining responsible for the child while on the job, the vast majority of the arrangements were informal (71% in Scotland), although some of them were paid. Nurseries and crèches accounted for one-sixth of all arrangements, and nannies, au pairs and childminders for one in eight. Mothers with full-time jobs were more likely to pay for childcare (54%) than those in part-time jobs (38%). Childcare tax credit reached 35% of those who paid for childcare in Scotland (compared with 49% in the UK as a whole). These estimates suggest that there could be room for expansion of the provision of formal childcare in Scotland, but there may be too few personnel qualified to care for children under the age of one. It is therefore all the more important for public policy to support the informal carers.

CONCLUSIONS

The process of political devolution in Scotland has increased the demand for evidence-based economic and social research concerned with Scottish-specific issues that are policy relevant. Such research (which has been sadly lacking in the past) is crucially needed to design and execute policy effectively. The analysis presented here of the Millennium Cohort Study has just scratched the surface of what can be done. It is our hope that this chapter will encourage others to delve more deeply into the first round of survey results. The cohort has been surveyed again at age three, and we will soon be able to gauge the progress made by those born at the start of the new millennium.

The early part of this chapter sketched a picture of Scotland's future demography that could be bleak indeed. Population ageing is going to present the Scottish people and government with serious economic and social challenges. If these challenges are not met through effective public policy, there is a real risk that the standard of living in Scotland will track the decline of the population.

Some argue that the ageing of the Scottish population can be slowed through increased immigration. Although this is technically correct, the scale of the immigration needed would be very large (see Wright 2004b). This is not to say that increased immigration or prevention of emigration will not make a valuable contribution to the Scottish economy, especially in the shorter term. For instance, it can help plug skill shortages. Immigration can also have other beneficial spillover effects on the wider economy. But the numbers needed to make a demographic impact over a longer period would have to be considerable.

It is low fertility that is the main cause of population ageing. An increase in fertility, on a sufficient scale, would have a favourable impact on population ageing. In this sense, policies successfully aimed at increasing fertility could be money well spent, although governments have seldom had much success in targeting the birth rate. Still, there may be scope by enhancing the compatibility of careers and parenthood for encouraging those with the lowest fertility and the latest starters, particularly the most educated, to bring births forward and in some cases eschew childlessness. Resources such as child tax credits and baby bonds may encourage people to embark on the responsibilities of parenthood, and there is scope for the labour market, education and other public services to be more consistently family friendly.

Even if the chances of encouraging Scottish people to have more children are somewhat uncertain, there is all the more need for policies to ensure those children who are born attain their full potential. Scotland needs to invest in all its people, including the newborn. The polarization of family circumstances suggests that some children are at risk of much poorer life chances than those born into the more advantaged families with older parents and somewhat fewer siblings.

Yet the more advantaged families should be just as concerned about what happens a generation down the line. The generation of women who are now avoiding or delaying motherhood will find in the mid twenty-first century that they have fewer of their own offspring around as potential providers of care. Where generations are lengthening, the women in the middle are more likely to find themselves in the uncomfortable 'pivot' position of simultaneous responsibility for elders and children.

The main social concern highlighted in this chapter, however, is the diminishing group who are still becoming mothers very early in their lives. Girls who become teenage mothers may lack a good many other skills apart from competence with contraceptives. Public concern about teenage mothers is not misplaced. Policies to make it easier to combine careers with motherhood are unlikely to encourage these largely unemployed young women to have their largely unplanned births any earlier; indeed it can be argued that they could create an incentive to develop a foothold in the labour market which at present seems relatively pointless.

The target group for interventions to support parenting should ideally not just be the inhabitants of particular areas (as in the local programmes of English Sure Start), and not just mothers of particular ages. The target should be all families who are struggling to provide a fulfilling upbringing to their offspring, and fathers as well as mothers may very well need this support.

The gradual improvement of the terms on which parenthood can be combined with employment—or to put it the Swedish way, the terms on which workers can be parents—has yet to trickle down the social scale and the age-at-motherhood gradient. It should not be taken as a prescription that everyone should earn their way out disadvantage and poverty while simultaneously raising, at a minimum, the 2.1 children needed for population replacement. While many women do combine paid and unpaid work, the alternative of specializing in the unpaid and often unacknowledged work of caring for young and old should also be a viable and valued option. Policies aimed at supporting 'workless' parents while at the same time enhancing the compatibility of the 'double burden' of parenthood and employment, would improve the standard of living of families in Scotland, contribute to a broader work/life balance, and arguably enhance the productivity or human capital of the next generation.

Such an approach might also bring about some demographic dividend in the form of a revived Scottish fertility rate, although this is hard to guarantee. It is also possible that the level or composition of net migration might be affected by the family friendliness of policies in Scotland as well as the buoyancy of labour markets. This consideration remains a speculation, but it is worth thinking about the possibility that the quality of life could have some impact on the quantity of people through migration as well as fertility. The parents and potential parents of the new century's children may not be the most vociferous political lobby, but they hold Scotland's future in their cradles. Policy that nurtures the nurturers is worth having for its own sake.

REFERENCES

Anderson, M. 2004. One Scotland, or several? The historical evolution of Scotland's population over the past century and its implications for the future. In *Scotland's demographic challenge* (ed. R. E. Wright). Scottish Economic Policy Network, Universities of Stirling and Strathclyde.

Brice J., N. Buck and E. Prentice-Lane. 2001a. British household panel survey user manual, vol. A: Introduction, technical report and appendices. Institute of Social and Economic Research, University of Essex, Colchester

Brice J., N. Buck and E. Prentice-Lane. 2001b. British household panel survey user manual, vol. B: Codebook. Institute of Social and Economic Research, University of Essex, Colchester

Bynner, J., H. Joshi and M. Tsatsas. 2000. Obstacles and opportunities: evidence from two british birth cohort studies. Occasional Paper, Smith Institute, London.

Dex, S. and H. Joshi. 1999. Careers and motherhood: policy for compatibility. *Cambridge Journal of Economics* 23:641–659.

Ekert-Jaffé, O., H. Joshi, K. Lynch, R. Mougin and M. Rendall. 2002. Fertility timing of births and socio-economic status in France and Great Britain: social policies and occupational profiles. *Population* E-57:475–508.

Ermisch J. and D. Pevalin. 2003. Does a teen birth have longer-term impact on the mother? Evidence for the 1970 British Cohort Study. Working Paper 28, Institute of Social and Economic Research, University of Essex, Colchester.

Feinstein, L. 2003. Inequality in the early cognitive development of British children in the 1970 cohort. *Economica* 70:73–98.

GAD. 2002. *National population projections: 2001-based*. London: Government Actuary's Department.

Graham, E. and P. Boyle. 2003. Low fertility in Scotland: a wider perspective. In *General Register Office for Scotland, Registrar General's review of demographic trends*, pp. 40–52. Edinburgh: General Register Office for Scotland.

Gregg, P., S. Harkness and S. Machin. 1999. *Child development and family income*. York: Joseph Rowntree Foundation.

GROS. 2003. *Registrar General's annual review of demographic trends*. Edinburgh: General Register Office for Scotland.

GROS. 2004. *Registrar General's annual review of demographic trends*. Edinburgh: General Register Office for Scotland.

Gutierrez Domench, M. 2003. Combining family and work in Europe: 1960–2000. PhD thesis, London School of Economics.

Hawkes, D. 2003. Education, earnings, ability and early child bearing: evidence from a sample of UK twins. PhD thesis, Queen Mary College, University of London.

Hobcraft, J. and K. Kiernan. 2001. Early motherhood and adult social exclusion. *British Journal of Sociology* 52:495–517.

Joshi, H. 2001. Is there a place for area-based initiatives? *Environment and Planning* A33:1349–1352.

Kiernan, K. 1997. Becoming a young parent: a longitudinal study of associated factors. *British Journal of Sociology* 48:406–428.

McCulloch, A. and H. Joshi. 2001. Neighbourhood and family influences on the cognitive ability of children in the British National Child Development Study. *Social Science and Medicine* 53:579–591.

——. 2002. Child development and family resources: an exploration of evidence from the second generation of the 1958 birth cohort. *Journal of Population Economics* 15:283–304.

Pevalin, D. 2003. Outcomes in childhood and adulthood of mother's age at birth: evidence from the 1970 British Cohort Study. Working Paper 31, Institute of Social and Economic Research, University of Essex, Colchester.

Plewis, D. 2004. The Millennium Cohort Study First Survey: technical report on sampling. Centre for Longitudinal Studies, Institute of Education, University of London.

Shaw, C. 2003. Interim 2001-based national population-based projections for the UK and constituent countries. *Population Trends* 111:7–9.

Shepherd, P., K. Smith, H. Joshi and S. Dex. 2003. The Millennium Cohort Study First Survey: guide to the SPSS data set. Centre for Longitudinal Studies, Institute of Education, University of London.

Smith, K. and H. E. Joshi. 2002. The Millennium Cohort Study. *Population Trends* 107:30–34.

Wright, R. E. 2002a. Can Scotland afford to grow old? *Scottish Affairs* 39(1):5–18.

———. 2002b. The impact of population ageing on the Scottish labour market. *Quarterly Economic Commentary* 27(2):38–43.

———. 2004a. Scotland's future demographic prospect. In *Scotland's demographic challenge* (ed. R. E. Wright). Scottish Economic Policy Network, Universities of Stirling and Strathclyde.

———. 2004b. Population ageing and immigration policy. Scottish Economic Policy Network, Universities of Stirling and Strathclyde.

PART 3
Governance

High-Quality Public Services

By Nicholas Crafts[1]

INTRODUCTION

Public services matter enormously: people care deeply about education and health, which can have profound effects upon their lives. By definition, public services cannot be efficiently provided by relying on the market alone, so the government has to intervene. At the same time, there is a general perception that public services have underperformed and have not always been well-managed. Expenditure has been increasing rapidly, but has this delivered the results we all want?

Improving the performance of public services assumes even greater importance in the problematic context of pressures on government budgets (see Chapter 5). Public expenditure in Scotland already amounts to almost 50% of GDP and pressures for further increases, for example, to support an ageing population, are considerable. Yet in a globalizing world, small open economies that adopt high tax and spend policies will face serious fiscal difficulties.

This chapter focuses on three closely connected topics. How do public services contribute to the growth of living standards? How well have public services performed? How can we get better value for money in public services? These are discussed with particular reference to education and health, with a view to drawing out policy implications for Scotland.

An important issue common to all three questions is that of the measurement of the benefits from public services. There is no consensus on exactly how this should be carried out; yet it is central to deciding how much to spend overall, to allocating expenditure across competing claims, to assessing performance, and to designing incentive structures for efficient delivery.

The chapter also stresses the pervasiveness of the 'principal–agent problem' in the provision of public services. As governments have increasingly realized, it is not enough simply to spend more; it is also crucial to motivate managers and workers in the public sector to deliver desired outcomes efficiently. The key issues in addressing the incentives facing these public sector workers revolve around the use of performance targets and the extent to which competition among providers also has a part to play. The chapter concludes with an assessment of the policy implications.

---

[1] I have had a great deal of help in writing this chapter and am very grateful to Wendy Alexander, Jo Armstrong, Brian Ashcroft, Diane Coyle, Jim Cuthbert, Margaret Cuthbert, Nicki Georgiou, Eileen Mackay, Brian Main, John McLaren, Alan Peacock and Andrew Walker. Needless to say I did not heed all their (sometimes conflicting) advice and I am responsible for all the remaining errors.

What Makes Public Services Special?

It is useful to start with a definition of public services. They should not be thought of simply as the traditional gamut of public-sector activities. For present purposes, public services comprise those activities where there is a basic rationale for public intervention because market provision is unlikely to be adequate (Besley 2003). The main reasons for this are the following: substantial externalities in consumption and/or production (positive spillover effects whereby individuals' choices affect other people as well); minimum service requirements (such as a wish to achieve, universal access regardless of income); badly informed choices by consumers who lack relevant expertise (there is asymmetric information between consumers and producers).

In any of these circumstances, social and private returns diverge; the private market economy will supply an inappropriate output mix and will not undertake all the projects that a social cost–benefit analysis would identify as desirable.

Clearly, the traditional public sector includes many activities, most obviously education and health services, which have these attributes. For example, society has a strong interest in ensuring that citizens acquire sufficient human capital to be self-supporting at an acceptable living standard rather than be a burden on the state; a minimum level of education can be regarded as a right; and the components of a good education may not be easy for everyone to recognize. Similarly, a great deal of specialist knowledge is required to know which medical inputs will be effective; failure to obtain medical treatment has consequences for the spread of disease; and enjoying access to good health services is acknowledged as a citizen's right. On the other hand, whether broadcasting can be described as a public service under this definition is quite doubtful, and publicly owned airlines, coal mines and power stations surely do not qualify.

Thus, public services are by definition characterized by problems of market failure. This justifies public intervention but what matters is efficient and equitable provision, not the mode of delivery per se. When it does provide a public service, the government has to decide whether to produce the service itself or purchase it from other producers: it has to confront the classic 'make or buy' decision which shapes the boundaries of the firm in the private sector. With regard to ensuring universal access to public services, there are likewise alternatives to direct provision free at the point of use to consumers such as empowerment through transferring purchasing power, for example, through vouchers.

The choice between state ownership of and state contracting for public services involves a number of difficult trade-offs. Generally speaking, incentives for cost reduction and innovation are stronger under private ownership especially under conditions of competition. On the other hand, quality of provision matters and may be hard to guarantee in purchasing from the private sector because it is difficult to write complete contracts which cover all contingencies and are readily verifiable. Guaranteeing 'non-contractible quality' is an important reason for public provision but it has to weighed against poor value for money. Decisions of this kind should be informed by awareness of the scope for innovation and the power of potential competition, and the extent to which fear of reputational damage will constrain chiselling on quality by private contractors (Schleifer 1998).

If cost reductions carry the risk of significant quality reductions, and quality is hard to protect contractually, then public provision is beneficial. On the other hand, if threats to quality are negligible, perhaps because it is easy to describe what is wanted and to monitor its delivery, then purchasing services from the private sector will generally be superior because of its greater incentives for cost reduction (Grout and Stevens 2003).

Although market failures do provide a rationale for state intervention in public services, they do not mean that consumers' needs and wishes should be ignored. Another important aspect of the provision of public services is how responsive they are to changing demands, and how poor performance can be eliminated. In private markets, innovations that match new wants can be rewarded by profits, while lack of attention to cost control or customer service can be punished through the exit of unprofitable firms. These mechanisms work primarily through consumer choice and competition. Similar incentive structures have been largely absent where public services are publicly provided. However, the problem is that empowerment of consumers in order to improve services risks greater inequality of outcomes.

Considerations of *market* failure need to be balanced by recognizing the likelihood of *government* failures in the delivery of public services. Two aspects of this are worth noting, both of which are related to vote-seeking behaviour. First, when provision is under centralized government control, innovation may be stifled and mistakes perpetuated. There may be no incentives for anyone to own up to 'white elephants'. Secondly, and probably more important, policies which improve efficiency, offering a very small potential benefit to each of millions of taxpayers, but nevertheless hurt well-organized groups (including producer interests) are unlikely to be vote winners.

Public services like education and health not only account for a large part of public expenditure, they also produce outputs that people value greatly. The evidence for this can readily be found in market behaviour. For example, after taking into account the other obvious factors that influence the property market, a good primary school in the neighbourhood has a substantial impact on house prices. Thus Gibbons and Machin (2003) found that a 10% improvement in test results of 11-year-old children would raise local house prices by 6.9% with the implication that a 1 percentage point rise in Key Stage 2 scores across England would be valued at £13.6 billion.

Even more striking is the high valuation that people place on reductions in risks of mortality. Empirical studies have repeatedly shown that danger money is substantial. The concept used in this literature (and in British government policy making) is the value of a statistical life (VSL), or the total amount that the population would be willing to pay for a safety improvement that reduced expected deaths per year by one. Recent estimates of VSL in Britain vary but all agree that it is large, for example, £7.3 to £9.0 million, according to Siebert and Wei (1994), and £17.7 million, according to Arabsheibani and Marin (2000).

Similarly, research into reported happiness indicates that the income loss equivalent to being widowed is huge (Blanchflower and Oswald 2001). It has become apparent in recent decades that having a poor education seriously jeopardizes employment prospects. In 2002 only 59.2% of men of working age with no qualifications were employed (33.0% inactive, 7.8% unemployed) compared with 85.4% of those with qualifications (Gregg and Wadsworth 2003, p. 88). Yet unemployment creates great unhappiness, way above the implications of loss of income, such that it has recently been estimated that it would require $60 000 to compensate the average American worker for loss of employment (Blanchflower and Oswald 2001). If the education system were more successful in achieving good outcomes for its students, there would be a large welfare gain on top of that conventionally captured by national income accounting.

The outputs of both education and health services can furthermore raise the rate of growth of real national income. This is generally recognized in the case of education where expenditure is seen as investment in human capital. The pay-off in terms of national income is quite well measured by the extra wages which people with more education command—about 8% for an additional year of schooling (Cohen and Soto 2001). For the typical OECD country where average years of schooling of the labour force has risen in the past 20 years by about 1.25 years, this has contributed about 0.2 percentage points per year to the growth of real GDP per person over that period (Bosworth and Collins 2003).

If improvements in life expectancy are highly valued, they can be regarded as equivalent to increases in material consumption and thus they contribute directly to growth of living standards seen from the perspective of consumers. This might be a quite considerable contribution. Nordhaus (1998), using estimates of VSL as the basis of his calculation, found that including this component as equivalent to consumption would have raised the growth of real personal consumption per person in the United States by 1.8% per year for the period 1975–1995, approximately doubling measured GDP growth.

Conventional models of economic growth do not embody this contribution but do suggest that expenditure on public services can affect the growth rate, positively through the supply of complementary factors of production such as transport infra-structure which enhance the returns to private investment, and negatively through the impact of taxation. The evidence for OECD countries suggests that an increase of 1 percentage point in the share of GDP devoted to productive public expenditures (but not transfer payments) on average raises the growth rate by about 0.1 percentage points. On the other hand, increasing direct taxation by 1 percentage point of GDP reduces the growth rate by about 0.1 percentage points, although increasing indi-rect taxation has no effect (Kneller et al. 1999). Applying this analysis to the 1998 UK Comprehensive Spending Review, Kneller (2000) estimated that the impact of greater spending of itself would have been to raise the growth rate by about 0.5 percentage points but this would have been almost entirely offset by the effects of the extra direct taxation levied to finance it.

In sum, public services are special because of the prevalence of market failures, the value of the services, the need to provide them efficiently and equitably, and the requirement for large amounts of tax to provide them. Taken together, this set of characteristics means that improving productivity in public services is exceptionally important.

How Well Have the Public Services Performed?

Measuring productivity in public services is unfortunately terribly difficult. The notion of productivity relates output to inputs: the fewer inputs used to produce a given volume of output, or the more output obtained from a given volume of inputs, the higher is productivity. In the private sector, output can be added up in monetary terms and the prices paid for goods and services can be interpreted as representing their value to consumers. Over time growth in the volume of output is estimated by deflating the current monetary value of production by a price index.[2] An index of the total volume of inputs is obtained from an average of the rate of growth of individual inputs, weighted according to their cost shares. Then the change in total factor productivity (TFP)—the additional output not explained by increases in the quantity of inputs—is estimated by dividing the output volume index by the input volume index.

Measuring output of public services is much harder because generally there are no prices available for these non-market activities and thus no obvious way to value one type of service in terms of another. Nor is there direct evidence of willingness to pay for different quality or effectiveness of what is provided.

Nevertheless, the Office for National Statistics has recently produced experimental measures of TFP change in UK public services, described in Pritchard (2003). The estimates show that while government expenditure increased by 48% between 1995 and 2002, output rose by only 15%. Over the period, there was in fact a considerable increase (29%) in the prices paid for inputs (primarily labour), higher than inflation in the economy as a whole, limiting the increase in the input volume; even so, the picture is one of a small decline in productivity.

Where possible (about 70% of the public sector), the ONS measure the volume of production in terms of the number of specific outputs (e.g. lessons in schools, treatments in hospitals). This replaces the traditional method of assuming that output grows at the same rate as employment, setting productivity growth to zero. In the absence of prices charged to consumers, aggregate output of each service is obtained using weights based on the relative costs of producing each type of output (e.g. police output is based on crimes investigated where an incident of violence against the person is assumed to be equivalent to five motor vehicle thefts based on relative demands on police time). Some of the ONS results are reported in Table 8.1.

On the face of it, the estimates seem to indicate serious cause for concern. It is probably best, however, to look at these results as a worrying diagnostic rather than proof positive of deterioration in public services productivity. As Pritchard (2003) himself points out, not all types of output have been covered and there is no allowance for improvements in the quality of output. A more serious drawback is that what people care about is *outcomes* rather than outputs as measured in this way; for example, not how many operations are performed by the National Health Service but how effective these are in improving the quality of life and averting premature death.

---

[2]There are serious issues involved in creating an appropriate index of prices; for a detailed discussion see Schultze and Mackie (2002).

Table 8.1. ONS productivity in public services, 2001 (1995 = 100).

	Inputs	Output	Productivity
Education	118	104.6	88.6
Fire	106	105.1	99.2
Health	122	116.6	95.6
Police	111	107.0	96.4
All	113.7	110.9	97.5

Source: Pritchard (2003); output is measured as a cost-weighted change in volume, volume of inputs based on cost-weighted change in labour, purchased inputs and capital consumption, and the productivity concept is total factor productivity (TFP).

Table 8.2. Borda scores for public-sector performance and output efficiency in OECD countries, 2000.

Borda scores		Output efficiency	
Canada	54	Japan	1.00
Sweden	54	United States	1.00
Japan	51	Ireland	0.93
Australia	49	Norway	0.93
Austria	48	Australia	0.92
Netherlands	47	Austria	0.92
France	39	Netherlands	0.91
Denmark	38	Denmark	0.87
United States	35	Sweden	0.86
Norway	33	Canada	0.84
Ireland	31	UK	0.80
Germany	31	Germany	0.79
UK	28	Spain	0.78
Spain	27	France	0.77
Italy	19	Portugal	0.70
Greece	13	Italy	0.68
Portugal	6	Greece	0.65

Source: Borda scores based on rankings of performance in terms of health, education, administration and infrastructure. Data from Afonso et al. (2003) except health, which is based on mortality amenable to health care; see Table 8.3 below. Output efficiency from Afonso et al. (2003).

Afonso et al. (2003) do measure efficiency using outcomes. They make comparisons between countries of various aspects of public-sector performance relative to the share of GDP taken by public expenditure. Using statistical techniques, they calculate efficiency scores, summarized in Table 8.2. The results suggest that some countries get much worse value for their public expenditure than others. The interpretation of the results shown is that public-sector performance in the UK is only 80% of the potential if inputs were used as well as in the most efficient OECD countries.

Again, this might be regarded as a worrying sign of shortfall in the management of public services in the UK. Here too, however, there are important problems which argue for a more cautious assessment. First, performance is evaluated across seven

Table 8.3. Overall mortality versus mortality amenable to health care.

	Infant mortality	Life expectancy		Amenable mortality
Sweden	3.4	79.3	France	75.08
Japan	3.8	80.6	Sweden	79.60
Spain	3.9	77.9	Japan	81.41
Norway	3.9	78.5	Spain	84.11
Denmark	4.3	76.4	Norway	87.51
France	4.4	78.5	Italy	88.13
Germany	4.5	77.0	Australia	88.36
Austria	4.8	77.9	Canada	91.80
Netherlands	4.9	77.7	Germany	95.90
Canada	5.2	78.2	Denmark	97.21
Australia	5.3	78.9	Netherlands	97.25
Greece	5.4	77.9	Greece	98.53
Italy	5.3	78.7	Austria	106.85
UK	5.6	77.3	USA	114.65
Portugal	5.5	75.6	Ireland	129.34
Ireland	5.9	76.3	Portugal	132.07
USA	7.1	77.1	UK	133.62

Sources: rankings and data based on infant mortality and life expectancy from Afonso et al (2003), mortality amenable to health care per 1 000 000 aged 0–74 from Nolte and McKee (2003).

indicators which are arbitrarily given equal weight. They include aspects such as economic stability that may be related to fiscal and monetary policy but are not public services in our sense. Secondly, the outcomes include standard measures of educational attainment and mortality which are, however, influenced by factors other than the provision of public services. Third, the outcomes are expressed relative to the OECD average which gives very little weight to variations in the performance of key sectors like health since the variance of infant mortality and life expectancy is very low in the OECD.

Unfortunately, however we look at the performance of the public sector by outcomes, the UK appears quite mediocre. As an illustration, Table 8.2 reports 'Borda scores' based on rankings in quality of administration, quality of infrastructure, test scores in OECD's PISA comparison of educational systems, and 'avoidable mortality'.[3] Out of the 17 countries in the table the UK ranked 10th in quality of administration, 12th in quality of infrastructure, 5th in educational achievement and bottom in avoidable mortality (see Table 8.3).

The World Health Organization's *World Health Report* (2000) assessed the performance of health systems in terms of five aspects: disability adjusted life expectancy (DALE) (weighted 25%), equality of DALE (25%), responsiveness to patients

---

[3] Borda scores are a useful way of aggregating non-commensurate data; they require only an ability to rank outcomes. The total Borda score is derived from summing the rankings achieved in the individual components. A perfect score in Table 8.2, i.e. best in everything, would be 68. For a fuller explanation and discussion, see Dasgupta and Weale (1992). 'Avoidable mortality' is mortality amenable to health care as defined by Nolte and McKee (2003).

195

(12.5%), equality of responsiveness (12.5%), and equity in financial contributions (25%), where the weights were chosen on the basis of survey evidence. The evaluation of efficiency of converting expenditure into these outcomes was then based on a statistical model. The UK ranked 18th in the world when all these aspects were considered, compared with 24th based on efficiency in delivering DALE alone.

Not surprisingly, this assessment is controversial (Pedersen 2002). The most serious criticism relates to the choice of DALE as the measure of health attainment as it is only partly a result of health care and is also affected by factors such as diet, other public policies, incomes, etc. Nolte and McKee (2003) propose that a superior measure is 'mortality amenable to health care'. This shows a much greater variance and a quite different ranking, as Table 8.3 reports. Sadly, on this basis the UK exhibits a much worse performance.[4]

It is, of course, also true that mortality is affected by lifestyle choices (most obviously, of course, smoking and drinking) and by deprivation. Or (2000) published an econometric analysis of premature mortality in OECD countries and concluded that consumption of sugar and alcohol and the effects of pollution were important reasons why death rates in the UK were higher than those in Japan (the leading country) while differences in health expenditures had only a small effect. Still, mortality in the UK, particularly for women, was found to be distinctly higher than expected, having allowed for all identifiable influences including both lifestyle factors and health expenditure, which may suggest inferior performance by the health service.

Turning to the evidence on health in Scotland, Leon et al. (2003) also concluded from a detailed survey of Scottish health that deprivation cannot fully account for the excess of mortality in Scotland compared with England, which is particularly noticeable for adults rather than infants. They noted that cancer survival rates in Scotland, especially for women, were low by international standards and that this suggests that failings in the health-care system bear some of the responsibility for Scotland's steady decline in the international life expectancy league table over the past 50 years.

In the case of education, there are similar difficulties in assessing performance. The most obvious performance measures are years of schooling of the population or trends in national examination results. However, the first clearly ignores improvements in the quality of education and the second is potentially contaminated by changes in standards—perhaps resulting from attempts to make performance look good. Accordingly, more weight probably should be given to the standards achieved by British students and workers in international tests of what they can do.

The most useful evidence on this has been provided by OECD (2000) in its assessments of the labour force and of schoolchildren in competence in reading, mathematics and science literacy. Some of the key results are summarized in Table 8.4. These show that the UK has scored well in the PISA assessments of school children, notably not only in terms of the average but also in terms of the bottom 25% of

---

[4]Nolte and McKee (personal communication) are currently working on an estimate of avoidable mortality for Scotland. On the basis of the evidence in Leon et al. (2003), it is unlikely that Scotland's performance is better than that of the UK as a whole.

Table 8.4. Literacy scores.

| | (a) 15 year olds, 2000 | | | (b) Population, 16–65 | |
	Average	25th percentile		% Level 1	% Level 4–5
Japan	543	490	Sweden	6.8	34.6
Canada	532	473	Denmark	7.9	20.1
Australia	530	465	Norway	8.3	24.8
UK	528	465	Germany	10.0	18.6
Austria	514	453	Netherlands	10.3	18.4
Ireland	514	456	Belgium	16.8	18.0
Sweden	513	451	Australia	16.9	18.5
Belgium	508	438	Canada	17.2	23.3
France	507	443	USA	21.8	20.9
Norway	501	439	UK	22.8	18.1
USA	499	431	Ireland	24.2	13.7
Denmark	497	434	Portugal	46.2	4.3
Germany	487	419			
Spain	487	426			
Italy	474	413			
Portugal	461	397			
Greece	460	392			

Sources: (a) OECD (2001) based on scores in all three of reading, mathematics and science literacy. (b) OECD (2000) based on scores in all three of prose, document and quantitative literacy. Level 1 indicates persons with very poor skills where the individual may, for example, be unable to determine the correct amount of medicine to give a child from information printed on the package while Levels 4–5 describe respondents who demonstrate command of higher-order information processing skills (OECD 2000, p. xi).

achievement. A standard criticism of British education in the past has been that it served the academic elite well but failed those of lesser academic ability miserably; on this internationally comparable standard the latter is now less evident. On the other hand, past schooling standards do indeed seem to have left much to be desired; part (b) of Table 8.4 reports a relatively large proportion of the UK population is only at Level 1 (very poor skills).

For Scotland, the picture appears to be similar to that for the UK as a whole, although the published data are less detailed. The average literacy score for 15-year-olds in the PISA study was 527 while the percentages at Level 2 or below in reading were 31.1 in Scotland compared with 32.5 in England. In the earlier study of 16–65-year-olds, Scotland recorded 23.0% at Level 1 and 15.3% at Levels 4–5, much the same as the UK as a whole (Carey et al. 1997).[5]

INCENTIVE STRUCTURES AND PRODUCTIVITY IN PUBLIC SERVICES

Given the disappointing evidence on the performance of UK and Scottish public services, even acknowledging the measurement problems, how might their productivity

---

[5]The percentage at Level 4–5 is reduced somewhat by greater outmigration from Scotland by those who attained the highest levels of competence.

be improved? The task is difficult because the provision of public services is characterized by pervasive *principal–agent problems*. These arise wherever one person, an agent, works on behalf of someone else, a principal, in a situation of incomplete and asymmetric information. The agent's own self-interest and that of the principal typically differ, and it will be difficult or impossible to observe the agent's effort, even when outcomes are observable. This leaves the principal unsure how far unsatisfactory performance is the fault of the agent rather than of circumstances. So the principal either has to monitor the agent closely and/or devise incentives to encourage the agent to perform better.

Public services often involve long chains of principal–agent relationships. Consider school education. The parents elect politicians, who set targets to be delivered by education authorities, who employ head teachers to supervise teachers, who are expected to deliver the parents' desired educational outcomes. At each link of the chain there is a problem ensuring that someone else works effectively.

In the private sector the driving force is pursuit of profit, which can be improved by reductions in costs or the innovation of attractive new products. These benefit shareholders, but depend on managerial effort. Frequently, productivity improvement can be a difficult process involving reorganization, job losses and plant closures. Thus, in UK manufacturing during the period 1980–1992, 50% of labour productivity growth and 80% of TFP growth came from entry, exit and reallocation of market shares between business establishments (Disney et al. 2003).

In general, shareholders have inferior information to the management as to whether costs could be lower or what the profit potential of innovations might be. Accordingly, managers have some leeway to postpone hard choices or to indulge their own whims, so costs are higher than they need be and productivity is lower than it could be. This is a principal–agent problem where the incentives of the managers (agents) are not fully aligned with those of the shareholders (principals).

But the agency problem is mitigated in the private sector, vitally by competition. First, it offers yardsticks for shareholders to alert them to underperformance by their own managers; and, secondly, managers can be incentivized through contracts that reward them for outperformance of their rivals, aligning their interests better with those of the shareholders. The empirical evidence relating to the private sector in the UK strongly supports this analysis (see Nickell et al. 1997; Aghion et al. 2002). Given these results, the strengthening of competition policy is rightly seen by the government as a major pillar of its productivity agenda for the private sector (HM Treasury 2000).

In the public sector, agency problems are both endemic and harder to mitigate. Consider school education, which is everywhere in the world mainly a public-sector activity. Research on pupils' attainments in international tests in mathematics and science shows that these are to a very large extent determined by the institutional arrangements in countries rather than the amount of resources provided per pupil. Better performance is stimulated by national examinations, an absence of teachers unions' influence on the curriculum, competition from private schools, and school-level decision-making on personnel and teaching methods (Woossmann 2003). These research findings are explicable in a principal–agent framework: do teachers have an incentive to perform well rather than to exploit their informational advantages over parents? The incentive structures determine the public service outcomes.

The self-interest of producers in the public sector may well lead to poor value for money for taxpayers. This is not necessarily to suggest that public sector workers do not work hard. The general problem is likely to be the lack of effective pressure for change that keeps them busy doing the wrong things while management remains in the comfort zone. The nature of public services makes agency problems more intractable than in the private sector. This is partly because the situation is typically one of multiple principals and multiple tasks for the agents; and also because competition may not be an appropriate antidote (Dixit 2002).

The UK government has chosen performance targets as the way to address the problem. The performance targets are set out in so-called Public Service Agreements (PSAs). The government claims that they will (HM Treasury 2003, p. 27) provide direction and focus by setting out objectives clearly; improve outcomes; increase accountability; and ensure equity in the sense that acceptable standards will always be met.

The potential downside of the targets is also apparent, however, and a considerable amount of anecdotal evidence has already emerged to suggest that these may be serious in the National Health Service, where the approach has been pioneered. These include skewing of efforts towards tasks which are measured and away from others; creative accounting to misrepresent performance; discouragement of increasing efficiency for fear of ratchet effects; and inhibition of desirable innovations which are not rewarded by the scoring system (Goddard et al. 2000). When there is asymmetric information, performance targets may actually make it better *not* to try hard to innovate because the downside risks if things go wrong exceed any rewards for achievement, while doing things the same old way will not attract criticism.[6]

It is too soon to conclude that PSAs have failed. They probably will prove superior to the previous approach of spend and hope. Monitoring performance against them may well provide useful information. However, a recent survey concluded that there is almost no evidence for the impact of public-sector performance targets on outcomes or efficiency, although there are good reasons to believe that in many cases the targets have been poorly designed and give too little weight to outcomes that final users care about (Propper and Wilson 2003). At the same time, the disappointing trends in public-sector productivity reviewed above suggest that PSAs may not be as effective as the Treasury claims. It remains unclear what are the sanctions on government departments for failing to achieve performance targets.

In Scotland, the situation is even less clear. The draft budget of October 2003 outlined 153 departmentally set targets to be agreed with Scottish Executive Finance. What the future status of these targets is uncertain, and ongoing responsibility for

---

[6]An acute version of a problem of this type is highlighted by Prendergast (2003). His example concerns the introduction of a new complaints procedure for the Los Angeles Police Department which led to a spectacular fall in the productivity of its officers. The reason was that turning a blind eye to offences does not produce complaints, whereas arresting offenders runs risks of accusations of maltreatment.

monitoring and enforcement is still opaque. Methods to strengthen the performance-monitoring aspects of the budgetary process are under consideration.

These shortcomings with targets suggest that it is important to explore the role of competition in the provision of public services as an alternative way of addressing agency problems. In the UK this might typically be competition between not-for-profit producers; this comprised the 1990s' experience of 'quasi-markets' introduced by the Conservative government. Not-for-profit firms have lower incentives to cut quality in order to reduce costs. But, at the same time, in the absence of competition they have fewer incentives to reduce costs than would a for-profit firm with strong shareholders, and are prone to favour worker interests over those of consumers (Bennett et al. 2003). They are therefore most likely to be appropriate where quality is vital but also difficult to contract for, most obviously in hospitals, and most likely to be efficient when exposed to competition (Glaeser 2002; Lundsgaard 2002).

But there are some serious downsides to consider as well. These include the possibility that ill-informed consumers make serious and at worst life-changing mistakes in choosing between providers; that inequality of outcomes increases and access to services becomes more unequal; and that costs of regulation exceed any productivity benefits. On top of this, voters may regard the process of competition as unacceptable because it is perceived as unfair (Besley 2003).

Evidence is accumulating from experiments with quasi-markets in public services. Competition has been allowed a limited role in school education with funding following students, devolution of budgets and some limited choice of school for parents. Empirical investigation of the results for English secondary schools has concentrated on outcomes (rather than productivity). It has found that greater competition within a school district is associated with better exam results, and with a tendency over time to a narrowing of performance differentials; but this greater competition may also have had some adverse effects on equity in that schools with good results have seen a small reduction in the proportion of pupils from poor families (Bradley et al. 2001; Bradley and Taylor 2002).[7] Commentators who were originally somewhat sceptical have been persuaded that these reforms have basically paid off, although in need of some refinement with regard to social exclusion (Glennerster 2002).[8]

A more radical experiment with competition has been quite successful in Sweden. There, since 1992, anyone can establish an independent school and receive state funding per pupil equal to 85% of the average cost in the municipality provided that the school is approved by the regulator on ability to deliver the state's curriculum, that there are no tuition fees, and no selection of students. The results of this reform have been to raise test scores for those who remain in state schools with no adverse effect on weak students. Sandstrom and Bergstrom (2002) estimated that an increase

---

[7]There was, however, no increase in 'segregation' measured on the basis of children eligible for free school meals; on the contrary, this fell slightly after parental choice rights were enhanced (Gorard et al. 2003).

[8]Outcomes in England at Key Stage 2 (age 11) have improved most in the previously worst-performing schools but Glennerster points out that many of the most deprived schools experience little competition and that more must done to compensate schools financially for admitting low-performing and difficult students (Glennerster 2002, p. 130).

of 1 percentage point in the share of students in a municipality going to independent schools produces an improvement in exam results in the other schools equivalent to that which might be expected from an increase in public expenditure per pupil of 5%.

The assessments of the internal market in the National Health Service are more equivocal. This was designed to split purchasers from providers of health care and to introduce competition among hospitals which were given Trust status. Purchasers were general practitioners (GPs) who elected to become fundholders, and District Health Authorities. In common with other countries which tried similar experiments, governments were reluctant to accept the full implications (and the risks) of operating a system of this kind wholeheartedly; and, after 1997, the Labour government abandoned much of it, though not the purchaser–provider split. Propper (1995) concluded that hospitals were so heavily regulated that incentives to increase efficiency were weak while the perception of inferior treatment given to the patients of non-fundholding GPs was a political liability. Nevertheless, Le Grand (2002, pp. 141, 142) points out that the period of the internal market saw modest productivity gains which have subsequently been lost.[9]

On the whole, the evidence is that purchaser–provider splits with contracts to reimburse hospitals for outputs *ex post* do reduce costs relative to integrated public health services with direct public funding of hospitals (Gerdtham and Lothgren 2001). In the specific case of the Swedish experiment of the mid 1990s, the reduction in costs was about 13% (Gerdtham et al. 1999). At the same time, competition among providers carries risks that if purchasers are not well-informed about and/or insensitive to quality, competition on price will lead to sub-optimal quality (Dranove and Satterthwaite 2000). There are grounds to believe that the NHS internal market had some adverse effects on the quality of care as there is evidence of a small increase in death rates after treatment for heart attacks in hospital subject to greater competition (Propper et al. 2003). On the other hand, in the United States, under the auspices of Health Maintenance Organizations as purchasers, both costs of treatment and mortality from heart attacks were reduced by competition among hospitals in the 1990s (Kessler and McClellan 2000).

In sum, although the empirical evidence is not decisive, it is clear that incentive structures matter for cost efficiency and productivity in the provision of public services. Complex principal–agent relationships are pervasive and there is no simple solution to better delivery. Two possible approaches to improving service delivery are increased monitoring through performance targets, and increased contestability in the provision of services. Both approaches address the problem of lack of appropriate incentives in the public sector. Present government policy in the UK and Scotland has stressed the use of performance targets rather than competition as a response to the problems. But it is not clear that the present mix of these two approaches is correct. It may be that too much faith has been placed in the former and too little in the latter.

---

[9]The productivity measure is a crude one which does not measure health outcomes and takes no account of the quality of care.

POLICY IMPLICATIONS FOR SCOTLAND

How Valuable Might Better Public Services Be?

In 2000 life expectancy at birth in Scotland, at 73.1, was 2.5 years lower than in England and Wales. Since 1981 the gain in life expectancy has been 4.6 years in England and Wales against 4.0 years for Scotland (ONS 2003). Applying the Nordhaus (1998) method, a ballpark estimate is that, if mortality risks in Scotland were overnight to fall to English levels, the consumption equivalent of the welfare gain would be £2912 per person or 21.3% of 2001 GDP.[10]

It would plainly be ridiculous to suppose that the differences in mortality between Scotland and England can be attributed entirely, or even mainly, to failings in the health-care system. Deprivation and lifestyle choices are major contributors. That said, however, the health service in Scotland enjoys 19% greater expenditure per person and the 30% more doctors per person than England and yet achieves worse outcomes, for example, lower cancer survival rates for women (Leon et al. 2003).

Leaving school with low standards of literacy has seriously adverse implications for subsequent life chances and, notably, for employment prospects. Controlling for a number of socioeconomic variables, OECD (2000) found that in the UK in the mid 1990s young men had a 45% risk of not being employed if they were at the 5th percentile of prose literacy compared with a 25% probability at median literacy. If the Scottish labour force had the same competence in prose literacy as the Swedish labour force, then the employment rate among Scottish men would be predicted to rise by about 5%. In 2001 that would have meant an extra 65 000 in employment. On the basis of the psychic costs of unemployment in Blanchflower and Oswald (2001), suppose that each of these men would have needed about £28 000 a year in compensation for their inactivity. Then the annual loss to Scottish males from their inferior literacy competence adds up to £1.82 billion.[11] Once again, weaknesses in the educational attainments of the Scottish labour force should not be seen as only or mainly the fault of the education system. Clearly, the socioeconomic background of children has a major impact on schooling outcomes.

These calculations should both be regarded as illustrative and subject to wide margins of error. Nevertheless, their message is that mediocre standards in public services can be very expensive and there is much to be gained from improvements. It would be quite wrong to be complacent about past performance; on the contrary, it appears that disappointing outcomes both in education and health have been costly to Scotland.

---

[10]To implement this calculation requires estimates of VSL and of age-standardized mortality differences between Scotland and England. Using the data in Miller (2000), I take VSL to be $132 \times$ GDP per person = £1.80 million. The difference in mortality rates standardized by the Scottish age structure is 1618/million, so the gain from eliminating the difference would be £1.80 $\times$ 1618 = £2912 per person.

[11]I do not wish to imply that women are unimportant but have confined the calculation to men simply because the econometric evidence relates to that gender. I have converted Blanchflower and Oswald's estimate by assuming the required compensation for unemployment is $2.0 \times$ GDP per person.

Taking Cost–Benefit Analysis Seriously

Social cost–benefit analysis is a well-established technique for investment appraisal in the public sector. It is invaluable as a way of taking account of the opportunity costs of public expenditure. In particular, it ensures that the cost of capital is recognized by discounting future spending, while the requirement to quantify marginal benefits in terms of the public's willingness to pay (rather than the untested assumptions of politicians) establishes value-for-money. In some parts of the public sector, for example, in the assessment of trunk road schemes, the details of how best to apply the technique have been finely honed over several decades. If desired, appraisals can weight differently the benefits accruing to, say, rich and poor, while externalities should be taken into account and quantified whenever possible. In principle, a major attraction of cost–benefit analysis is the contribution that it can make to allocating funds between different uses at the margin (allocative efficiency).

Yet frequently UK policy disregards the results of well-designed cost–benefit calculations. Some of the most blatant recent examples can be found in the actions of the Westminster government in the transport sector. In 1998, road schemes whose benefits were estimated to be on average well over three times costs were jettisoned (Glaister 2002). Similarly, road congestion charging at peak times in large urban areas would be strongly recommended by cost–benefit analysis (Glaister and Graham 2003) but has been introduced (belatedly) only in central London. On the other hand, the 10-year transport plan announced in 2001 proposed that the vast majority of investment in transport infrastructure should go to railway projects for which independent analysts believe costs exceed benefits (Affuso et al. 2003).

How might taking cost–benefit analysis seriously affect Scottish health and education? With regard to health, cost–benefit analysis is not used, although, if it were, it might well justify shifting resources into the sector from elsewhere in the public sector given the high value that the public places on reduced mortality risks. The present criteria for adopting new health technologies appear to be based on cost per quality adjusted life year (QALY), which can be translated into a benefit–cost criterion based on VSL. This would be well worth doing. It would reveal whether a lower (implicit) valuation is given to VSL in the health sector than in, say, railway safety or road improvement schemes, which might open the way to asking whether the available evidence would justify that relative valuation.[12] Unless, health sector decisions are transparently made in the same broad framework applied elsewhere in the public sector the scope for misallocation of resources is considerable (Loomes 2002).

With regard to education, one obvious question to be asked is whether the adoption of a target of 50% of 18-year-olds going to college (rather than other transitions to work) can be justified by cost–benefit analysis. The teenagers are compelled to add four years to their education (and sacrifice four years of earnings) to do jobs for which

---

[12]A great deal more needs to be discovered about public perceptions of and attitudes to risk with a view to quantifying the benefits of reductions of different types of hazard. However, what is known does not seem to justify the huge premium currently placed on railway safety (Chilton et al. 2002).

they are 'overqualified'; the alternative might be becoming genuinely well-trained to do traditional craft occupations (Wolf 2002).

Another curious aspect of public-sector decision-making which a more consistent use of cost–benefit analysis would highlight, is its treatment of the opportunity cost of time. In the analysis of transport projects, time savings are typically a major component of the benefits. A recent survey of the evidence confirmed that this is appropriate, for example, the value of time savings to employers in the mid 1990s from faster journeys was around £17 per hour (Wardman 1998). The National Health Service, however, generally behaves as if the cost of patients' time is zero both in terms of the way appointments are handled and in terms of the unavailability of GPs at the weekend and after office hours. Not only is this very inefficient from the point of view of both employers and workers but it is also likely to result in inequity of access.

Improving Health

The internal market is alive and well, after some remedial surgery, in England, where experiments to increase consumer choice and a price list for common operations are intended to put pressure on providers to reduce costs. In contrast NHS Scotland has returned to something close to the original NHS design. In particular, health care in Scotland will be provided through a public integrated public health system through NHS Health Boards. There will be more generous funding and much heavier use of central guidance and monitoring compared with the 1980s. The new Performance Assessment Framework has 109 indicators.

The Scottish Executive promises that it 'will intervene when serious problems or deficiencies arise which are not being resolved quickly enough at local level' (2003a, p. 62). Yet the implication of earlier sections is that this may not be the best direction for health policy in Scotland if the aim is to pursue cost-effectiveness in obtaining the maximum health gains for the additional public expenditure. Indeed, it flies in the face of evidence-based policy. There seems to be an overemphasis on performance indicators coupled with an undue reluctance to consider a greater role for competition within the public sector in delivering improvements in productivity.

First, it is unclear that the 109 performance indicators are well-designed. Relatively few of them involve quantified targets and there is little reference to international best practice as opposed to keeping up with the Scottish national average. It is also surprising that there is no sense of priority across these disparate aspects of performance.

Secondly, there is no indication that the control of expenditure within NHS Scotland is going to be informed by cost–benefit analysis. Since little attention will be paid to the extent to which patients' health outcomes and quality of life would actually be improved by alternative uses of resources within the NHS budget, the performance assessment framework is unlikely to ensure cost-effective health care, especially given the ever-present threat of political interference.

Thirdly, it would be quite understandable if the potential role of competition were regarded with great caution; but it is disappointing that the Scottish Executive's attitude is apparently one of complete antipathy. This stance runs the risk of increasing costs and ignores the evidence that integrated public health systems are relatively expensive in delivery of health care. Even economists who are deeply sceptical of the role of competition, and who argue that non-contractible quality issues loom very large in parts of the health-care services, accept that there are many aspects of elective surgery for which there are good measures of outcome and well-understood technologies. In these areas careful experiments in competitive provision, even involving suppliers from outside the NHS, may be an appropriate way forward (Smith 2003).

Improving Education

The Scottish Executive has a laudable determination to raise educational attainment in Scotland while also recognizing the importance of education for social inclusion and citizenship. Its approach relies heavily on 47 performance targets across five dimensions, of which 19 are quantified (Scottish Executive 2003b). In the event of underperformance there are also to be increased powers for the Minister of Education to intervene by compelling the local authority to take action (Scottish Executive 2003c). The language is of systematic planning, monitoring and enforcement.

As with health care, there are question marks about this system of performance assessment. The priorities are unclear and many of the outcomes will go unmeasured. Critics worry that, in practice, the emphasis will be entirely on educational attainment and teachers' efforts will be skewed to 'teaching to the test' (Ozga 2003).

What is particularly striking, however, in recent Scottish education policy is the lack of emphasis on extending parental choice and making education provision more contestable. The evidence is that moving in this direction tends to raise educational attainment for a given amount of public expenditure. The Scottish experience was that the introduction of greater parental choice in the 1980s did not worsen segregation in schools (Paterson 2001) while parents were quite active in requesting a school other than that designated where geography was conducive to this, i.e. in cities (Willms 1997).

Looking for ways to increase the role of parental choice within a non-selective state school system surely deserves more attention. A more radical move would be to consider emulating the Swedish experiment of increasing contestability by making available state funding for all viable independent schools while outlawing selection and tuition fees, a policy which might extend the benefits of potential competition to parents outside the big cities.

Better Information

It is highly desirable that better quality information relating to public services productivity in Scotland is developed. This should go beyond the use of performance indicators as control/management tools or the estimation of crude measures of outputs per unit of input along the lines that the ONS produces for the UK. These may be useful diagnostics but, taken too seriously, they respectively run the risk of distorting effort and understating achievement.

What is really needed is a much more serious attempt to quantify the outcomes that public services deliver and the contribution that they make to well-being. This requires giving serious thought to eliciting the public's valuation of the benefits. In order to facilitate better decision-making, this has to be expressed in monetary terms using the concept of willingness to pay. The Atkinson Inquiry is addressing these issues for ONS and its findings should be a high priority for discussion, and possible implementation, in Scotland.

CONCLUSIONS

Public services contribute more to the growth of living standards than is generally recognized. Effective provision of health and education can reduce risks of mortality and unemployment and this is worth a great deal if quantified as its equivalent in terms of additional income per person.

Only by grasping the nettle of monetary valuation of the outcomes delivered by public services will it be possible to assess their performance adequately and to allocate resources efficiently across alternative uses.

Running public services well is important not only because of the contribution that it makes to living standards but also because of its fiscal implications. Getting the best outcomes from public expenditure requires both the allocation of funds on the basis of benefit–cost comparisons and also the creation of incentives that encourage the efficient use of inputs. In other words, productivity in public services matters.

Improvement in the productivity of public services has proved elusive in the past. This stems from a combination of weak incentives to producers, poor data collection and monitoring by those responsible for ensuring good results, and an absence of competition or contestability in provision.

For the effective delivery of public services it is crucial to structure the incentives facing service providers so that the interests of the users are paramount. Performance targets and greater competition among potential providers are alternative ways of addressing this issue. The Scottish Executive is giving great weight to the former and neglecting the possibilities of the latter. This is an act of faith rather than evidence-based policy.

REFERENCES

Affuso, L., J. Masson and D. Newbery. 2003. Comparing investments in new transport infrastructure: roads vs railways? *Fiscal Studies* 24:275–315.

Afonso, A., L. Schuknecht and V. Tanzi. 2003. Public sector efficiency: an international comparison. European Central Bank Working Paper 242.

Aghion, P., N. Bloom, R. Blundell, R. Griffith and P. Howitt. 2002. Competition and innovation: an inverted U relationship. National Bureau of Economics Working Paper 9269.

Arabsheibani, G. R. and A. Marin. 2000. Stability of estimates of the compensation for danger. *Journal of Risk and Uncertainty* 20:247–269.

Bennett, J., E. Iossa and G. Legrenzi. 2003. The role of commercial non-profit organizations in the provision of public services. *Oxford Review of Economic Policy* 19:335–347.

Besley, T. 2003. Making government responsive. In *Public services productivity* (HM Treasury), pp. 7–10. London: HMSO.

Blanchflower, D. G. and A. J. Oswald. 2001. Well-being over time in Britain and the USA. Warwick Economics Research Papers 616.

Bosworth, B. P. and S. M. Collins. 2003. The empirics of growth: an update. *Brookings Papers on Economic Activity* 2:113–206.

Bradley, S. and J. Taylor. 2002. The effect of the quasi-market on the efficiency-equity trade-off in the secondary school sector. *Bulletin of Economic Research* 54:295–314.

Bradley, S., G. Johnes and J. Taylor. 2001. The effect of competition on the efficiency of secondary schools in England. *European Journal of Operational Research* 135:545–568.

Carey, S., S. Low and J. Hansbro. 1997. *Adult literacy in Britain*. London: HMSO.

Chilton, S., J. Covey, L. Hopkins, M. Jones-Lee, G. Loomes, N. Pidgeon and A. Spencer. 2002. Public perceptions of risk and preference-based values of safety. *Journal of Risk and Uncertainty* 25:211–232.

Cohen, D. and M. Soto. 2001. Growth and human capital: good data, good results. Centre for Economic Policy Research Discussion Paper 3025.

Dasgupta, P. and M. Weale. 1992. On measuring the quality of life. *World Development* 20:119–131.

Disney, R., J. Haskel and Y. Heden. 2003. Restructuring and productivity growth in UK manufacturing. *Economic Journal* 113:666–694.

Dixit, A. 2002. Incentives and organizations in the public sector. *Journal of Human Resources* 37:696–727.

Dranove, D. and M. A. Satterthwaite. 2000. The industrial organization of healthcare markets. In *Handbook of health economics* (ed. A. J. Culyer and J. Newhouse). Amsterdam: Elsevier.

Gerdtham, U.-G. and M. Lothgren. 2001. Health system effects on cost efficiency in the OECD countries. *Applied Economics* 33:643–647.

Gerdtham, U.-G., C. Rehnberg and M. Tambour. 1999. The impact of internal markets on health care efficiency: evidence from health care reforms in Sweden. *Applied Economics* 31:935–945.

Gibbons, S. and S. Machin. 2003. Valuing English primary schools. *Journal of Urban Economics* 53:197–219.

Glaeser, E. 2002. The governance of not-for-profit firms. NBER Working Paper 8921.

Glaister, S. 2002. UK transport policy, 1997–2001. *Oxford Review of Economic Policy* 18:154–186.

Glaister, S. and D. Graham. 2003. *Transport investment and pricing in England*. Southampton: Independent Transport Commission.

Glennerster, H. 2002. United Kingdom education 1997–2001. *Oxford Review of Economic Policy* 18:120–136.

Goddard, M., R. Mannion and P. Smith. 2000. Enhancing performance in health care: a theoretical perspective on agency and the role of information. *Health Economics* 9:95–107.

Gorard, S., C. Taylor and J. Fitz. 2003. *Schools, markets and choice policies*. London: Routledge Falmer.

Gregg, P. and J. Wadsworth. 2003. Labour market prospects of less skilled workers over the recovery. In *The labour market under new Labour: the state of working Britain* (ed. R. Dickens, P. Gregg and J. Wadsworth), pp. 86–97. New York: Palgrave Macmillan.

Grout, P. A. and M. Stevens. 2003. The assessment: financing and managing public services. *Oxford Review of Economic Policy* 19:215–234.

HM Treasury. 2000. *Productivity in the UK: the evidence and the government's approach*. London: HMSO.

———. 2003. *Public services: meeting the productivity challenge*. London: HMSO.

Kessler, D. P. and M. B. McClellan. 2000. Is hospital competition socially wasteful? *Quarterly Journal of Economics* 115:577–615.

Kneller, R. 2000. The implications of the comprehensive spending review for the long run growth rate: a view from the literature. *National Institute Economic Review* 171:94–105.

Kneller, R., M. Bleaney and N. Gemmell. 1999. Fiscal policy and growth: evidence from OECD countries. *Journal of Public Economics* 74:171–190.

Le Grand, J. 2002. The Labour government and the National Health Service. *Oxford Review of Economic Policy* 18:137–153.

Leon, D. A., S. Morton, S. Cannegieter and M. McKee. 2003. *Understanding the health of Scotland's population in an international context*. Edinburgh: Public Health Institute of Scotland.

Loomes, G. 2002. Valuing life years and QALYs: 'transferability' and 'convertibility' of values across the UK public sector. In *Cost-effectiveness thresholds: economic and ethical issues* (ed. A. Towse, C. Prithcard and N. Devlin), pp. 46–55. London: King's Fund.

Lundsgaard, J. 2002. Competition and efficiency in publicly-funded services. OECD Economics Working Paper 331.

Miller, T. R. 2000. Variations between countries in values of statistical life. *Journal of Transport Economics and Policy* 34:169–188.

Nickell, S. J., D. Nicolitsas and N. Dryden. 1997. What makes firms perform well? *European Economic Review* 41:783–796.

Nolte, E. and M. McKee. 2003. Measuring the health of nations: analysis of mortality amenable to health care. *British Medical Journal* 327:1–5.

Nordhaus, W. D. 1998. The health of nations: Irving Fisher and the contribution of improved longevity to living standards. Cowles Foundation Discussion Paper 1200.

OECD. 2000. *Literacy in the information age*. Paris: OECD.

———. 2001. *Knowledge and skills for life*. Paris: OECD.

Office for National Statistics. 2003. *Population trends*. London: HMSO.

Or, Z. 2000. Determinants of health outcomes in industrialized countries: a pooled, cross-country, time series analysis. *OECD Economic Studies* 30:53–77.

Ozga, J. 2003. Measuring and managing performance in education. Edinburgh University Centre for Educational Sociology Briefing 27.

Paterson, L. 2001. Education and inequality in Britain. Paper presented to British Association for the Advancement of Science Annual Meeting, Glasgow.

Pedersen, K. 2002. The World Health Report 2000: dialogue of the deaf? *Health Economics* 11:93–101.

Prendergast, C. 2003. The response of the Los Angeles Police Department to increased oversight. In *Public services productivity*, pp. 19–21. London: HMSO.

Pritchard, A. 2003. Understanding government output and productivity. *Economic Trends* 596:27–39.

Propper, C. 1995. Agency and incentives in the NHS internal market. *Social Science and Medicine* 40:1683–1690.

Propper, C. and D. Wilson. 2003. The use and usefulness of performance measures in the public sector. *Oxford Review of Economic Policy* 19:250–267.

Propper, C., S. Burgess and D. Gossage. 2003. Competition and quality: evidence from the NHS internal market 1991–1999. University of Bristol CMPO Working Paper 03/077.

Sandstrom, F. M. and F. Bergstrom. 2002. School vouchers in practice: competition won't hurt you. IUI Research Institute of Industrial Economics Working Paper 578.

Schultze, C. L. and C. Mackie. 2002. *At what price?* Washington, DC: National Academy Press.

Scottish Executive. 2003a. *Partnership for care: Scotland's health white paper*.

——. 2003b. *National priorities in education: performance report.*

——. 2003c. *Ensuring improvement in our schools.*

Shleifer, A. 1998. State versus private ownership. *Journal of Economic Perspectives* 12(4):133–150.

Siebert, W. S. and X. Wei. 1994. Compensating wage differentials for workplace accidents: evidence for union and nonunion workers in the UK. *Journal of Risk and Uncertainty* 9:61–76.

Smith, P. 2003. The case against the internal market. In *Can market forces be used for good?* (ed. J. Dixon, J. Le Grand and P. Smith), pp. 18–31. London: King's Fund.

Wardman, M. 1998. The value of travel time: a review of British evidence. *Journal of Transport Economics and Policy* 32:285–316.

Willms, J. D. 1997. Parental choice and education policy. Edinburgh University Centre for Educational Sociology Briefing 12.

Wolf, A. 2002. *Does education matter?* London: Penguin.

Woossmann, L. 2003. Schooling resources, educational institutions and student performance: the international evidence. *Oxford Bulletin of Economics and Statistics* 65:117–170.

Committing to Growth in a Small European Country

By John Bradley[1]

> Do I dare
> Disturb the universe?
> In a minute there is time
> For decisions and revisions which a minute will reverse.
>
> T. S. Eliot

INTRODUCTION

To be offered the opportunity of reflecting on the Scottish economy is a particular pleasure for an Irish economist. We Irish follow the fortunes of the economies of the Celtic 'fringe' of the United Kingdom with singular interest, having been constitutionally part of that fringe until 1922, and remaining locked into close business and economic relationships with Great Britain from then until well into the 1970s. After independence, British and Irish people continued to enjoy the benefits of a common work area, travelling back and forth unhindered by passport controls, with a frequency born of long-standing familiarity.

Ireland parted company from the UK in 1922 and embarked on the task of running its own political affairs and building its own institutions. My grandparents remained convinced that the break had been a dreadful mistake. As a young child in the 1950s, they would take me on bus rides to the seaside south of Dublin, and to my excruciating embarrassment, would loudly ask the conductor for tickets to 'Kingstown', a place-name that Irish nationalists had long since changed to 'Dún Laoghaire'.

But, however familiar the British–Irish link remained to ordinary people, it proved more difficult to regularize at an official level. It was not until the advent of the European Common Market that this was finally resolved. A modest externality of the European movement, grown out of the ashes of World War II, was that it provided an encompassing framework within which Anglo-Irish political and economic relationships could become more relaxed, cooperative and mutually beneficial. Today it seems very natural to discuss the economies of Scotland and Ireland not only within

---

[1]The editorial group around the Allander Series of lectures provided an extraordinarily stimulating environment within which this chapter was commissioned, written and revised. My sincere thanks go to Wendy Alexander, Jo Armstrong, Brian Ashcroft, Diane Coyle and John McLaren, for sharing their enthusiasm and insights into the challenges facing Scotland and helping me see Ireland in a different light. They improved the chapter beyond measure. My ESRI colleagues, John Fitz Gerald and Danny McCoy, were also an invaluable sounding board for ideas.

this context, but also as archetypes of the kinds of entities that make up the European Union: small states and regions.

Scotland is a typical region of a great nation state, whose political institutions embed it in that state, but leave its local policy makers with a degree of autonomy. Scotland relates to the outside world mainly through the institutions of its encompassing nation state, even after devolution. This is so obvious and natural that it goes almost unnoticed. Yet it colours the way that Scotland views the world and responds to global opportunities.

Irish independence in 1922 gave it the potential for considerable policy autonomy. But before the 1960s the carry-over of dependency on Great Britain placed severe physical and psychological restrictions on the practical exercise of autonomy. One symbol of dependence was that British and Irish notes and coins circulated freely alongside each other, at a strict one-to-one parity. Almost all of the mainly agricultural Irish exports were sold to Britain. Only after 1960 did the Irish economy begin to succeed in restructuring, diversifying and converging.

But the detailed bilateral comparison of the economic performance and potential of the Scottish region and the Irish state is not this chapter's central theme. It is more useful to focus on each of them as European archetypes of small regional and national economies, and to reflect on the implications that this has for the design of successful growth strategies. Within the European context, the economies of small nation states and regions have more in common than is often recognized. In earlier research on the Irish growth experience, Paul Krugman stressed the need for a better balance between a purely regional paradigm, with growth driven by an export base, and the kinds of macroeconomic and productivity-driven issues that matter for national economies, even small ones (Krugman 1997). He explored the extent to which one has to look inside an economy, at its internal macroeconomic mechanisms and business interrelationships, in order to understand it. Ireland today has adjusted to thinking about its economy in national as well as regional contexts. Scotland is still engaged in that exercise.

The next section presents a brief interpretation of the recent Irish growth experience, since this has attracted attention in Scotland. The relevance for Scotland of the experience of a small country that converged from relative poverty to the EU average standard of living in less than 15 years is not obvious, though. Even if I sometimes detect an air of pessimism in Scotland about its future, remember that in modern times it has never strayed very far from UK living standards, which are exactly at the EU average. Scotland has never had to grapple with the challenge of convergence. Rather, it faces the more complex challenge of renewal.

I then reflect on the fact that policy makers, in particular, regional policy makers, who think that they are pragmatists, seldom work in an intellectual or political vacuum. In the famous words of Keynes: 'The ideas of economists and political philosophers, both when they are right and when they are wrong, are more powerful than is commonly understood.'

Developing this theme, David Henderson, in his 1985 Reith Lectures coined the phrase 'do-it-yourself' economics, by which he meant ideas and beliefs which owe little to economics textbooks, yet influence policies, people and events. And Paul

Krugman recently had some harsh things to say about 'policy entrepreneurs', those who offer unambiguous diagnosis, even when professors are uncertain, and easy answers where professors doubt that any easy answers can be found.

Since there is scope for misunderstanding the role of economic ideas, it is worth reviewing the history of growth strategies as they have been implemented over the past few decades in a small state like Ireland. The point I stress in this chapter is that the actual facts of underdevelopment are seldom in dispute. What is crucial is the way that local (and sometimes international) policy makers and analysts think about those facts. In other words, the conceptual frameworks that underpin policy actions are all-important. Failure to develop is usually associated with incorrect conceptual frameworks rather than with the absence of hard work. On the other hand, an appropriate framework seems to have the power to energize people.

Then I turn to a wider European aspect of convergence, or, to use the EU term, 'cohesion'. It is a defining characteristic of European policy making that the demands of efficiency and equity are both taken seriously. Since the late 1980s the EU has implemented a major programme of regional investment aimed at promoting 'cohesion' among the poorer member states. The member states whose performance lagged most—Greece, Ireland and Portugal—as well as the poorer regions of Spain, Italy, Germany and the UK, received generous levels of development aid. Ireland had the good fortune to be at the precise point in its development strategy that ensured optimal use of EU development aid. But in the case of Scotland, the role of the EU in the area of regional policy may simply be a distraction from challenges that would be best treated by the more effective use of Scotland's much larger local resources.

Then I turn to the challenges of today, where both Scotland and Ireland find themselves with a broadly similar standard of living.[2] Ireland is newly promoted into the Premier League. Scotland has been in it for a long time—but I detect a fear of relegation. Both economies now face a similar challenge: how to stay in the Premier League. The experience of small EU countries suggests that success is almost always associated with a far wider range of overlapping and mutually reinforcing strategic approaches than are normally used by economists; and that strategy best operates within robust and appropriate institutional frameworks that must be carefully designed and implemented. I conclude with some reflections on the characteristics of good regional governance.

Perhaps I should signal up-front a perception that colours my analysis. Over the past decade, as I have interacted with Scottish and other UK regional economist colleagues, I have detected an unwillingness, sometimes an inability, to think of Scotland's potential in a truly international way. I interpret this as a mindset induced by the sheer strength of the centripetal intellectual and financial pull of London, combined with the fact that Scottish Ministers, their advisors, and academics do not regularly have to sit around tables in Brussels and Frankfurt explaining themselves

---

[2]The assertion of similar Scottish and Irish standards of living has to be heavily qualified. It is a statement about the approximate equality of Scottish GDP per head and Irish GNP per head (smaller than GDP due to profit repatriation by foreign firms). Consumption per head remains higher in Scotland, but not spectacularly higher.

robustly to their peers, and listening in turn to other national and regional narratives. Nobody denies that the Edinburgh–London axis must remain a vital one for Scotland. Indeed, the Dublin–London axis also continues to be important. But the Irish Taoiseach (or Prime Minister) is also obliged every few years to act as EU President for six months, and ministers as well as the entire civil service must perform on the EU and world stage. I hasten to add that nobody is foolish enough to imagine that Ireland is very influential in this role. But the process has an electrifying effect on the country and exposes it to a vast array of international challenges that might otherwise pass it by.

REFLECTING ON IRELAND'S 'GREAT LEAP FORWARD'

Let me start with a somewhat downbeat interpretation of Ireland's convergence story. Since my purpose is to discuss policy frameworks for growth, it is appropriate to examine Irish economic performance in terms of the 'Lisbon Agenda'. This important initiative arose out of a nagging realization on the part of the European Commission and the major EU states that the Single Market, established in the late 1980s and early 1990s, was not delivering as dynamic a growth performance as had been expected. Based on a wide range of indicators, many of the European economies were failing to catch up with the US, and some were even falling further behind.

These concerns came to a head at the Spring European Council meeting held in Lisbon in 2000, where an ambitious programme was launched, entitled *An agenda of economic and social renewal for Europe*. After ten years of strong growth, we Irish were initially a little complacent about the Lisbon Agenda. After all, we had dynamic clusters of high-technology sectors (mainly computers, software and pharmaceuticals); our growth had accelerated dramatically in a sustained way; we had slashed our unemployment rate from one of the highest in Europe to one of the lowest; and we believed that we had improved our social protection systems beyond recognition. But our complacency was not to last very long.

As a means of giving substance to the task of monitoring progress on the Lisbon Agenda, the European Commission began to publish regularly a set of over 100 socioeconomic indicators, gathered into six main areas: general economic performance, employment creation, innovation and research, structural reforms, social cohesion and care of the environment. If you stand back from the details of the indicators, some fairly robust conclusions emerge. Using the most recent data, Figure 9.1 shows the frequency of appearance of each of the 15 EU states in the top and in the bottom three ranks for each structural indicator. In terms of appearance in the top three, the international pecking order is Sweden, followed by Finland, Denmark, Ireland and the UK. In terms of appearance in the bottom three, the order is Greece, followed by Portugal, Spain, Italy and the UK.[3]

But if you move down to a more detailed level, a less comforting picture of Ireland emerges. Eighteen of our twenty-five 'top three' scores arise in the areas of 'general

---

[3] Unfortunately, the Lisbon indicators are not yet published at the EU regional (or NUTS 2) level, so we cannot pinpoint Scotland's performance.

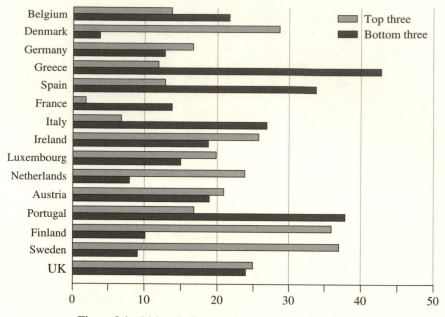

Figure 9.1. Lisbon indicators of performance: frequency of appearance in the top/bottom three structural indicators.

economic performance' and 'employment performance'. One can designate these two areas somewhat loosely as 'outturn' indicators, i.e. growth, exports, jobs. In the other four main areas, which might be loosely designated as 'input' indicators, Ireland achieves very few 'top three' scores, but many 'bottom three'. So we are presented with something of a paradox. Ireland is apparently delivering a top-class performance in terms of a series of outturn indicators, while simultaneously displaying modest to mediocre performance in a series of indicators of quality inputs. The three Nordic countries—Finland, Sweden and Denmark—performed excellently in both output and input indicators.

What then drove Ireland's top-class 'outturn' performance, propelling it to convergence in terms of GDP/GNP per head? It was clearly not the expected Lisbon Agenda drivers: innovation, structural reforms, social cohesion and the care for the environment. How did Irish policy makers manage to leverage top-class growth and jobs out of apparently so few top-class inputs? Are there useful lessons for other states and regions?

To answer, we need to examine three interrelated issues:

(i) the quest for smart policies that maximized the use of the limited policy autonomy and the constrained resources available to a small state like Ireland as it attempted to converge;

(ii) the returns to a strategy of taking full advantage of an orientation towards EU policy initiatives and European markets at a time of great change and dynamism in the world economy;

(iii) the sustainability of high performance in the longer term, as well as the pay-off that can come from integrating all the different strands of policy making within a coherent national strategy.

The first of these issues might appear to be of limited interest to Scottish policy makers, but it serves to highlight the importance of having an appropriate strategic policy framework. The other two are as important to Scotland as they are to Ireland.

IRELAND'S CONVERGENCE: WHY IT WAS NECESSARY, HOW IT WAS DONE?

Although the flashy performance of Ireland over the past decade attracts most attention, the origins of its successful convergence lie in the 1960s. The rapid recovery and growth of the main economies of Western Europe, after an initial period of post-war reconstruction, had cruelly exposed the stagnation of the Irish economy. Policy thinking until the early 1960s had been dominated by a decision taken in the 1930s to attempt to build an Irish industrial base behind high tariff barriers. Recall that the partition of the island in 1922 had split off the only heavily industrialized region, centred on Belfast, leaving the then Free State with the very modest remainder. The simple, unqualified and dogged embrace of protection by Irish policy makers appeared to offer exactly what the country needed at that time, and was in tune with an unfolding political and economic drama being played out in the rest of the world as it lurched towards war.

In April 1933, at a lecture in Dublin, John Maynard Keynes commented favourably on the Irish switch to protection, declaring that 'Ideas, knowledge, science, hospitality, travel—these are the things which should by their nature be international. But let goods be homespun whenever it is reasonably and conveniently possible, and, above all, let finance be primarily national' (Keynes 1933). He concluded: 'If I were an Irishman, I should find much to attract me in the economic outlook of your present government towards greater self-sufficiency'.

What is seldom quoted is what immediately followed, and heavily qualified, these remarks.

> But as a practical man and as one who considers poverty and insecurity to be great evils, I should wish to be first satisfied on (some) matters. … I should ask if Ireland is a large enough unit geographically, with sufficiently diversified natural resources, for more than a very modest measure of national self-sufficiency to be feasible without a disastrous reduction in a standard of life which is already none too high'.

Ignoring Keynes's caveats, inward-looking import substitution policies were pursued into the post-war period, and continued until the late 1950s, with disastrous consequences. In the absence of a competitive and export-oriented industrial sector, there was very little that could have accelerated an economic decoupling from the UK, and the consequences followed inexorably. In the words of the Norwegian sociologist, Lars Mjøset (1992): 'Ireland became a free rider on Britain's decline, while Austria and Switzerland were free riders on Germany's economic miracle'.

The 1950s in Ireland were disrupted by a series of serious balance-of-payments crises because of the fundamental lack of competitiveness of the manufacturing sector. This was exactly what Keynes had warned about back in 1933. Ireland was simply too small to continue as an inefficient producer of goods where it had no comparative advantage.

The policy changes that evolved during the crisis-wracked 1950s were consolidated in 1958 in a seminal report, *Economic Development* and codified in a government White Paper, *First Programme for Economic Expansion* (Pr. 4803, The Stationery Office, Dublin, 1958). With the benefit of hindsight, we can recognize this period as a transition between old and new perspectives, and not a whole-hearted embrace of a modern view of the economy. For example, the zero rate of corporation profits tax, combined with the liberalization of trade and foreign investment as well as the freedom to repatriate profits, were to become crucial factors in a process that would inexorably lead to the decline of much of the inefficient indigenous manufacturing sector and the rise and eventual dominance of a new foreign-owned sector. Yet the corporation tax initiative lay buried in an appendix of *Economic Development* and was not even mentioned in the main text, which was mainly concerned with proposals concerning agriculture and the agri-food sector.

We also now understand better that, when a mainly agricultural country attempts to modernize, the primary requirement is for the farming sector to shrink as a proportion of the overall economy, and for the manufacturing sector (and elements of services) to expand and develop in a way that drives export growth through improvements in cost competitiveness. Given Ireland's dismal record of native entrepreneurship in the post-war period, this involved attracting direct investment from America. Yet the vision of *Economic Development* was mainly agriculture-led export growth, with a continuing mainly indigenous manufacturing base. The official aim was to emulate Denmark. In fact, 30 years later we had become a bit like Massachusetts! While the official rhetoric stressed continuity with the agricultural past, the newly created state development agency (the Industrial Development Authority, or IDA) buzzed with excitement at the potential offered by the new policy regime (Mac Sharry and White 2000).

The policy changes introduced in the 1950s were a mix of a commitment to trade liberalization, a range of direct and indirect grant aid to private firms, and the incentive of zero corporation profits tax on exports. Luckily, this policy mix was precisely what was needed to ride the coming tidal wave of American foreign direct investment, in contrast to the declared aim of reviving inefficient domestic industry on the back of an expanding indigenous agri-industrial base. The policy thrust was uniquely appropriate to Ireland's development challenge, but the outcome eventually produced by these policies turned out to be very different from what was anticipated. This provides a nice illustration of the distinction between the factors that influence the design of policy and how the business community actually exploits the new freedoms.

The strong web of dependency between Ireland and the UK that had endured relatively unchanged from independence until the late 1950s only began to weaken after the shift to foreign direct investment and export-led growth. Starting from a

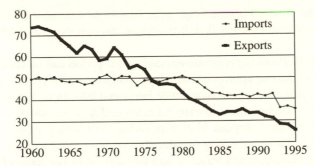

Figure 9.2. Irish trade with the UK: export and import percentage shares 1960–95.

point in the 1950s when about 90% of Irish exports still went to the UK, the share declined steadily thereafter, and stabilized at about 20% by the mid 1990s (see Figure 9.2).[4]

The opening of the economy and the removal of tariff barriers were necessary policy kick-start. Free trade with the UK happened in the mid 1960s. Free trade with Europe came later when Ireland joined the then EEC in 1973. Irish economic policy making since the late 1950s has always emphasized the need to face the consequences of extreme openness, to encourage export-orientation towards fast-growing markets and products, and to be aligned with all European initiatives. Thus, we joined the European Monetary System in 1979, breaking a long link with sterling and its deep economic and psychological dependency. We embraced the Single Market of 1992, the Social Chapter of the Maastricht Treaty, and most recently, Economic and Monetary Union from January 1999. The enthusiastic embrace of openness has provided the enduring strategic backbone of our economic planning since the 1950s.

Of course, the Scottish economy is also as open as the Irish, measured in terms of the ratio of exports to GDP (Fraser of Allander Institute 2001). But almost half of these 'exports' are external sales to the rest of the UK. In this sense the rest of the EU market is simply not as important as it is to Ireland. Combined with the pervasive 'eurosceptic' views of many UK policy makers, it is easy to see why Europe and EU initiatives are likely to play a weaker role in the UK regions.

An attractive corporation tax rate and the absence of tariffs were only a start, and would not in themselves have made Ireland a major host for high-quality foreign direct investment. Other factors came together to reinforce Ireland's eventual economic convergence and interacted to create a virtuous circle of superior performance. Educational standards in the Irish work force had lagged behind the world. Policies were urgently needed to bring about a steady build-up of the quality, quantity and relevance of education and training, and farseeing educational reforms were

---

[4]Figure 9.2 also neatly illustrates the fact that the Irish share of imports from the UK declined only marginally over the 35 years between 1960 and 1995. Over their history, the Irish had developed a strong taste for British goods that only the recent strength of sterling against the euro has eroded. Exports, on the other hand, were to be an engine of convergence, and diversification beyond the UK market was essential.

initiated in the 1960s. These reforms were later to be extended by the emphasis given to scientific and technical skill formation through the use of EU Structural Funds from the late 1980s.[5]

The Irish policy-making environment during this period can be characterized as having shifted from one appropriate to a dependent state on the economic periphery of the UK to that of a region more fully integrated into an encompassing European economy. Foreign direct investment renovated and boosted Irish productive capacity. The Single European Market provided the primary source of demand. All that remained was for a long overdue 'big push' on improvement in physical infrastructure, education and training, and this arrived in the form of a dramatic innovation in regional policy at the EU level, with the advent of Structural Fund aid from the late 1980s.

It is clear that there were some special circumstances surrounding the Irish switch to trade liberalization and active encouragement of inward investment. First, the manifest failure of the previous protectionist policies had been so obvious that no political party or domestic lobby favoured their retention. Second, the range of abilities and expertise available within the Irish public sector was considerable, but there was a willingness to learn from European experiences, in particular, the indicative planning experiences of France (Chubb and Lynch 1969). Third, the completion of European reconstruction, and the growth in importance of the EEC, provided the opportunity to capture some of the rapidly expanding flow of American investment into Western Europe. Fourth, rapid advances in technology and declining transport and communications costs during the 1960s facilitated the process of foreign investment by multinational corporations, which flourished spectacularly from the late 1980s.

Why is the example of the Irish policy inflection point of the early 1960s relevant to discussions today? In the confusion of daily political life, one can live with a certain lack of coordination; one can switch direction many times and experiment; one can be inconsistent. Tactical policy mistakes and errors can usually be detected before too much damage is done, and revised policies implemented in a learning game of trial and error. However, this is only the case when the strategic thrust of policy has been set correctly. Getting the medium-term strategy right is vital mainly because change is very difficult and errors are very costly, and sometimes terminal. Could the paradox be that the extreme peripherality and vulnerability of the Irish economy forced its policy makers to become more thoroughly international in their outlook, while Scotland, a region with an enviable record of post-war modernization and success by comparison, had to change less and was less aware of shifting global forces?

---

[5]A Polish journalist recently asked me to explain how the Irish were so prescient as to prioritize investment in human capital over all other investments in the first two EU Structural Fund programmes during the Celtic Tiger years, 1989–1999. None of the other recipient states or regions had done so, preferring to focus on physical infrastructure. I could only reply that education and skill formation had been strategically prioritized as far back as the 1960s. It would have been simply inconceivable *not* to have prioritized human capital in the Structural Fund programme.

COHESION FOR ALL: THE EU TAKES ACTION

The desire for equitable development is expressed in the Treaty of Rome, but prior to the late 1980s the EU budget was largely dominated by the need to finance the Common Agriculture Policy (CAP). The redistribution of the EU budget to reform and expand EU regional aid policy into a sophisticated system of National Development Plans was driven by two main factors.[6] First, the progressive enlargement of the EU after its foundation in 1956 brought about an ever-increasing degree of socioeconomic heterogeneity with the accession of Ireland (1973), Greece (1982), Portugal and Spain (1986). In addition to the process of enlargement, the parallel evolution from a common market into a more integrated economic union obliged EU policy makers to aid the weaker states and regions to meet the competitive challenges of the Single Market and Economic and Monetary Union.

While all nation states had previously operated internal regional policies, what was different about the new EU regional initiatives was that very significant financial aid was made available by the wealthier member states (including the UK) to co-finance national and regional policy initiatives in a limited number of the poorer member states and regions. After 1989 there was a major shift of resources from the CAP to regional development aid directed at a limited number of countries, while remaining within a budgetary envelope of about 1.25% of EU GDP.

In Scotland (as well as in Northern Ireland), experience of EU regional aid has been as a rather minor addition to the much larger financial transfers that take place between the regions of the UK. For example, the EU contribution to the Highlands and Islands Structural Funds programme for the period 1994–99 was only 293 million euro, and total expenditure (EU, local public and private) was 696 million euro (ECOTEC 2003). It has even been claimed that

> The Structural Funds, often regarded as a means of regional emancipation, in fact have the opposite effect. Since the UK does not recognise additionality at the territorial level, the effect of structural fund designation is to earmark a part of the block grant deemed to represent the European contribution and oblige the devolved administrations to allocate another tranche as 'matching funds'. These moneys are then ring fenced and unavailable for allocation to other priorities.
>
> (Keating 2001)

Ireland, together with Greece and Portugal, being considerably less developed than Scotland, obtained a much higher level of EU co-finance. The magnitude of the financial aid, combined with the requirement to take a medium-term strategic approach to public investment planning, brought about a sea-change in the way the Irish public sector approached this crucial aspect of development.

What was special about the Structural Fund policies was their ambition to implement policies whose explicit aim was to transform the underlying structure of the beneficiary economies. Policies moved far beyond a conventional, demand-side,

---

[6]For simplicity, we will henceforth refer (somewhat inaccurately) to EU regional aid as 'Structural Funds'.

Table 9.1. Main economic categories of Irish structural funds (percentage shares of total).

Economic category	CSF 1989–93	CSF 1994–99	CSF 2000–06
Aid to productive sector	56.0	47.0	16.0
Human resources	25.0	32.0	36.0
Physical infrastructure	19.0	21.0	48.0

cyclical stabilization role of public expenditure, and were directed at the promotion of structural change, the acceleration of medium-term growth and the eventual achievement of real convergence mainly through efficiency or supply-side improvements.

EU financial aid required explicit multi-year investment programmes. A more strategic approach to planning public investment could be taken, allowing a break with annual capital budgeting in the Irish case.

Recent advances in the study of economic geography imply that the conditions required for automatic convergence to take place do not often hold in practice (Krugman 1995; Fujita et al. 1999). Policy has come to focus on the importance of such factors as the initial level of regional physical infrastructure, local levels of human capital, or on the fact that regions that start off at a structural disadvantage may never converge in any reasonable time period. Research has even suggested that the removal of barriers to trade and factor movements may lead to a relative deterioration rather than an improvement for some regions.

The EU-inspired Structural Funds came to dominate Irish policy making during the 1990s, and had three main priority areas of investment. Direct support for productive investment improved the environment for enterprises. Infrastructure expenditure offset structural and geographical disadvantages. Spending on human resources augmented human capital. The Structural Funds have influenced the evolution of the Irish economy over the past 15 years while the evolution of the economy in turn influenced the redesign of successive programmes. Table 9.1 shows the percentage shares of each of the three main categories of public investment, for each of the three cycles of Irish Structural Funds that have operated since 1989.

The first programme focused heavily on direct aid to the productive sectors, with a strong emphasis on human resources, and a substantial programme of investment in physical infrastructure. It was designed at a time when the economy had not fully emerged from the crisis of the 1980s, and direct aid appeared to offer the fastest and best immediate return. By the time of the second Structural Fund programme, the increased emphasis on human resources (up from 25 to 32%) reflected concerns about the continuing high level of unemployment, and had a strong 'equity' element that complemented the earlier 'efficiency' element. The third programme was designed at a time when the convergence of the Irish economy was apparent. By the late 1990s Ireland had moved to what was effectively full employment, and major infrastructural deficits had been exposed by the rapid growth in the volume of traffic on the congested road systems both in the major cities, and connecting these cities. In order to address these bottlenecks, there was a major shift to infrastructure invest-

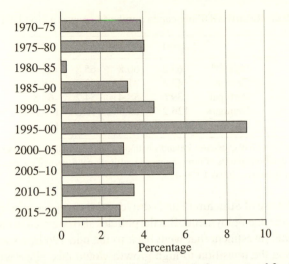

Figure 9.3. Irish GDP growth, before and after structural funds (including forecasts). *Source:* Bergin et al. (2003).

ment, the share going to human resources also increased, with a focus on upgrading skills, and there was a reduction in direct aid to the now-booming productive sectors.

Not all the step-change in economic performance (Figure 9.3) can be assigned to the Structural Fund interventions. In fact, their impact in isolation is relatively modest, but when added to the impact of the Single Market, foreign direct investment and fiscal reforms, the effects are much larger (ESRI 1997). Analysis suggests that a ranking in terms of effectiveness is topped by Ireland, followed by Portugal, Spain, and with the smallest impacts on Greece (ESRI 2002). In the EU 'macro' regions (the Italian *Mezzogiorno*, Northern Ireland and East Germany), the Structural Funds appear to have had only modest impacts. It has been suggested that the effectiveness of Structural Funds depends on 'conditioning' variables, and the most important of these is economic openness (Ederveen et al. 2002). The Irish economy is the most open in the EU, measured by the ratio of exports to GDP. The Scottish economy is as open as that of Ireland, but the UK effect dominates. Portugal is also quite open, relative to its size. Spain is less open, but Greece is the least so.

After almost a decade and a half of Structural Funds and the Single Market, how have the so-called 'cohesion' countries performed? Table 9.2[7] shows the convergence experience of three of these countries, with the UK and Denmark as additional benchmarks.

In the context of a draconian fiscal restructuring in the late 1980s which provided the basis for nominal convergence (in terms of inflation, interest rates, borrowing, etc.), the combination of adaptation to the competitive rigors of the Single Market

---

[7]Scotland's performance on this uniform EU basis is not available. But the UK Regional Accounts show that its GDP per head tracks at about 95% of the UK average, and the UK itself is just above the average of EU GDP per head. Since there are unlikely to be differences in purchasing power parity between the British regions (i.e. differences in regional price levels), this is probably a good measure of Scottish performance on the EU basis.

Table 9.2. Relative GDP per capita purchasing power parity: EU15 = 100.

	1960	1973	1986	2003
Ireland[a]	63.2	60.8	65.8	122.4
Greece	43.8	71.1	62.9	68.4
Portugal	39.6	58.4	54.2	68.8
Denmark	126.2	120.9	117.8	113.8
UK	123.3	104.2	101.1	104.4

[a]It should be noted that GDP overstates Ireland's national income (or GNP) by about 15%, due to large-scale outflows of corporate profits of foreign-owned multinational firms that operate in Ireland. *Source: European Economy* (2003) 4:120–121.

and the efficient use of Structural Funds drove real convergence (in terms of growth, income levels and unemployment). But the policies also operated in the wider context of human capital investment that went back to the mid 1960s, a social partnership that ensured that the transition to high growth would take place with harmonious industrial relations, and a determination to move towards deeper monetary union in Europe. This distinguished Ireland from, say, Greece, which faced a broadly similar convergence challenge, but which was very late in embracing internationalization.

Looking at the way poorer countries and regions in the EU can seek to accelerate their growth rate in order to catch up, the Irish experience suggests a process involving interlocking beneficial externalities:

(i) There was an initial clustering of similar industries, kick-started in Ireland early in the 1960s by incentives based mainly on very low rates of corporate taxation, and a range of other attractive incentives towards investment and training. Two such clusters grew strongly in the 1980s: pharmaceuticals and computer equipment. Although mainly foreign-owned, local suppliers of specialized inputs grew as well.

(ii) These clusters generated a Marshallian local labour market for skilled workers which further facilitated growth. The early focus on human capital during the 1960s and 1970s was enhanced during the 1990s. Remember that most children in the 1950s and 1960s were the first generation to grow up in an urban environment. Education in traditional 'grammar' schools was the norm, since the apprentice training schemes typical in UK's industrial cities were non-existent. Farmers' children tend to have a more utilitarian attitude to education and training, particularly when the private returns to technical and business skills are high.

(iii) Spillovers of information and skills from the high-technology clusters further encouraged growth in high-technology areas and provided the basis for additional clustering effects, often in traditional areas that could benefit from new technologies in their supply chains (e.g. food processing, music and films, high fashion clothing, etc.). This made it important to facilitate internal transport and communications, and the improvements in physical infrastructure supported by the Structural Funds became crucial.

(iv) Finally, the efficiency externalities operated against the background of a consensual social partnership, put in place to ensure that there were as few losers as possible in the fiscal and wider economic restructuring required to drive a virtuous circle. The result was that growth was less likely to be choked off by industrial unrest.

Thus, openness to the full rigors of competition in the international marketplace was a necessary condition for Irish economic success, but was not sufficient. Nor did the availability of EU development aid guarantee rapid convergence, as the comparison of Ireland with Greece illustrates. The barriers to faster growth needed to be correctly identified, a broad growth-promoting policy environment had to be put in place, and the specific Structural Fund public investment policies had to be appropriate, efficient and effective.

The sheer complexity of the convergence challenge meant that in small peripheral countries like Ireland, it became important to develop and articulate a culture of excellence in economic and business analysis so that realistic policies could be identified which would command broad agreement among the Social Partners. Regional policy *within* EU member states, on the other hand, often tends to be palliative, in the sense that it attempts to make the regional disparities easier to endure rather than making any serious attempt to eliminate them. The main policy instrument used is income support transfers from richer to poorer regions, a process that does not exist to anything like the same extent between richer and poorer countries of the EU. It appears to be politically difficult to design regional policies that introduce fundamental differences between regions of a nation state other than in terms of the level of income redistribution. But if the Scottish economy is to be renewed in Krugman's 'second wind', big innovations are precisely what are needed (see Chapter 2).

STAYING AHEAD: TOUGHER THAN CONVERGENCE?

Today on the global economic map, the lines that matter are those defining 'natural' economic zones, which can be regions or states. With falling transportation and telecommunication costs, economies have become increasingly interdependent, and

> The real economic challenge… [of the nation or region]… is to increase
> the potential value of what its citizens can add to the global economy,
> by enhancing their skills and capacities and by improving their means
> of linking those skills and capacities to the world market.
>
> (Reich 1993)

This process of global competition is organized mainly by multinational firms and not by governments. Production tends to be modularized, with individual modules spread across the globe so as to exploit the comparative advantages of different regions. Hence, individual small nations and regions have less power now to influence their destinies, other than by refocusing their economic policies on location factors, especially those which are relatively immobile between regions: the quality of labour, infrastructure and economic governance, and the efficient functioning of labour markets.

Thus far we have been using a mainly economic framework of analysis. But there are severe limitations to a purely economic perspective on transformation and renewal. In the case of a UK region like Scotland, one constraint on its freedom of action is the rather limited range of significant policy instruments that it can use, since Scotland is integrated into the UK fiscal and monetary union. But does a small state like Ireland, a member of the European Monetary Union, really possess many policy options that would be denied to Scotland? A low rate of corporation tax? This was essentially a one-off Irish initiative taken almost half a century ago, at a time when the economy was one large green field, and the population was emigrating in droves. The tax changes since then have been modest, and largely dictated by EU law.

Indeed, the low rate of corporation tax condemned the long-suffering Irish taxpayer to decades of penal rates of direct and indirect taxation. The personal choice was that you could have a job in Ireland with a foreign-owned multinational (rather than in London, Manchester, Glasgow or Boston), but you paid for it by high personal taxes. Is there much else that an Irish government can do in the economic sphere that could not also be done by a Scottish government today, without necessarily incurring the wrath of the UK Treasury? In a recent report of the Scottish Executive, attempts were made to achieve lower Scottish tax rates by persuading the UK government to reduce UK tax rates. These proposals were slapped down by the Treasury in a peremptory fashion (Scottish Executive 2003).

Rather than searching for cleverer fiscal tricks, I believe that a better way ahead for Scotland is to accept the constraints of being in the UK fiscal union, and to broaden the debate beyond the strictly economic issues. Economic policy research tends to be directed at issues and challenges that arise at the level of regions, nations or even groupings of nations such as the EU. Business policy research, on the other hand, is focused on the performance of individual firms or groups of firms, and Michael Porter has stressed that it is more helpful to consider firms as competing in *industries*, not in *nations* (Porter 1990). This simple insight lies at the heart of the differences between the mainly regional/national-based perspective of economic researchers, and the mainly firm-based perspective of business researchers, particularly in matters concerning the design and execution of industrial strategy. This is particularly relevant in small countries and regions, where the economic research agenda is often heavily influenced and distorted by trends in international monetary and macro economics, and where regional problems, including industrial strategy, tend to be neglected. For example, the experience of the Scottish Economic Policy Network (Scotecon) over the past few years suggests that it may be difficult to persuade Scottish economists to direct their research towards tackling important regional problems. The UK-wide Research Assessment Exercise (RAE) also tends to crowd out local topics in favour of more 'publishable' national topics.

One might characterize a key challenge of industrial policy making in any small nation or region as that of blending the techniques and insights of the predominantly *economic* analysis of what one might call the 'outer' business environment with those of the *business* analysis of the 'middle' ground of strategy. These two areas are often studied in isolation from each other by non-overlapping groups of researchers.

Seldom are the two different perspectives looked at as being entirely complementary. Seldom are they both invoked to guide policy makers.

At the level of the individual firm or corporation, strategy is usually formulated in a context where government policies are largely exogenous, and firms address the challenges of assessing the business portfolio and identifying strategic goals. The crucial role of management is to formulate a corporate strategy aligned with the nation's or region's wealth-building strategy. So this issue is usually examined largely from the point of view of domestic or of regional companies adjusting to national strategy.

In Ireland, however, causality as often as not runs in the opposite direction. In other words, the Irish industrial development agency—the IDA—constantly scans the world for inward investment in high-technology sectors, even when the domestic environment is not sufficiently attractive to persuade leading-edge firms to locate in Ireland. But information on firms' expressed needs are fed back to the Irish government by the IDA, and major policy changes can be executed quite rapidly. A case of information feedback was the transformation of the Irish university system in the mid 1970s, when massive resources were put into the enhancement of electronic engineering and chemistry to create a skilled labour force for potential inward investors (Mac Sharry and White 2000). A more recent example was the provision of generous resources to the university system to fund basic research in the areas of electronics and biotechnology, when a lack of such skills was identified as a potential bottleneck to future investment.

Thus the national wealth creation strategy in Ireland often adapts to the requirements of firms in the global corporate environment, and not the other way around. The strategic challenges facing small open economies like Ireland and also Scotland are thus very different from those facing large developed nations like the US, Japan, Germany, France and the UK. A question that one might ask is whether Scottish Enterprise has quite so close and symbiotic a relationship with the highest policy-making levels in the Scottish government as the IDA has had with Irish policy making. How quickly can the Scottish administration develop the cross-economy networking skills that were less in demand before devolution but will be crucial in future?

The success of Irish industrial strategy was due in large part to the innovative and flexible behaviour of government policy makers as well as to the expertise and dynamism of the state's development agency (the IDA). However, policy makers are usually most effective when they are swimming with the tide of events rather than against it. Irish policy making is, to a considerable extent, pragmatic and opportunistic. But it is characterized by a form of pragmatism that appears to be singularly in tune with the best thinking on international industrial policy frameworks. The strategy is not so much 'picking winners' as 'picking winning environments'. A winning environment is essentially a public good, and is a legitimate target of public policy.

Sophisticated policy making requires sophisticated policy makers. I find it difficult to believe there is much difference in the level of administrative and technical competence as between Scotland and Ireland. Indeed, given the greater number, and world-class nature of Scottish universities, one might expect a higher level of expertise in Scotland. But Brussels is much further away from Dublin than London is from Edinburgh: perhaps what Irish policy makers lack in terms of narrow administrative and technical expertise they more than compensate for in terms of a willingness to test the extent of their limited autonomy and experiment with novel solutions to apparently intractable problems. If one plays broadly according to the international rules, Brussels seldom interferes. But more pervasive checks on policy innovation in Scotland may extend beyond Whitehall's blocking role. For example, Whitehall could not prevent the evolution of an innovative form of Social Partnership in Scotland. But local trade unions, employers' organizations and politicians could and possibly would.

Luck also plays a large part in industrial strategy. The expected external conditions needed to support success do not always conveniently arrive, and their absence may frustrate otherwise admirable policy initiatives. Nor is the true significance of the internal elements of a strategy always fully understood even by its own designers (as discussed above). But chance is best handled within well-thought-out frameworks which take full account of the nature of the external environment (opportunities and threats) as well as realistic views of domestic capabilities (strengths and weaknesses). Industrial policy frameworks such as those of Raymond Vernon, Michael Porter and Michael Best do not provide all the answers.[8] But they can help policy makers in both the public and private sectors to bring focus and synergy to the disparate policies that make up broad industrial strategy in small open economies like Scotland and Ireland.

At the risk of oversimplification, the recent industrial performance in Ireland shows that the intelligent combination of economic policy and business strategy has generated huge synergies in terms of rapid national growth and convergence. Economic policy needs to exploit opportunities and remedy weaknesses shown up by frameworks such as Porter's and Best's. Ireland was lucky in that it could build a growth and convergence strategy around its Structural Fund programmes, and articulate them in National Development Plans. Perhaps in Scotland circumstances were never quite so dreadful as to precipitate a dramatic sea-change in the direction of policy. Could it be that an unwritten and perhaps subliminal condition of funding the Scottish public sector through a Barnett-type tax-sharing formula (i.e. fair shares for all), is Scotland is not meant to be too innovative about the way it spends the money?

CHARACTERISTICS OF GOOD REGIONAL GOVERNANCE

Perhaps the most striking aspect of the Irish development experience is that it has assigned such an important role to the public sector in an era when the dead hand of government interference is almost universally castigated, at least in the Anglo-American world. Yet the role of government as 'strategic organizer' in a global economy driven by market forces is very different from the previous role of Communist governments as 'central planners'. Government as strategic organizer carries

---

[8]For policy frameworks, see Vernon (1979), Porter (1990) and Best (2001). For a description of how the three business strategy frameworks can be used to illuminate Ireland's experience, see Bradley (2002).

out its functions in *collaboration* with private businesses and not as a *substitute* for the market economy. An Irish government must decide its own strategic policy priorities, since there is nobody else waiting to carry out the task. The Scottish situation is made more complicated by the division of responsibilities between London and Edinburgh. What are the major strategic tasks that any Scottish government needs to tackle? There are four key elements:

(a) *Assessing Strengths and Weaknesses*

The state must play a crucial role in shaping and reshaping the conditions within which the market operates, through providing public goods and promoting research, analysis and dialogue. In Ireland this is perhaps easier to implement politically than in Scotland, since Irish politics is only weakly differentiated on a left–right axis. Irish political parties (with the exception of Sinn Féin) tend to present themselves as national managers of a mainstream globalized economy. The great nationalist debates are now over, and there never was much of an ideological debate. There is a broad understanding of the strategic needs of the economy, and governments are judged on how well they appear to be implementing the agreed strategy.

Drawing on a wide range of local policy research, it is clearly understood in Ireland that concepts of national competitiveness need to embrace local inputs of infrastructure, skills and entrepreneurship, and that many of the foreign firms that came in the 1980s will move offshore to lower-cost locations. Successful Irish-owned firms are themselves becoming international investors as the Irish business environment continues to restructure in the global economy. Thus, EU enlargement is seen both as an opportunity (new markets for Irish firms) and a threat (other small states are rapidly upgrading their infrastructure and human resources).

Irish economic policy researchers tend to regard the local economy, the global economy, and the relationship between the two, as defining the scope of their work. Universities and research institutes play a vital role in this process, both with EU academic collaborators and in association with the local business community. Academic economists quickly learned to market their work for international publication in terms of the analysis of a small, open economy (which is of universal interest), rather than in terms of Ireland (which is not). My experience of Scotland suggests that the integration of the Scottish university system in the UK-wide RAE may induce a reluctance to explore Scotland's strategic challenges through policy research, because it is thought to be of lesser status or of limited interest to other European regional economists. This needs to change radically if Scottish administrations are to build on the possibilities of devolved power.

(b) *Recognizing Trade-offs between Policy Options and Building Coalitions for Action*

The dilemmas to be faced here are complex, and involve issues such as efficiency (or growth) versus equity (or redistribution); sectoral diversification versus sectoral concentration; the optimal pace of change and renewal (shock versus gradualism);

inward investment versus domestic 'bootstrapping', and so on. Policy frameworks must be put in place to support these market decisions. Political decisions are not always to the liking of economists, but seldom entirely ignore the implications of solid research. Good research makes it harder for policy makers to get away with bad decisions.

For example, during the 1960s there was a major public debate in Ireland about whether inward investment ought to be concentrated into a few large cities, with a view to reaping agglomeration economies. But the efficiency benefits of growth poles were rejected at that time in favour of greater spatial equity (Bradley 1996). More recently, the rise of urban agglomerations about Dublin and Cork has revived this debate, as it becomes obvious that certain sectors (computers and software in Dublin and pharmaceuticals in Cork) only thrive in large urban areas. Spatial policies are central to economic success, but are the most difficult to implement in practice.

(c) *Building a Healthy Business–Government Relationship*

When this relationship is with locally owned businesses, political tensions can easily arise. But in the case of Ireland, the crucial internal relationships are between government and the social partners (i.e. trades unions and employers' organizations) on the one hand, and with foreign multinational firms, on the other. The Irish and Scottish experience shows that this relationship can be mutually beneficial and these firms have a long record of providing long-term, secure and well-paid employment. In exchange, they expect that their requirements will be taken seriously, and lines of communication will work efficiently. In Ireland, the internal Social Partnership underpins the efficiency of the economy, mainly by ensuring that conflicts are discussed and resolved (where possible) in a context where the costs of failure are widely understood.

There is a huge pay-off to such formalized relationships in terms of disseminating information throughout the economy. Students have a better understanding of where the job opportunities might be, and select careers accordingly. Educators find it easier to design relevant courses. Researchers have a ready audience for their output, and get better feedback. Employers have better information to feed into their business planning. Foreign investors become more familiar with how the region functions, and can take very long-term decisions in a more predictable environment. Policy makers, who are most in need of guidance, tend to make more sensible decisions. In a Smithian way, all these actors pursue their own self-interest, but somehow the outcome seems to be better than if relationships are adversarial and knowledge is hoarded or absent.

(d) *Enhancing Government–Government Cooperation*

Government–government cooperation in Ireland takes place almost entirely under the auspices of the EU, where Irish government ministers and civil servants negotiate with other member states, and are part of external EU negotiations where their domestic interests are affected. With the exception of Structural Funds (which are coming to an end in Ireland), and the CAP price supports (which are applied to all EU member states), the Irish relationship with Brussels deals more about policy than directly about money. Scottish policy makers have to deal with London in a very different context: one where major decisions on fiscal matters are decided over their heads. But the price for loss of fiscal autonomy is a guaranteed share-out of UK tax revenues. No such arrangement exists at the EU level.

As I review the performance of successive Irish governments, these are the four key strategic issues I monitor. We in Ireland are very conscious that the European Union has been enlarged by 10 new states, many of which have made rapid and successful transitions to liberal policy regimes, and will soon become remarkably attractive alternative locations for inward investment. The quality of Irish strategic thinking as much as the efficiency of its businesses will be what determines future performance.

How is strategic thinking likely to evolve in Scotland? Will it continue to focus on its role within an encompassing UK-wide policy context, and try to extract the maximum benefits from this relationship through UK regional policy instruments? I hope that I will not be misunderstood if I call this an 'easy' option, one that is likely to guarantee a performance and a standard of living that is only modestly below that of the UK as a whole. Is that an acceptable goal for Scottish policy makers? Alternatively, will they increasingly exploit existing devolved powers or take on and exploit greater local powers, and use them to diversify within the UK in a wider European context?

If Scotland takes the second, more challenging, option, then there is much detailed work to be done that would be impossible to explore in this chapter. But I conclude by highlighting three themes that will be crucial.

(a) Scottish growth, development and renewal strategies need to be placed at the centre of government activity, and clearly distinguished from the day-to-day activities of social ministries. If this is done, as with the EU-aided National Development Plans and Structural Funds in Ireland, there is a real chance of a step-change in economic performance. But such strategies need to be animated by careful research rather than considered merely as aspects of allocating public expenditure (Burnside and Wakefield 2003).

(b) The apparently high level of educational qualifications in Scotland should not blind policy makers to the necessity of continuing to prioritize human resources in all aspects: education, technical skills, re-integration of the socially excluded, basic business research and training, etc. What matters in today's globalized economy is as much the 'software' of human capital as the hardware of fixed investment. Optimizing this 'software' is probably the single most important act of any modern government.

(c) Strategic regional economic policy design needs to be linked with industrial and service sector strategic policy thinking, and every effort made to ensure

229

that they are mutually reinforcing. Within the EU there are dramatic differences between the approach adopted by the successful small Nordic states (e.g. Finland, Denmark and Sweden), based on building indigenous industrial strengths, and the path taken by Ireland, based mainly on success in attracting high-quality foreign direct investment. Scottish researchers and policy makers need to engage in this European debate, rather than drawing mainly from the narrower UK regional policy agenda.

REFERENCES

Bergin, A., J. Cullen, D. Duffy, J. Fitz Gerald, I. Kearney and D. McCoy. 2003. *Medium-term review: 2003–2010*. Dublin: The Economic and Social Research Institute.

Best, M. 2001. *The new competitive advantage*. Oxford University Press.

Bradley, J. 1996. *An island economy: exploring long-term economic and social consequences of peace and reconciliation in the island of Ireland*. Dublin: Forum for Peace and Reconciliation.

———. 2002. The computer sector in Irish manufacturing: past triumphs, present strains, future challenges. *Journal of the Statistical and Social Inquiry Society of Ireland* 31:25–71.

Burnside, R. and S. Wakefield. 2003. Cross-cutting issues: economic development. SPICe briefing, 03/80, 2 October.

Chubb, B. and P. Lynch (eds). 1969. *Economic development and planning*, vol. 1: *Readings in Irish public administration*. Dublin: The Institute of Public Administration.

ECOTEC. 2003. Ex-post evaluation of the Objective 1 Programme 1994–99: UK member state report. Report submitted to DG Regional Policy, ECOTEC, October.

Ederveen, S., J. Gorter, R. de Mooij and R. Nahuis. 2002. *Funds and games: the economics of European cohesion policy*. The Hague: CPB Netherlands Bureau for Economic Policy Analysis.

ESRI. 1997. *Single Market review 1996: aggregate and regional aspects: the cases of Greece, Ireland, Portugal and Spain*. London: Kogan Page. (In association with the Office for Official Publications of the European Communities, Luxembourg.)

———. 2002. The ex-post evaluation of Objective 1, CSF 1994–1999: states and macro-regions. Report prepared for DG Regional Policy, Brussels.

Fraser of Allander Institute. 2001. Tracking the bigger picture: baselines, milestones and benchmarks for the Scottish economy, 2001. Report produced for the Scottish Enterprise Network by the Fraser of Allander Institute, March.

Fujita, M., P. Krugman and A. Venables. 1999. *The spatial economy: cities, regions, and international trade*. Cambridge, MA: MIT Press.

Keating, M. 2001. Devolution and Public Policy: Divergence or Convergence? Report on a joint IPPR/ESRC Devolution Programme project, Department of Social and Political Sciences, European University Institute, October.

Keynes, J. M. 1933. National self sufficiency. *Studies* 22:177–193

Krugman, P. 1995. *Development, geography, and economic theory*. Cambridge, MA: MIT Press.

———. 1997. Good news from Ireland: a geographical perspective. In *International perspectives on the Irish economy* (ed. A. Gray). Dublin: Indecon Economic Consultants.

Mac Sharry, R. and P. White. 2000. *The making of the Celtic Tiger*. Cork: Mercier Press.

Mjøset, L. 1992. The Irish economy in comparative institutional perspective. Report 93, Dublin: National Economic and Social Council.

Porter, M. 1990. *The competitive advantage of nations*. London: Macmillan.

Reich, R. 1993. *The work of nations: a blueprint for the future*. London: Simon and Schuster.
Scottish Executive. 2003. Update to Scottish Executive response to nurturing wealth creation: a report by the Scottish manufacturing group. Department of Enterprise and Lifelong Learning, November.
Vernon, R. 1979. The product cycle hypothesis in a new international environment. *Oxford Bulletin of Economics and Statistics* 41:255–267.

Conclusions

The contributors to this book between them cover a vast amount of evidence on the Scottish economy, with wide-ranging implications for policy. Clear conclusions emerge. These include general imperatives that should guide policy makers in all small economies committed to improving growth, opportunity and governance; the particular character of Scotland's economic challenges; and, finally, some possible first steps for Scotland.

IMPERATIVES FOR GROWTH IN A SMALL ECONOMY

At James Heckman's seminar in the Allander Series, one enthusiastic participant asked, 'Professor, if we do everything you recommend, how will Scotland be different in five years time?' He paused before replying, 'If Scotland successfully implements the most vital policy—i.e. the best combined pre-5 and parenting programme in the world—then in five years' time what Scotland will have is many better-behaved seven-year-olds!'

Therein lie two profound insights: the really important choices are not necessarily the most obvious ones; and it can take a long time to achieve results. On the first point, only the kind of scrutiny of the evidence detailed in Chapter 6 by Heckman and Masterov would lead to a policy focus on under-fives and the quality of parenting. Armed with such evidence, policy makers need to be willing to educate the public about it and demonstrate its causal links to better policy. Good evidence makes it harder for policy makers to get away with bad decisions. On the second point, a policy focused on the early years exemplifies the different time horizons of professors on the one hand and politicians and public on the other. The latter are unduly short compared with the scale of policy challenges, which might not pay off for a generation. Consequently, the Scots and others need to countenance some short-term sacrifices, risk-taking and slow progress in the service of greater ambitions.

Ten general lessons can be drawn from our contributors (see Table 10.1).

IMPERATIVES FOR GROWTH

The first and most fundamental lesson emerging from this book is that public policy can have an important impact on regional growth rates. But just as markets can fail, so too can policy and policy makers. Successful policies require an understanding of

Table 10.1. Ten general lessons.

1.	Public policies matter for long-term growth.
2.	Growth must be the principal strategic policy priority.
3.	Policy must emphasize the underlying rationale for growth—greater opportunity—to build a coalition of support.
4.	Evidence is essential in order to design better policies and build support for them.
5.	Policies for small economy growth are frequently common to advanced nations.
6.	Openness is key to building capabilities and improving growth.
7.	Setting appropriate incentives is vital.
8.	Competition and contestability are often needed to shape appropriate incentives.
9.	Reforms need to be designed so they can overcome entrenched institutional barriers.
10.	Public sector efficiency matters as much as private-sector efficiency, both in its own right and in order to implement policies effectively.

not only the processes of economic growth but also the need for an effective policy process. Hence the second imperative, that growth cannot simply be yet another policy objective among many competing priorities. As John Bradley highlights in Chapter 9, the facts surrounding any nation's economic performance are rarely disputed; rather, what is contested is the framework of action that guides policy. Get the strategic framework wrong and no amount of hard work can compensate. Get it right and it has the power to energize the entire nation.

The strategic priority given to growth must be tempered by recognition of a third lesson, namely that building a commitment to improved growth rates means demonstrating the link to enhanced opportunity and ensuring effective governance. Making the linkages between improved growth, expanded opportunity and effective governance is a pressing task for public figures, whether leaders in business, politics or society. Interestingly, the consensus among our external contributors was that while Scotland's recent growth performance has been satisfactory by the standards of many other advanced regions and nations, Scotland's record on realizing the opportunities is more worrying, which is the reverse of the assumptions many Scots might have made.

For example, with respect to Scotland's cities Edward Glaeser noted that the one challenge to the Edinburgh–Glasgow corridor becoming a high human capital economy is the legacy of poverty created by the decline of manufacturing. Tackling the poverty is a prerequisite to improving opportunity and also to enhancing growth because, as Glaeser bluntly puts it, the skilled fear living among the poor. The same argument applies to the growing social polarization in motherhood and the impact this has on early life chances, which in turn decisively shape economic opportunities over a lifetime. Moreover, as Nicholas Crafts suggests, on performance and delivery Scotland's public sector falls some way short of international best practice. The

233

fact that contributors diagnosed shortfalls in social and economic opportunity and often ineffective public governance is sobering given Scotland's social democratic political consensus and large public sector. In all small economies, policy makers should repeatedly return to the underlying rationale for seeking faster growth when trying to overcome institutional barriers to change. In the battle for public support for reform, as important as *what* to do to increase growth is *how* to do it (governance) and *why* (opportunity).

Too often the nature and pace of reform is dictated by what is politically feasible—the path of least resistance—rather than what is most important in terms of its potential impact on growth. Crucial to building a momentum for change, particularly in the absence of a crisis, is the role of evidence. Without either a crisis or a powerful evidence base, progress will be slow indeed. As Nicholas Crafts stressed in his chapter, making 'variance visible' matters.

So, a fourth imperative is to create a relevant evidence base and invest it with the authority to shape policy. This is no simple or technical matter. As our contributors have demonstrated, the available evidence is too often patchy and frequently at such a high level of abstraction that the implications for policy are far from clear.[1] This is all the more unsatisfactory when policy makers have inadequate managerial capabilities and/or insufficient resources. Constantly striving for better evidence—based on measuring what consumers, rather than producers, value—can improve the quality of decision-making. However, some existing evidence offers an immediately compelling case for policy reform. For example, Scotland has a fivefold variation in productivity and a long tail of underperforming companies in many sectors, which makes it straightforward to be convincing about the difficulty in creating or maintaining enclaves of high-efficiency activities in a sea of wider inefficiencies, whether public or private.

One important insight that forms the basis of the next, fifth, imperative is that growth policies for advanced regions and small nations differ little. Macroeconomic stability is a prerequisite for growth, although not sufficient. Recent evidence from the OECD[2] demonstrates the importance of sound macroeconomic policies such as a low and stable inflation rate, openness to international trade and a moderate tax burden. Given that context, the policy prescriptions of Paul Krugman in Chapter 2 and William Baumol in Chapter 3 mostly transfer to any small, open, regional economy. Perhaps more surprisingly, the political economy hurdles noted by Edward Glaeser in Chapter 4 and Nicholas Crafts in Chapter 8 are also less contingent on a specific region or nation's history and geography than one might expect. The lessons for Scotland transfer well.

---

[1] Crafts discusses the complexity of evidence with respect to the role of competition in health services. In some circumstances an extension of competition or contestability is appropriate, e.g. for routine procedures, and in other circumstances it is not, e.g. for the management of chronic conditions or emergency care. Similar complexities arise in attempting to stimulate innovation and technology entrepreneurship—what is the right balance between policies that promote international technology transfer and efforts to strengthen the commercialization efforts of domestic institutions through research funding, patent reform, IP regulations and so on?

[2] *Understanding economic growth*, OECD, 2004.

The sixth imperative is that smaller economies, national or regional, must recognize and exploit the consequences of their openness. Relatively small movements of labour or capital—in or out—can have a significant overall economic impact. Hence for small economies relatively small changes in regional attractiveness and amenity can lead to marked shifts in economic performance over time through the attraction of mobile labour and capital. And, in turn, the higher productivity associated with these mobile factors of production can generate important spillover effects. Thus exogenous factors can have a more far-reaching impact in a small and highly open economy than a larger one, where the focus must of necessity be overwhelmingly on domestically generated productivity growth.

Promoting greater openness is a vital ingredient in maximizing the potential for growth in small economies like Scotland. As interregional growth rates are much more sensitive than international growth rates to differences in efficiency, regional policy makers cannot afford to neglect the 'small stuff' that can affect regional competitiveness. This means getting the basics right: communications and transport, schooling and higher education, and attractive general amenities. Embracing openness should strengthen the local culture of entrepreneurship, help retain talent and encourage the 'buzz' associated with a dynamic economy. It also has implications for policy towards innovation, internationally mobile investment and migrant flows. Innovation will continue to be of prime importance for economic growth. The globalization of R&D means a region's capacity to source new technology globally through effective technology transfer will be increasingly important. As William Baumol argues in Chapter 3, this will require any country to ensure that it is a skilled imitator as well as an effective innovator. And this is even more important at the regional level when technology is increasingly sourced globally.

Improving regional competitiveness also requires appropriate incentives across the whole spectrum of economic activity. Without exception the book's contributors underline the crucial role of incentives, our seventh imperative. These include incentives to raise the level of entrepreneurial activity, including minimizing the stigma of failure, as well as to increase innovation, R&D and technology transfer. Even at the level of the national fiscal settlement, incentive structures matter, as Paul Hallwood and Ronald MacDonald demonstrate in Chapter 5. Similarly, extending opportunity requires the right package of incentives to encourage support for childbearing, offering all children the best start in life, and to improve work–life balance.

Getting incentives right may be most difficult in public services, given the extent of adverse incentives arising from principal–agent relationships throughout the public sector. Both target-setting and contestability can counteract the tendency to producer domination. But poorly designed targets can distort behaviour, so policy makers must focus on the value users place on a service.

The effectiveness of incentives is typically enhanced in a competitive market, the eighth imperative. Competition stimulates change and the introduction of new technologies in the private sector. Recent evidence indicates that the utilization of new technologies and investment in IT in particular is positively associated with productivity growth in the US, the UK and Sweden.[3] Managed competition and contestability can also drive change in the public sector, as Chapters 6 (Heckman and Masterov) and 8 (Crafts) emphasize. Competition stimulates innovation, particularly through opportunities for new entrants, although temporary differences in the quality of provision will inevitably arise as the overall quality of service increases. Hence in those areas where the citizen is an informed consumer, the extension of opportunity may be best served by an extension of managed competition within the public sector rather than through the more conventional target-setting approach.

The evidence on how far managed competition improves the quality and productivity of public services is still incomplete, and there are areas such as the provision of emergency services for chronic or complex conditions where it is not appropriate. Nevertheless there is a pressing need for collecting better evidence, rather than sticking with an ideological starting point. The advantages of introducing contestability rather than target-setting typically include the speedier reallocation of production to higher productivity suppliers, increased weight placed on users' needs, better information for public-sector agencies purchasing services, and firmer budget constraints. The degree of contestability in public services in Europe is unrelated to the level of public spending. For example, Sweden, with the highest level of public spending in Europe, has high levels of contestability in schooling, and similar patterns are found elsewhere in Scandinavia.

However, while being open, competitive and setting appropriate incentives are generic essentials for economic success, these forces operate in the context of an economy's specific challenges and capabilities. Our penultimate and ninth policy imperative concerns the role of institutions in the growth process. Pro-growth policies need to overcome the entrenched institutional and political barriers to change. These challenges go a long way towards explaining the disappointing progress across the EU on the Lisbon Agenda for growth and structural reform. There is a striking degree of expert agreement about the right policies, but implementation has typically proved difficult for exactly these contextual reasons. This is not a new problem— but perhaps exacerbated by the intangible nature of the type of investments now required. For example, in the past new infrastructure investment was a visible gain with few losers, while the gains from advancing contestability in public services are less visible and often encounter significant producer resistance. So there are issues about how the most important reforms can command public support. The creation of a better evidence base for policy is an important contribution to overcoming institutional barriers—but, for exactly that reason, the accumulation and interpretation of evidence can be both controversial and contested. Hence it is important to ensure evidence is in the public domain, forming a narrative well-articulated by the government and important interest groups.

The final lesson, therefore, involves recognition of the potentially limiting and liberating role of the public sector in the small economy growth process. There is a need to focus on the efficiency of public services, not only in order to enhance the well-being of citizens, but also as a condition for improved growth. Many of

---

[3] *Understanding economic growth*, OECD 2004, pp. 23–27.

the chapters emphasize the key role of the public sector, particularly in European economies where the state is typically responsible for spending approaching 50% of GDP. In these advanced and relatively high-cost locations, the drag-anchor of widespread public-sector inefficiencies cannot easily be dismissed. Producer dominance in the public sector not only hinders efficiency or quality gains in public services themselves but can also act as an impediment to private sector initiative. Conventional consultations on policies typically rely on existing interest groups, typically themselves established producer interests. Not surprisingly, the outcome often avoids the tough decisions which might be right from a consumer or productivity perspective. Hence Scotland and other small economies need to consider how to develop an institutional architecture committed to advancing effective reform, and willing to champion policies characterized by more vigorous competition and able to assess the value of any service to the consumer.

This list, challenging enough, omits some important policy concerns. These include environmental sustainability, trends in the distribution of income and inequality, the burgeoning debate about quality of life and well-being in advanced economies, the nature of work, and the future of pensions in an ageing society. All are vital issues for policy makers, but lie beyond the scope of this book. Our emphasis, and these ten lessons drawn from the earlier chapters, focus on economic growth.

THE SCOTTISH GROWTH CHALLENGE

Where should Scottish policy makers begin, in the light of these general conclusions? As several of our contributors pointed out, Scotland's economic performance in terms of both absolute and per capita GDP growth is not disastrous by international standards. Despite recent reverses, Scotland did appear to enjoy a 'second wind' from the 1960s, which saw GDP per capita rise to parity with the UK. However, the attraction of inward investment, and the rapid growth of domestic financial services led by banking, does not appear to have produced important productivity spillovers, or stimulated enterprise and innovation across the wider economy. As Chapter 1 showed, Scotland's long-standing productivity weaknesses include relatively low levels and quality of capital investment; a reluctance to innovate; ambivalence towards globalization and widespread suspicion about the benefits of competition. With some notable exceptions, Scottish business is still insufficiently international in its outlook yet Scotland's small domestic market means early internationalization is vital to significant success.

Scottish policy makers need to display a greater awareness that *policies matter* for long-term growth. While growth is accepted as the top *strategic policy priority*, it is not clear that its implications, whether for regulation, planning, infrastructure, education, innovation policy or public services, have been followed up across the whole gamut of Scottish Executive policy.

Both the UK and Scottish governments have been developing an awareness of the need for useful and useable research for some time. There is a now a greater appreciation of the need for an *evidence-based* approach in making policy recommendations and developing policies. But Scotland does in this regard appear to lag the UK.[4] Scottish policy makers need to understand that, without evidence, policy proposals reduce to applied ideology and ultimately prejudice. John Bradley, during his Allander Series lecture, wryly noted that the Scottish Executive would win a beauty competition for the ubiquity of its strategy statements, but these seem to have had limited impact on day-to-day decisions.

In terms of *openness*, Scotland needs to think harder about how to attract, and then retain, both highly mobile labour and high-value mobile investment embodying the latest technology and ideas. Today the single most important ingredient in keeping firms in a region, and attracting new ones, is to make sure that the region has plenty of skilled workers. Scotland currently educates many skilled workers, only to see them leave or face underemployment at home.

The absence of sufficient challenging professional opportunities helps explain the high outward migration of many graduates of Scottish universities, both native and foreign-born. Yet despite the talent drain Scotland's political classes are too willing to ascribe a lack of evidence of skill shortage as a *successful* policy outcome, and are failing to address systematically the underlying reasons for the lack of opportunities available to highly skilled people. Here better evidence can help win the battle for hearts and minds, and shape Scotland's understanding that systemic inefficiencies, no matter how comfortable, bear a cost.

Nevertheless, the emergence of human capital as the key constrained resource also creates opportunities for Scotland. As Edward Glaeser emphasizes, the location choices of highly skilled people are increasingly driving the location of mobile capital—not the other way around, as was typically the case in the past. Hence the quality of life in Scotland's major cities, Glasgow and Edinburgh, is becoming a major determinant of future success.

However, policies to attract mobile labour and capital cannot succeed in isolation. A region's infrastructure such as the transport network, the cost and availability of broadband, or general amenities need to compare well in international terms. And, as noted in Chapter 1, questions have been raised about the quality of Scotland's infrastructure. Chapter 1 also highlighted how foreign direct investment had a beneficial effect on the Scottish economy in the second half of the twentieth century. This success is an example of Paul Krugman's second-wind hypothesis, although the absolute decline in productivity as significant parts of this FDI moved away from Scotland after 2000 indicates that the spillovers were too limited.

Scotland's relatively poor performance in generating or exploiting such spillovers has led policy makers to focus more on attempts to raise the productivity of domestic activities. As William Baumol stresses, domestically focused efforts should con-

---

[4]After the new Labour government came to power in the UK in 1997, it appointed additional special advisers and set up several bodies concerned with the generation of knowledge and ideas for policy— the Performance and Innovation Unit, the Centre for Management and Policy Studies, and the Social Exclusion Unit—and it routinely commissions external experts to examine key policy areas. In addition, private think tanks close to government such as the Institute for Public Policy Research and Demos, prospered (W. Solesbury, *Evidence based policy: whence it came and where it's going*, ESRC UK Centre for Evidence Based Policy and Practice, 2001). These developments have not yet been mirrored in Scotland.

tinue. He suggested policy recommendations to boost generic technology transfer into Scotland: scholarships for Scots to study key subjects abroad; ensuring Scotland's overseas network prioritizes technology-transfer activities and the study of the technology-transfer measures adopted by other governments. Meanwhile, Scotland should not abandon the contest for internationally mobile labour and capital. The recent record in both cases, FDI and net migration flows, indicates that Scotland needs to reconsider both incentives and the priorities of the institutions charged with these tasks.

Finally, in terms of *competition*, we have already highlighted the risks in both public and private sectors of thin, protected markets. Scotland's public sector often relies upon top-down, monopolistic delivery mechanisms for its universally available public services. In these circumstances of a high level of central control or the reliance on centrally set targets, the absence of appropriate published measures of Scottish public-sector productivity is short-sighted. At a minimum there should be the application of cost–benefit analysis to make explicit the opportunity costs of public expenditure and the quantification of marginal benefits.

But in addition to these generic challenges contributors also pointed to *specifically Scottish policy challenges*. In particular, it needs to become much more willing to face up to the consequences of the extreme openness that characterizes today's global economy, especially for small economies. Scotland cannot boast the internationally experienced workforce of nations such as Ireland, where 40% of professional and managerial workers have worked abroad.[5] And, its population is very homogeneous by Western European standards. Put bluntly, despite the fact that global migrant and investment flows are increasing elsewhere, immigrants within Europe and in the UK have been saying no to Scotland.

Despite this there are areas of economic activity where Scotland is world class, for example, in oil and gas, financial services and biosciences. In these areas Scotland already offers a sufficiently thick market in skills to attract and hold highly skilled labour. This contrasts with other sectors with thinner labour markets where the absence of sufficiently exciting professional opportunities limit the inward migration of talent.

Hence Scotland must think more deeply about how to create an environment conducive to the sort of activity that will attract and retain the highly skilled. And while attracting the highly skilled is important so is migration in general, to temper if not arrest the decline in Scotland's population and so help address the social costs of an ageing population and moderate higher dependency ratios. Scotland is already in many ways an attractive place to live and work. Recent initiatives such as GlobalScot (a business network of expatriate Scots) and the Fresh Talent Initiative (measures to boost inward migration and retain overseas students after graduation) are important parts of the policy mix, but so will creating a growth-promoting environment, a matter to which we return below in the context of Scotland's productivity performance.

---

[5]In the Irish case, overseas includes the United Kingdom, but even on a comparable basis Scotland still cannot match this level of returnees.

The experience of Ireland and many other countries demonstrates that migrants are attracted to growing economies. When growth accelerates, for whatever reason, it is easier to attract returnees, new migrants or others with links with the country in question. The good news for Scotland is that her global and even UK diaspora provides a rich vein of potential immigrants.

But migration alone cannot solve Scotland's population challenges. As Heather Joshi and Robert Wright note in Chapter 7, women in Scotland are choosing to have fewer children than those in the rest of the UK and comparable northern European countries. The provocative response from some demographers is that the evidence suggests that fertility rates are lowest in those developed countries where women find it hardest to combine child-rearing with a career. Scotland is not an international leader on childcare. In Germany, Spain and Italy there are efforts underway to change the cultural and socioeconomic climate towards child-rearing, Scotland must also get in step. In principle, growth in GDP per head can occur with a declining population, but as Paul Krugman notes there are few real world examples. A falling population will probably reduce absolute growth in GDP per head as external economies and spillovers are lost. So Scotland needs to arrest its population decline.

The virtuous circle of growth poses a characteristic chicken and egg problem for policy makers: people and capital will be attracted to a growing economy; growth depends on attracting skilled people and mobile capital. A good starting point for evidence-based policy is recent productivity performance, but using structural policy reforms to achieve faster growth has proved notoriously difficult around the world. The frequent domestic gloom about Scotland's economic performance often reflects impatience with the time horizons required for supply-side interventions to pay dividends in terms of measured outcomes. A case of James Heckman's better-educated seven-year-olds writ large! If the contributors to this book have a message for Scottish policy makers on how to address this dilemma, it is that the best chance for sustained growth, a 'third wind', is to focus on three areas: capabilities, innovation, and public-sector efficiency.

Strengthening Capabilities

Scotland's existing set of capabilities, like those of any nation or region, are determined by its legacy of place and history. This inheritance, and the ability to build new capabilities, determine its capacity to stimulate growth. Many contributors urged Scottish policy makers to devote their energies to building on the foundations of strong capabilities rather than shoring up real or perceived weaknesses in capabilities.

For example, Edward Glaeser is upbeat about the potential of both Edinburgh and Glasgow but cautions Edinburgh against constraining development by becoming a 'boutique town' and urges Glasgow to understand the necessity of becoming more like Boston, skills and amenity-led, rather than looking back to past traditions and in the manner of Detroit. Recognizing the Glasgow–Edinburgh corridor as the focal point of Scotland's future growth implies profound changes in order to achieve coherent planning, housing and transport infrastructure and connectivity.

Raising the Rate of Innovation

William Baumol assessed Scotland's capabilities in terms of entrepreneurship and innovation. In business R&D Scotland lacks vital capabilities despite the existence of UK-wide incentives. Scotland's universities exhibit strong underlying research capabilities but weaker incentives to commercialize the outputs of this R&D success-fully. Scottish management must be willing to take innovation sufficiently seriously, and to formalize the process to enhance their competitive advantage. The woefully low level of spending on R&D by business, and the weakness of the innovation process from 'blue-sky' research through to commercialization, form serious barriers to growth.

Both the private sector and policy makers in Scotland need to see more clearly that successful growth comes in the main from the rapid diffusion, adoption and adaptation of new technologies and products developed elsewhere, described by Baumol as the capability to imitate. In addition a raft of incentives to support innovation and entrepreneurship, access to and efficiency of capital, and entry to competitive growing markets will be needed.

Improving Public-Sector Efficiency

Government can no more neglect its own efficiency than can any other economic agent. Scotland cannot hope to raise its productivity significantly if the business climate is characterized by widespread public-sector inefficiency. A key theme emerging from this book is that in smaller economies, with inevitably thinner markets, it is *more* not *less* important for policy makers to be clear about the role of competition in public services in benchmarking performance and stimulating innovation.

In Scotland, as elsewhere in Western Europe, lip service is often paid to a reform agenda but concrete action is painfully slow. The coalition of resistance to reform, usually producer-led, remains too influential in the policy-making process. The more diffuse coalition of consumers and citizens who would benefit from structural reform are too often ignored in conventional policy making and, in the absence of evidence and experimentation, typically unaware of the nature of the potential gains foregone. Nicholas Crafts challenged the shortcomings of an overwhelmingly target-driven approach to performance management, citing the 109 metrics for each of Scotland's 15 area health boards and the 47 targets for each school. Centralized approaches to the provision of services fail to provide the necessary spur to either efficiency or innovation.

Herein lies a real opportunity for using experimentation and evidence to accomplish reform. Scotland's smaller scale certainly offers advantages; after all, it is easier to turn a rowing boat around than it is a supertanker.

EARLY STEPS

The Scottish experience illustrates that policy makers know more about what should happen than how to make it happen. Creating public support for change is easier in circumstances of crisis, but true crises are rare in advanced European economies.

In the absence of crisis, change must come in part from compelling evidence that creates a broadly based 'pull' for change and in part from a 'push' from political, civic and business leadership. Inevitably, any coalition for change will only gather momentum over time.[6] The existence of stubborn institutional or political barriers to change requires clear signals of intent from policy makers, first steps that can shift the collective mindset and demonstrate the links between higher growth and expanded opportunity.

In addition to these long-term and systemic changes, good candidates for early action are those areas where the evidence base is clearest. The implication for policy makers is to focus on areas where you know you can make a difference. Thus Edward Glaeser contrasts the relative clarity about how to tackle crime, using the advances in intelligence-based policing to create safer and more competitive cities and also address the diminished opportunities of poorer people living in high-crime areas, with the opaqueness of policy solutions for tackling relative disadvantage in education.

If high-amenity cities can help beyond this to retain or attract skilled workforces, the straightforward policy implications include a pro-development planning regime for Scotland's cities and their surrounding regions, providing affordable housing for middle-income families, and car-friendly commuting options (incorporating road pricing) as well as public transport. Adair Turner, Vice-Chairman of Merrill Lynch (Europe), commenting on the final seminar in the Allander Series, highlighted Scotland's comparative advantage of space compared with other parts of the UK and Europe where population densities are much higher. This could be better exploited by linking Glasgow, Edinburgh and their dozen or so adjacent local authorities into one cohesive urban core (reassessing what services are managed at this spatial level and which are best tackled at the more local level). Such institutional innovations would inevitably bring about closer cooperation and connectivity between the two cities, vital to achieving economic scale on the European stage.

Despite the lesser clarity about how to achieve long-term objectives in education, James Heckman and Dimitriy Masterov strongly argue that strengthening a nation's human capital capabilities addresses not only growth objectives but also opportunity objectives. They provide clear evidence that the highest returns are associated with the earliest interventions, when both cognitive and non-cognitive skills take shape. A central ambition of policy should be to 'water the seed' by directing the marginal pound of government expenditure to the early years, in preference to prohibitively costly attempts at later remediation. Schooling is only part of the skills formation process. In future, policy should also recognize the central role of the family in skills formation and hence seek to enrich family life and assist the development of the whole person. Public policy has taken the existence of healthy families for granted, yet 1 in 20 children under 16 in Scotland have a problem drug-using parent,

---

[6]For example, a majority of Edinburgh residents arguably oppose the relaxation of planning regulations, thereby restricting both house building and commercial development. But in the absence of evidence, people will not appreciate the costs of not building new homes. Evidence—on comparative house prices, building costs, developments foregone, the necessity of scale for global success—may make it possible to combat Edinburgh dooming itself to economic irrelevance.

some 41 000–59 000 children in all.[7] As families (rather than schools) are the major source of skills, it is vital that struggling families are supported if the children are not to be disadvantaged for life. An inclusive pre-school skill building and parenting programme from the first weeks of life should be considered, drawing on lessons from the Perry Preschool Program. Thereafter, Heckman and Masterov urge the need for rigorous cost–benefit analyses to rank alternative educational investments, with a strong focus (based on suggestive evidence from outside Scotland) on teaching quality, mentoring through the teenage years, and a determined assault on the long tail of illiteracy.

To address the impact of population decline on Scotland's human capital and growth, the following initiatives commend themselves: attracting both skilled and unskilled migrants, expanding the net inflow of students from the rest of UK and overseas, integrating refugees and economic migrants better, and attracting back Scots from the rest of the UK and overseas. Evidence on the ability of policy to influence the decline in fertility rates is limited as it has only recently become a focus of policy interest, but it will be important to monitor results in those societies seriously engaging with the dilemmas of parents trying to manage both work and family responsibilities.

Finally, we have highlighted the need to take sheer efficiency in public services more seriously and to introduce greater choice, contestability and competition into the Scottish public sector, while strengthening the government's ability to measure the value of services to the user. As Paul Hallwood and Ronald MacDonald, as well as Nicholas Crafts, argued, the Scottish government needs to develop a stronger core finance and performance management function. A fundamental review is also required of the current 'make or buy' decisions of the Scottish public sector, in areas such as the provision of water services.

Beyond improving the evidence base, and the government's measurement and monitoring capacity, it is just as important to develop a greater implementational capacity. With the focus of recent decades on Scotland's constitutional options and then on the bedding down of those new institutions, the development of a better delivery capability has not had a high enough priority. Remedying this and catching up with best practice elsewhere will require increased specialist expertise within the civil service, and the greater use of private-sector expertise at senior levels. As John Bradley noted, efficient business-friendly governing structures do offer a vital competitive advantage: more sophisticated systems of economic governance, a greater growth orientation of public spending and regulation and a fiscal regime supporting these objectives.

In recent decades, Scotland has been too focused on constitutional preoccupations, notably its relative position within the UK, and too little concerned about its global position. That is changing: contemporary Scotland is cautiously starting to view its challenges in an international context. Seen from this perspective it has much in common with other small advanced economies. This book has sought to

---

[7] *Hidden harm: responding to the needs of children of problem drug users.* The Report of an Enquiry by the Advisory Council on the Misuse of Drugs, HM Home Office, June 2003, p. 2.

contribute to the endeavour of responding to these common challenges. Its most encouraging conclusion is that policy makers in small economies will be able to improve economic performance and thereby improve opportunities for their people. We hope the people of Scotland will benefit, in the decades to come, from the lessons drawn here.

Policy makers in Scotland and elsewhere will only make progress on economic reform if they can convince their electorates that such reform will bring about a more prosperous and fair society. Measures such as better childcare, faster planning decisions, improved public services and safer streets have a direct and welcome impact, yet reform is all too often characterized as a cause of insecurity and harmful competition. A programme of reform must therefore be characterized as a coherent package offering greater opportunity and empowerment. The policy programme outlined in this book would, if implemented, improve the growth rate and boost confidence in a virtuous circle. However, as noted in the recent report by Wim Kok,[8] 'Facing the challenge of reform in Europe', competitiveness is a diagnosis of the vitality of an economy and society, rather than an abstract economic indicator.[9]

---

[8] The report is available at http://europa.eu.int/comm/lisbon_strategy/pdf/2004-1866-EN-complet.pdf. On the disappointing progress on the Lisbon Agenda it notes (p. 6): 'This disappointing delivery is due to an overloaded agenda, poor co-ordination and conflicting priorities. A key issue has been the lack of determined political action.'

[9] Governments must not duck their responsibilities: they must engage citizens in the process of economic reform. Nothing less than their future well-being is at stake.